Contents

Preface

NICOLAUS SCHAFHAUSEN & MIRJAM ZADOFF

This text has been produced in the second year of the pandemic and during a lockdown. Public spaces—streets, squares, museums, educational institutions, theaters—have been out of reach or out of order, could not be accessed or used for social interchange. Conversations, lectures, performances, and all forms of assembly have either taken place digitally or been canceled. Like all other institutions, the Munich Documentation Centre for the History of National Socialism, with its exhibits, events, and seminar rooms, has been closed more often than not in the past 18 months. In late 2019, however, visitors had crowded into the now empty spaces to view a new exhibition that critics described as "astonishing and groundbreaking," and in which they saw a "sign of a new culture of remembrance" and an "invitation to participate in a culture of political commemoration."[1]

The exhibition *Tell me about ~~yesterday~~ tomorrow* focused on opening up new approaches in the discussion of memory with a collaboration between art and scholarship. It served as a point of departure for contemplating ways of speaking and thinking about the past in the future. Its intention was not to present fixed notions about future models of remembrance, but rather to provide an altogether open catalogue of questions intended to trigger discussion and social engagement regarding the roles of art, scholarship, and the public in the politically contentious question of who interprets the past and in what way.

Remembering Nazism—writing and speaking about the atrocities—was at first an act of resistance, one mostly performed by survivors themselves or by isolated initiatives and for a long time ignored. It was only over the course of the 1980s and 90s that these traumatic recollections were given broader exposure—in memoirs and exhibitions and at memorials and commemoration sites. Though today one may occasionally have the feeling that official remembrances are all too ritualized, these rituals are important and justified, and continue to be an essential political obligation. Remembrance of these crimes has always taken place—as it does to this day—in a culture marked with violence against Jews, against gays and lesbians, against Roma and Sinti. So, it is an affront to survivors to hear politicians who foment fear and hatred mouthing the phrase "never again." In the last 30 years it has been largely left up to survivors, witnesses to the era, to urge us to learn from history—warning us with their biographies, their memoirs, their simple presence. But now many of them are no longer with us, or have been forced to remain out of sight by the pandemic.

1
Jörg Häntzschel, "NS-Dokumentationszentrum: Wie zeitgenössische Kunst die NS-Geschichte erzählt," in: *Süddeutsche Zeitung*, November 30, 2019; Timo Feldhaus, "So etwas sah man noch nie," in: *Der Freitag*, December 5, 2019; Roberta DeRighi, "Die Schau 'Tell me about yesterday tomorrow' im NS-Dokuzentrum," in: *Abendzeitung*, December 12, 2019; Uwe Mattheiß, "NS-Dokumentationszentrum München: Erinnern, um die Welt neu zu denken," in: *Der Standard*, December 12, 2019.

16

Worry about their silence occasionally leads to seemingly helpless actions, for example when the loss of contemporary witnesses is compensated for with holograms, augmented reality, or elaborate renovation projects, as in Nuremberg.

Even more than 75 years since the end of the war, the memory of National Socialism is on many levels closely associated with current political developments. In early 2021 *The New Yorker* published a report on a huge, forgotten, and largely unknown army depot in Virginia where Nazi "art" is stored, hidden from the eyes of the public. In 1945 the U.S. Army hoped to prevent the various busts, portraits, and history paintings projecting the aesthetics and ideology of the Nazi movement from falling into the wrong hands and spurring a revival of Nazism. The U.S. Army's present chief curator, Sarah Forgey, rejects the idea of making the depot accessible to the public. "Look at the world today. That rationale seems more valid in 2020 than it's been in a long time," she explained.[2] A few days later a deluded mob stormed the Capitol in Washington, D.C.

2
Quoted from Dexter Filkins, "Inside the U.S. Army's Warehouse Full of Nazi Art," in: *The New Yorker*, January 4, 2021.

Fear of the supposedly auratic remains of the Nazi regime was also behind the Munich Documentation Centre's decision to display no originals in its permanent historical exhibit *Munich and National Socialism*. Like all memory projects, this exhibit also reflects a specific moment in time—the way Nazi history was remembered in the early 2000s, namely with a rational eye, trusting on the instructive power of facts, with a focus on the criminal apparatus and certain well-known perpetrators. From our present perspective, we are inclined to consider additional gray areas, the shockingly banal histories of the followers, the mediocre characters who profited from the regime—and ultimately the question of when and how empathy and solidarity within society eroded. When the Documentation Centre was established, the guiding question was, "What does that have to do with me?" Today, more than 75 years after the end of the war and in the light of other challenges, the question needs to be rephrased. What have we learned from this experience? How does the past affect our social behavior in the present day? Who should be initiating discussions of memory, and how does memory function in a diverse and digitally connected society?

From such considerations we developed the idea of this exhibition as a collaboration between scholarship and contemporary art, which we put together with Juliane Bischoff as co-curator, Anke Hoffsten as project manager, and the entire staff of the

Documentation Centre. The art works aim to investigate and process how historical and present-day conditions are related. Post-migrant artists who focus on German memory discourse serve to welcome a diverse public. Post-migrants are not only understood as recipients of a German memory culture, but as its proponents.

Within the framework of the exhibition, art, memory, and scholarship were to be presented in a common space so as to provide new perspectives in the discussion of memory, perspectives containing both analytical as well as individual and personal approaches. The outbreak of the Covid-19 pandemic in March 2020 meant that most of the planned events and presentations had to be canceled; discursive formats, gatherings, and public performances were no longer possible. In June 2020 we responded with a digital program, the *Assembly*, centered on the podcast series *History is not the Past*—with contributions on contemporary issues and future scenarios by scholars, journalists, curators, artists, writers, and musicians.[3] The relevance of memory for the future of our democracies was dealt with in terms of history, society, and culture. For the future shaping of society a look at the past is essential, for without memory we lose our future.

With the present volume we wish to reconnect with that series and take up the thread where the digital discussion program led us. The result is a textual presentation that carries the themes and questions of *Tell me about ~~yesterday~~ tomorrow* beyond the period of the pandemic. It presents writers from various disciplines with different ways of thinking and perspectives—historians, contemporary artists, art historians and critics, philosophers, scholars in gender, memory, and media studies, and museum curators. Their contributions are accompanied by a documentation of the exhibition as presented in the galleries of the Documentation Centre and nearby venues—the Basilica of St. Boniface, the Zentralinstitut für Kunstgeschichte, the Kunst-Insel am Lenbachplatz, and the façade of the Strafjustizzentrum.

In her essay on the structure of prophetic speech, the poet Monika Rinck questions the notion that time is linear and ceases to exist once it has passed. With respect to the title *Tell me about ~~yesterday~~ tomorrow* she argues that both the past and narratives of the future are based on present-day conditions, and are thereby constantly being renegotiated and defined.

In a speech delivered on International Holocaust Remembrance Day, historian Dirk Rupnow, who lives in Austria, discusses developments in contemporary history and memory

3
URL: >https://
yesterdaytomorrow.
nsdoku.de/history-
is-not-the-past<
(accessed June 21,
2021).

cultures over the last few decades and considers how memory of the Holocaust can be preserved despite our increasing temporal distance from it. Géraldine Schwarz describes the complexity of European memory cultures of the postwar period, and suggests that their different perspectives can help us examine historical perceptions with greater subtlety. The German-French journalist feels that the resulting reflections can also be applied to other chapters in European history. In his poem cycle *von der wiederkehr (of return)*, Max Czollek presents a vision of the present poised between an uncertain future and a traumatic past. The poet and journalist is convinced that the German language itself conveys historical continuities and references to the catastrophe of the Holocaust. Philippe Sands is a lawyer, specialist in international law, and writer. In his research on the past of a Nazi governor of occupied territories in Eastern Europe he advocates the incorporation of personal experiences in one's view of history so as to augment it with multiple perspectives. The curator and historian Niko Wahl considers the parallels between individual and collective memories. He sees that by carefully relating different narratives to each other, regardless of their different contexts, it is always possible to stimulate socially responsible engagement and the need for focused political action.

Andreas Huyssen speaks with the artist Doris Salcedo about the depiction of violence, artistic abstraction, and collective memory in the southern hemisphere. Her commemorative work *Fragmentos* is dedicated to the civil war in Colombia, and was created for the National Museum in Bogotá together with women who were victims of sexual violence during the war years. The historian Andrea Pető then wonders why with but few exceptions there are no visual narratives that make it possible to commemorate wartime victims of sexual assault in the places where they are remembered. In conversation with the architecture theorist Karamia Müller, the artist Simon Denny discusses colonial entanglements whose continuing presence is manifested in both family histories and social structures. In response, the two point out ways the arts can generate opposing narratives. The philosopher and artist Marina Gržinić offers glimpses into a research project that compares the different ways memory is preserved in Austria, Belgium, Croatia, and Bosnia and Herzegovina. She emphasizes the importance of dealing with the present and history in any discussion of the future of society, and points to the relevance of transnational memory discourse.

Referring to her own curatorial, research, and teaching activity as an example, Clémentine Deliss makes it clear what fundamental changes are required to open up institutional structures. Her approach describes the museum as a place for active engagement, one in which the public itself develops an approach to and way of dealing with archives, collections, and presentation methods. The curator Vanessa Joan Müller stresses the relevance for the present of continuous analysis and contextualization of historical works of art. Using the example of Emil Nolde, she shows how blurred the lines dividing an artist and his work can be. Although the Nazis banned Nolde's works as "degenerate" and "un-German," the artist himself was an avowed National Socialist. Yet for a long time after the war he was considered an untainted example of German rectitude. Catrin Lorch, an editorial writer for the *Süddeutsche Zeitung*, deals with the half-hearted provenance research in Germany. The Gurlitt Case, especially, was a missed opportunity to discover the importance of the theft and expropriation of art to the Nazi regime. Dorothea Schöne, director of the Kunsthaus Dahlem, examines the question of how institutions housed in National Socialist buildings deal with the cultural tension without letting their mission be overwhelmed by it. Schöne's curatorial approach takes certain aspects of the architecture as a starting point, and offers them as referents to the exhibited art. Nora Sternfeld describes the confrontation of Okwui Enwezor's curatorial program with the Nazi architecture of Munich's Haus der Kunst as para-monumental. To the art and cultural historian, para-monuments are distinguished by the fact that they do not mask their powerful monumentality but actively confront it.

Next Ismail Küpeli shows how Turkey's current president Recep Tayyip Erdoğan employs anti-Semitic narratives in order to express his political conservatism and Islamic nationalism on a cultural level. The political scientist particularly recalls a play produced by Erdoğan in 1975 that was unmistakably aimed at an imagined communist-Zionist enemy. On the basis of numerous examples, the Polish curator Piotr Rypson analyses the authoritarian transformation of Polish cultural policy since the Law and Justice Party came to power, and how its focus on nationalist themes has had drastic material, financial, and personal consequences for history museums, art institutions, and public-law media.

The art historian and critic Sven Lütticken devotes his essay to artistic autonomy and the role of works of art in political activism. He focuses on works produced both before and after the Second World War that warned against the rise of fascism or its revival. Dieter Lesage, a philosopher and curator, examines the concept of "the many" throughout history. Starting with the Greek "hoi polloi," he also discusses more recent forms of activism such as the "occupy" movement, and in doing so demonstrates the political relevance and interpretation of the concept through the centuries.

The journalist Georg Diez provides a blueprint of digital and democratic change, and shows that new technology can be considered not as an unpredictable fate but rather as a manageable and progressive alternative for strengthening democratic structures. The artist Liam Gillick defends in his essay the complexity of contemporary forms of art, and rejects supposedly undemanding works that are readily understandable and seemingly universal. Instead, he argues that to really make the art world more accessible it will be necessary to rethink administrative and bureaucratic structures. Finally, the painter Brenda Draney relates her experiences during the pandemic, with its travel restrictions, quarantines, and disinfectants. Between the "end of the world" and the "danger of hope" she describes how seemingly fragmentary thoughts and experiences fit together into a complex and willful narrative that also fundamentally affects her work as an artist.

* * *

In the present situation it is difficult to formulate definite conclusions. We find ourselves in the midst of a process that most of us, including the writers of this preface, had not anticipated. The pandemic points to open and unresolved questions in our daily lives. And all the more to the social, political, and even aesthetic questions raised by the exhibition *Tell me about ~~yesterday~~ tomorrow*. What might a social model look like that takes up the essential achievements of the period after 1945 by protecting the democratic foundations, the rights of freedom and participation in a diverse society? Institutions like the Munich Documentation Centre have the dual aim of suggesting intellectual approaches and stimulating further engagement. They encourage constructive engagement with a complex, often conflict-filled present and a look at the past that has given rise to it.

A burgeoning populism has had such a lasting effect on our society in part because it establishes concepts, images, and a style of political engagement that alter people's level of perception and block a reflective view of the past. Populist ways of thinking and speaking are adopted, sometimes unconsciously, and seep into everyday discourse, where they reveal their true and lasting effectiveness.

The interaction of latent authoritarian attitudes among the populace and ideologies like those espoused by adherents of the "Querdenken" movement or Alternative for Germany politicians is one of the greatest challenges of our time. It can lead to a further division of society, the loss of common purpose or further depoliticization of broad levels of society, or even to a political force of its own. Right-wing populist movements are already exploiting existing resentments, reinforcing polarization, stoking prejudices, and responding to subjective feelings of uncertainty with supposedly simple solutions. In a complex, globally-oriented present with its tendency toward individualization, with their appeal to a supposedly homogeneous "we" (as opposed to the despicable "others"), populists are able to attract increasing numbers of followers. Also, a strategically deployed populist rhetoric of emotionalism and simplification that eludes rational argument and relies on exclusion and calculated scandal is being increasingly echoed in the everyday media.

This trend is perceptible again and again in the realm of art as well, when institutions are mainly judged on the basis of visitor numbers and not on how well they present their holdings in context, or when they are quick to succumb to populist simplification and polarization. Relevant contemporary art comments on the present day, and formulates alternatives to existing conditions quite apart from pragmatic or strategic considerations. It is a seismograph of the present with a view to the future, and protests against complacency and forgetfulness toward the past. But to develop its force it requires a receptive, critical counterpart—in the case of the present publication and the exhibition that preceded it that counterpart is the historian's scholarly view of the German past. One of the main interests of *Tell me about ~~yesterday~~ tomorrow* was accordingly presenting art as just such a constructive partner, one that derives perspectives for the present and the future from reflection on the past. Art is able to be effective in that it not only depicts social diversity but accepts it as a matter of course.

* * *

We are grateful to all those who supported this exhibition project. St. Boniface's Abbey, the Zentralinstitut für Kunstgeschichte, and the Strafjustizzentrum München placed their spaces and structures at our disposal, and helped us mount individual exhibits of works by Ydessa Hendeles, Sebastian Jung, and Harald Pickert. The exhibition was sponsored by the German Federal Cultural Foundation and the Canada Council for the Arts. The present publication was realized thanks to the attentive editorial collaboration of Lukas Graf and Andreas Eichmüller. Lastly, our sincere thanks to all the contributing writers and artists who made this project possible.

Olaf Nicolai, *Viele, die eine Ahnung haben… (Many People Who Are Aware…)*, 1999
Installation view, *Tell me about ~~yesterday~~ tomorrow*

Munich Documentation Centre for the History of National Socialism, View from Königsplatz Munich

Exterior view of the Munich Documentation Centre for the History of National Socialism, *Tell me about ~~yesterday~~ tomorrow*

Casting Shadows. A Few Thoughts on the Structure of Prophetic Speech

Tell me about ~~yesterday~~ tomorrow. Doesn't that mean skipping the present? No, I don't think so. Because the present is the moment when I am called upon to speak about tomorrow. In my mind I picture it exactly halfway between *yesterday* and *tomorrow*. If I wish to respond to this call—*tell me*—then surely I must ask myself how the experiences of the past can be extended into the future. Or is that the wrong question? Another try: Does the imaginary extension of an experience into the future necessarily assume the events in question to be part of a forward-moving linear process? By putting the question like this, the ways I think about time will have become spatialized. What do these spaces of time look like?

> *"expecting gruffness we had appeared uncombed and shy*
> *even lonely the first sentences finished us off and would*
> *vanish with us en passant"*[1]

The common conception of the future as a timespan that lies ahead contrasts with notions like Walter Benjamin's "angel of history", the cognitive model of the Aymara language (with a spatial construction that locates the future not in front of but behind us, at our backs, where we cannot see it),[2] or the shift in most African sign languages where the gesture denoting futurity points backwards, as Helga Nowotny mentions in her essay on the concept of innovation in a fragile future. The future, she continues, surrounds us, it is in front of us, behind us, around us—all at the same time.[3] These descriptions take the usual structure of metaphorical time to task. The notion of a timeline is well known, but maybe a time basin or time pool would be the more precise image. These are not merely questions of style. "Since we cannot think other than in the medium of our language, we always already move within categories and semantic relations defined by words."[4]

So is it even possible to conceive of time beyond spatial metaphors, regardless of whether I privilege a linear or a cyclical model? Can I improve these metaphors in which the mental image takes shape? For it is this mental image that determines the structure of my telling, that defines the narrative and, more fundamentally, the interpretation of time sequences, the linking of past, present and future.

FACTUAL SHADOWING

The Christian Bible begins with the Judaic Genesis and ends with the Christian Apocalypse. This story has been told. But its interpretation is still ongoing. For centuries, from the Church Fathers to the present day, Christian theology has assigned the Hebrew Bible,

1
Charlotte Warsen, *Plage. Gedichte.* (Berlin 2019), p. 4 (trans. Nicholas Grindell). In her long-form poems, Warsen works masterfully with repetitions and variations of individual lines, musically, using fugues and permutations. The texts are spread across the page, as if seeking to combine the linearity of reading with the variable eye movement of visual perception. Recurring particles that suddenly appear in an entirely different context make it seem as if the poet had to keep on presenting an idea, over and over.

2
Rafael E. Núñez, Eve Sweetser, "With the Future Behind Them: Convergent Evidence From Aymara Language and Gesture in the Crosslinguistic Comparison of Spatial Construals of Time", in *Cognitive Science* 30 (2006), pp. 401–450.

3
Helga Nowotny, *Insatiable Curiosity: Innovation in a Fragile Future* (Massachusetts 2008), p. 2.

4
Aleida Assmann, *Formen des Vergessens* (Göttingen 2016), e-book, unpaginated (trans. Nicholas Grindell).

the Tanakh, a subordinate status, treating it solely as a prefiguration of the so-called New Testament. The Christian practice of typological allegoresis viewed the Jewish tradition as no more than a preview of the Gospels that called for exegesis. The direction was fixed.

A book that played an important part in my reflection on this topic is Michael André Bernstein's *Foregone Conclusions. Against Apocalyptic History,* in which he looks at the way literary and historical texts about the (pre-)history of the Shoah are written.[5] In addition to the well-known rhetorical device of foreshadowing—casting a shadow ahead, in the sense of a premonition or portent—he develops two other forms of factual shadowing: backshadowing and sideshadowing.

Sideshadowing refers to a kind of attention that focuses on unrealized possibilities of the past, not as a way of flanking facts with fictions, but to disrupt the claims of a view of history for which everything that perishes must be doomed to perish from the outset—a clear case of ominous backshadowing. Resisting such constructions, often made using the future perfect tense, can help us "not to use our knowledge of the future as a means of judging the decisions of those living before that (still only possible) future became actual event."[6] To project oneself into a time when the Shoah has not yet taken place in order to describe its prehistory without knowing what will follow—is an impossibility.

Here is what could happen. That cannot be. But what is the relationship between the unthinkable and the unlikely? Unfortunately it is not the case that the more unthinkable an event is, the less likely it becomes. People who do not suffer great adversity are not so strongly compelled to change their habits of thought. They are not forced to imagine the unimaginable, simply because it has not befallen them. Bernstein asks a different question: How can something be unthinkable and unavoidable at the same time?

"On a historical level, there is the contradiction between conceiving of the Shoah as simultaneously unimaginable and inevitable. On an ethical level, the contradiction is between saying no one could have foreseen the triumph of genocidal anti-Semitism, while also claiming that those who stayed in Europe are in part responsible for their fate because they failed to anticipate the danger. On a narrative level, the contradiction is between insisting on the unprecedented and singular nature of the Shoah as an event and yet still using the most lurid formal tropes and commonplace literary conventions to narrate it."[7]

Although the contrast between narrative models and the events portrayed is especially stark here, it is also seen in other cases.

5
Michael André Bernstein, *Foregone Conclusions. Against Apocalyptic History.* Berkeley 1994.

6
Bernstein, *Foregone Conclusions*, p. 16.

7
Ibid., p. 23.

20

Sequences of events take shape in retrospect, pushing memory into the background; mere chronologies parade as causal connections. Bernstein quotes an appalling passage from a Kafka biography in which grammar itself takes on an ominous quality. When in doubt, resorting to dubious logic is clearly preferable to accepting something as nonsensical. On closer inspection, conventional narrative models in particular are more unrealistic than experimental forms that do without a concluding gesture, like Heimrad Bäcker's *nachschrift*, two volumes that work with a distillation of Nazi language, quoting it, rearranging it, effectively laying it bare on the page. "Realism", writes Friedrich Achleitner in his afterword to *nachschrift*, "lies not in how close an approximation of reality is achieved, but in distance to reality, in the chance to render its dimensions accessible to thought and experience".[8]

I am also interested in ongoing, sometimes stuttering associative processes that manage to establish contact with an as-yet-unfixed future, as in Charlotte Warsen's collection *Plage*, or the long poem *kommen sehen* by Anja Utler,[9] a post-apocalyptic monolog from an impossible future. "It is a strange realism, but it is a strange reality."[10]

PREDICTION

Which sequences of events take shape in foresight? Interpretation plays a vital role here. The Oracle of Delphi preferred to speak in obscure lines of verse. "In their ecstasy the oracular Greek mediums speak the language of the Gods. This language differs from the common language of humans."[11] The fits of mania and manifest madness of the sibyls contributed to a levelling of categories such as conceivability and likelihood. Those who consult the Oracle ponder what they are told at length in the historical present. In this way, the Oracle's speech obliges its future-hungry clientele to get involved in its interpretation. It is they who bring the Oracle's prophesy into the present of its application.

Many legendary attempts by the ancients to dissolve the mists that lay over the future led to terrible dilemmas, however, or even right into the midst of the very misfortune they were seeking to avoid. What will happen? No one knows. But one can state the following: What has happened once can happen again. Once it has happened, it has been proved to be possible. No further evidence is needed.

"expecting gruffness we had appeared uncombed and shy even lonely the first rays of sunlight finished us off and would vanish with us en passant"[12]

8
Friedrich Achleitner, "Über die Beschreibbarkeit des Unbeschreibbaren oder der Versuch eines Nachworts zur nachschrift", in Heimrad Bäcker, *nachschrift* (Graz 1993), p. 132 (trans. Nicholas Grindell).

9
Anja Utler, *kommen sehen* (Vienna 2020).

10
Ursula K. Le Guin, "The Carrier Bag Theory of Fiction", in *Dancing at the Edge of the World* (New York 1989), e-book, unpaginated.

11
Kai Trampedach, Politische Mantik. *Die Kommunikation über Götterzeichen und Orakel im klassischen Griechenland* (Heidelberg 2015), p. 206 (trans. Nicholas Grindell).

12
Warsen, *Plage*, p. 5, (trans. Nicholas Grindell).

In one of the last known prophecies of the Delphic Oracle from the third century AD (361/2), it seems to speak of its self-abolition. Was the Oracle aware of its own liquidation when it informed the Emperor that its magnificent hall had fallen to the ground, that Phoibos no longer had his house, nor his mantic bay, nor his prophetic spring, that the water had dried up?[13]

Apart from the future—Iranian poet Pegah Ahmadi said recently, paraphrasing Maurice Blanchot—nothing is impossible anymore.[14] In the meantime, as all plans have been put on hold by the global pandemic, the number of predictions has multiplied. Statistical calculations and forecasts now determine people's everyday lives, while speculations about the unfolding of events over the next eighteen months are broadcast as regular news bulletins. In this context, I was interested to read Carlo Caduff's book *The Pandemic Perhaps, Dramatic Events in a Public Culture of Danger*.

"Pandemic prophesy both looks forward to the future and back to the past. In fact, anticipations of the future and recollections of the past can become almost indistinguishable in prophetic discourse. It is a characteristic feature of such discourse that its disrupts our sense of time. Prophecy can address future events in the past tense, as if they had happened, and past events in the future tense, as if they are about to happen."[15]

Prophetic speech, he later writes, does not produce a future, but robs us of the present.[16] I'm not so sure. Perhaps it is not the present that vanishes under the tension of prophetic speech. The biblical prophets, for example, predicted a horrific future in order to turn their audience around, with the goal of preventing the calamity described in such detail from coming to pass. Evoking an endangered future served to bring about change and thus, ultimately, to save the present. For this reason, too, prophesy is an eminently political genre. Futurephilia is not necessarily to be treated with scepticism because of its ability, in its zeal, to lose touch with the present (something that also applies, incidentally, to its opposite, futurephobia). Instead, what I find suspect is the way both tend to cut off links to the recent past, obscuring the continuity of inhumane ideologies in a storm of predictions.

It was the protests against racist police violence in the United States that put an end to the monopoly of pandemic prophesies in Germany, breaking open the strange cocoon of a single prevailing discourse. And this happened just a few months after the racist attacks in Hanau on 19 February 2020 that have been more or less totally overwritten (drowned out) by predictions concerning the global

13
Kristin M. Heinemann, *The Decadence of Delphi. The Oracle in the Second Century AD and Beyond* (Abingdon, New York 2018), e-book, unpaginated.

14
Pegah Ahmadi, "(W) Ortwechsel. Brief Nummer 12": https://weiterschreiben.jetzt/wortwechseln/pegah-ahmadi-monika-rinck/ (accessed August 5, 2020).

15
Carlo Caduff, *The Pandemic Perhaps: Dramatic Events in a Public Culture of Danger* (Oakland, 2015), p. 7.

16
See Maurice Blanchot, "Prophetic Speech," in *The Book to Come* (Stanford 2003), pp. 79–85.

spread of Covid-19. The longing for plannability in the disrupted new normal had banished the attacks of February from the minds of large parts of the population. *Tell me about ~~yesterday~~ tomorrow.*

In Germany, debate is currently getting underway on the subject of German colonialism, something that has to date been presented in school curricula as an insignificant episode. This debate was prompted, among others, by the toppling of the memorial to Edward Colston in Bristol—the removal of a bronze figure from the past that had survived in the space of the present.[17] Did this set free repressed memories? The toppled memorial may leave behind a void that facilitates an engagement with the crimes of (German) colonialism by withdrawing them from "defensive and complicit forgetting".[18] But this can only work by looking back and analysing the severed or repressed links with the colonial past and then drawing useful conclusions. It is not enough to look into the future. Nothing that can be remembered is over.[19]

AN ALLIANCE WITH OPENNESS

Tomorrow! What's coming? If I wish to make serious predictions, I need a broad empirical basis, large sets of well structured data, reliable mathematicians, outstanding intuition and an informed political awareness, ingenuity, knowledge of the past, perhaps even good algorithms and a friendly artificial intelligence to do the work for me. Alternatively, I could generate a system within which nothing can surprise me. This, however, would be a classic paranoid system that would also need to possess some of the flexibility of conspiracy theories in order to adapt reality to my forecasts should the need arise. Then I'm in the picture, I've foreseen everything, and I need only write last words in which everything has always been clear. Period.

> *"expecting gruffness we had appeared uncombed and shy even lonely the last rays of sunlight leaned casually on the mountain range (and would vanish with it)"*[20]

The future is always both: horrific and promising, desolate and expansive. There is no paradigm shift. Even the notion that it might make sense to plan the future is an expression of privilege. In some parts of the world, it is almost never possible to speak realistically in the future tense.[21] With the experience of the pandemic, the reach of this phenomenon has increased somewhat. Has this openness magnified or diminished the future as an idea?

17
Tobias Grahlke, "Mehr als 'nur symbolisch' – Statuensturz, Hashtag-Proteste und konnektives Erinnern." Guest contribution on *54 Books*, 22 June 2020: https://www.54books. de/mehr-als-nur-symbolisch-ueber-den-statuensturz-von-bristol-hashtag-proteste-und-konnektives-erinnern/ (accessed August 5, 2020).

18
Assmann, *Formen des Vergessens*, e-book, unpaginated (trans. Nicholas Grindell).

19
See Klaus Heinrich, *Psychoanalyse Sigmund Freuds und das Problem des konkreten gesellschaftlichen Allgemeinen* (Frankfurt 2001), p. 59.

20
Warsen, *Plage*, p. 6 (trans. Nicholas Grindell).

21
Ali Araghi, "Reckoning with an Uncertain Future in Iran, and Outside It", in *The New Yorker*, 16.3.2020; https://www.newyorker.com/culture/personal-history/possible-futures-in-iran (accessed August 5, 2020).

Good literary writing favours opening up, not the prior knowledge of the paranoiac. It looks for a just form—for the knowledge of the ongoing conflicts of the past in the present, for memory as an arena, for the unfinishability of historical processes that are never linear: "I studied and overrode the hierarchically divisive tendencies of linear writing […] so that connections which had previously remained mute (obscure) appeared in the mirror of language and perpetually gave rise to new connections (realizations, aspects, insights, overviews)."[22] This is how the poet Elke Erb describes her approach.

22
Elke Erb, "Erinnerliche, ins Bewusstsein gekommene Vorstufen", in *Kastanienallee* (Salzburg 1988), p. 85 (trans. Nicholas Grindell).

But how should one imagine a non-linear continuity? Perhaps it would help to look back to the start of this essay where we discussed the extent and position of the metaphorical spaces of time that shape our thinking and for whose narrative representation Bernstein coined the term sideshadowing. This is about more than just a retroactive insertion of contingency. It's about the fact that the past is not fixed, that it changes with what we learn in the present; it's about the possibility of giving utopia a place and time in history and identifying false conclusions as such.

Elke Erb speaks of new connections. Even today, not only in artistic discourse, the new is still accompanied by the pathos of progress: the promise of new descriptions and new definitions, more usually referred to in English as re-description, re-definition. The fact that new does not necessarily mean better is obvious. New forms of interpretation may just as well mean: developments for the worse, the prevalence of faux-apolitical apocalyptic discourse, racist impulses, poems with a chauvinist tone. But none of this is new. These things have been with us for centuries. A world without them—now that really would be something new!

So: Tell me about yesterday AND tomorrow.

Late June 2020

Exterior view of the Munich Documentation Centre for the History of National Socialism, *Tell me about ~~yesterday~~ tomorrow*

Annette Kelm, *Verbrannte Bücher (Burned Books)*, 2019 | Installation view, *Tell me about ~~yesterday~~ tomorrow*

Emeka Ogboh, *Sufferhead Original – Munich Edition*, 2019 | Installation view, Kunst-Insel at Lenbachplatz Munich

Memorial Address on the Occasion of International Holocaust Remembrance Day, 2020

DIRK RUPNOW

Honored Memorial Assembly
Ladies and Gentlemen

I thank you most sincerely for the invitation to speak to you here today. January 27 is International Holocaust Remembrance Day, and exactly 75 years have passed since the liberation of the concentration and extermination camp at Auschwitz.[1] That name has become synonymous worldwide for the crime against humanity set in motion across Europe by Germans and Austrians and their henchmen. It is unquestionably a great honor to be here, but also a burden.

As whom, and in which capacity, have you chosen me to speak to you? The question has nothing to do with self-interest. In view of our subject and its challenges, a frank understanding strikes me as not only appropriate, but absolutely necessary. You have presumably invited me as a historian who engages in research and teaches at an Austrian university, and who has long grappled with the history of National Socialism, the Second World War, and the Holocaust— as well as with the history of antisemitism reaching further back, and finally with the consequences of all these that have by no means come to rest—in a manner of speaking, the omnipresence of this history. But of course I am also a German of my generation, born 27 years after the end of the war. I am someone whose grandparents lived during the "Third Reich" and were involved in the history we are talking about—and specifically, though not especially prominently, on the side of the bystanders, beneficiaries, and perpetrators, as I have to confess. No matter what your thinking was when inviting me, for me, naturally, the two aspects are inextricably interrelated.

For my generation the historical event lies at a certain distance in the past, but we feel a direct familial tie to it: it has to do with our grandparents. It is not as far in the past as it is for the generation of my present students, to whom it now seems just as remote as the Middle Ages—or at least that is my impression at times. When I was at school in Germany during the 1980s the subject was already very much discussed, thanks to the commitment of my teachers. Moreover, my school years coincided with the heyday of political and social debates; we have only to think of the so-called "Historians' Dispute" of 1986/87 (while the Waldheim debate was raging in Austria). My university years and the beginning of my academic career then overlapped with global recognition and the high point in scholarly engagement with this event.

To be clear: it is not an eye-witness speaking to you, as you might have expected at commemorative affairs of this kind heretofore,

1
This address was delivered on January 27, 2020, at the invitation of the president of the regional parliament of Styria, Manuela Khom, in the assembly room of the statehouse in Graz.

but rather someone born after the fact. Not that there are no surviving witnesses, though they are now becoming fewer and fewer. As a historian, I am able to speak about the past, of course, albeit in a very different way than an eye-witness might. There is an unbridgeable difference, and sometimes even competition for attention and credibility, between witnesses and historians. We must ask ourselves whether that difference necessarily expresses itself in such a way that witnesses speak moralistically while narrating their memories, whereas historians approach the past soberly and objectively in their research. To German historians this distinction has always been of great importance. It also allowed them to denounce and denigrate Jewish historians from the eye-witness generation and to conceal their own involvement. Witnesses from the time have played, and continue to play, a special role as go-betweens with the past, mediators whom we historians cannot replace, whom nothing will be able to replace in the future, not even technology. The end of firsthand testimony has long been discussed, yet it seems to be difficult to assess what the consequences will be before long, once it is upon us—despite the substantial collections of video interviews. What is past is past. And without personal recollections the past is never directly accessible. The frequently touted objectivity of historians in their specific approach to the past is meanwhile not only a presumption on the part of scholars themselves, but also a seemingly unavoidable expectation of scholarship on the part of non-scholars.

Ultimately, it is a matter of adopting still another position: Am I speaking as a proponent and actor or as a distanced contemporary and observer of the memory culture and the politics of history? Historians can be both. Perhaps the two roles cannot even be readily separated. And perhaps they need to be both at the same time in order to do justice to their task. So in the year 2020, 75 years after the end of the war, what can be said about the history of the Holocaust?

As a historian at home in the field of contemporary history, it seems to me that the most productive years in Holocaust research now lie behind us. For decades the Holocaust was for most—naturally not for all—more of a marginal issue in their engagement with the National Socialist era. Then, in the 1990s, Holocaust research experienced an enormous upswing. In 1990 Raul Hilberg's pathbreaking study *The Extermination of European Jews* appeared in German with the title *Die Vernichtung der europäischen Juden*, in an affordable paperback edition in three volumes in S. Fischer Verlag's so-called "Schwarze Reihe", edited by Walter Pehle. Hilberg had been born in Vienna in 1926, had fled with his family by way of France and Cuba to the United States in 1939. He returned to Europe as a U.S. soldier, participated in the liberation of the concentration camp at Dachau, came across portions of Hitler's private library in Munich, and finally worked in the "War Documentation Department." He was thus involved in the search for documents that could be of service in the pursuit of war criminals.

Once back in the United States, he started writing a dissertation in New York on the destruction of European Jewry. His supervisor was the German political scholar and exile Franz Neumann, who had himself published a first scholarly study during the war (1942/1944) of the structure and practice of National Socialism under the title *Behemoth*. In the mid 1950s, to be sure, no one was interested in Hilberg's richly detailed work on the extermination process: he had little success in finding an American publisher for it. Hannah Arendt gave it a negative appraisal, though she quietly took inspiration from it for her report on the Eichmann Trial in Jerusalem in 1961. A German translation was initially foiled by Munich's Institut für Zeitgeschichte. In the early 1980s it was finally published by a small, unknown Berlin firm—in a small edition and at a high price. Hardly anyone read it or became aware of it. Only with the S. Fischer edition in 1990 could the book begin to play its role as the universally praised standard work. Raul Hilberg, who died in 2007 in Vermont, where he had taught political science for decades, has meanwhile come to be widely known as the father of Holocaust studies

At the same time, after the upheavals of the year 1989, East European archives were opened, and with them a whole new access to the scenes of Holocaust crimes became possible. With Christopher Browning's book *Ordinary Men / Ganz normale Männer* (1992 / German edition 1993) and Daniel Goldhagen's *Hitler's Willing Executioners / Hitlers willige Vollstrecker* (1996), as well as the so-called "Wehrmachtausstellung" (Wehrmacht Exhibition) at Hamburg's Institut für Sozialforschung in 1995, research on the perpetrators began. Countless special studies on the most varied aspects of the historical event have since appeared, countless biographies of perpetrators at all levels of the National Socialist hierarchy, countless investigations of the operations in specific regions, countless works on individual institutions—in all possible languages of relevance to the subject, in all the affected countries and beyond.

My impression is indeed that the high point of interest has already passed, though I cannot definitively document this. Naturally there will continue to be research on the Holocaust, but the most intensive phase likely lies behind us. For some time now,

German-language scholarship in contemporary history has shifted its focus to the postwar period. To a number of my colleagues the Holocaust is not even part of "contemporary history" any longer, simply because there are so few witnesses still among us.

But after all the research results of the last three decades, are we better able to answer the fundamental question that concerns all who expose themselves in their study to the horror (Hannah Arendt speaks of the necessity of "dwelling on horrors"[2])? To explain how what "ought not to have happenend"[3] (again quoting Hannah Arendt) nevertheless happened, simply could happen? Explain how human beings could do such things to other human beings—without taking refuge in the comfortable assertion that the perpetrators were not human beings at all but simply demons? How societies can carry out such horror or permit it? Today we naturally have a better understanding of the processes and course of events, the determining factors, the institutions and persons involved. We naturally know more than before. But at the same time there are also more divergent appraisals. Was the Holocaust simply the conclusion of a long development of antisemitism, from antiquity and the Middle Ages to the racist antisemitism of the late 19th century and to the genocidal or deliverance antisemitism of the Nazis? Was it owing to the delusions of enemies of the Jews and antisemites? Or should we rather see the Holocaust as the greatest mass robbery-murder in history, committed for purely economic reasons? Was the Holocaust the product of a too-powerful state or of failed states? Was the specific dynamic of events—the killing of roughly six million Jews in roughly three and a half years—set in motion at the center of power or at the periphery?

And finally: Are we always really in agreement about what we mean when we speak of the Holocaust? Are we only talking about the fate of European Jewries, also referred to as the "Shoah" (catastrophe)? Or do we as a matter of course include other groups of victims? Ultimately, we know from scholarship that the mass crimes against various groups were in part very closely interrelated. Are we also thinking of the Roma, who called the systematic persecution and extermination directed against them "Porrajmos" (the Devouring)? Are we also thinking of Soviet prisoners of war, Polish civilians, homosexuals, Jehovah's Witnesses, the politically persecuted? Are we now also commemorating the people who were regarded as sick and disabled, therefore "unworthy of living," and had to die in the course of "euthanasia campaigns"? After all, National Socialist euthanasia was a separate complex of crimes, to be sure, but we know how closely it was connected to the Holocaust on a personal, organizational, and ideological level.

2
Hannah Arendt, *The Origins of Totalitarianism*, New York 1951, p. 415.

3
Hannah Arendt, "What remains? The language remains": a conversation with Günter Gaus, Zur Person, ZDF Television, Germany, October 28, 1964, translated by Joan Stambaugh, in: Hannah Arendt, *The last interview and other conversations*, Brooklyn–London 2003, pp. 1–38, 23.

As historians, we naturally now have a number of socio-psychological explanations for the murders as well—but in spite of all the insights we have gained, don't we ultimately have to admit that we still cannot understand and explain the Holocaust? That at bottom there is still something incomprehensible that—if we are completely honest—shocks us or even shocks us all the more, the longer we occupy ourselves with all the details? That, at least, is my own personal response. Unless we choose to say in resignation: that's just the way people are? You are aware, of course, of how ambivalent any attempt at "understanding" actually is. As Madame de Staël put it: "To understand everything is to forgive everything."

What can be said now, in the year 2020, 75 years after the end of the war, about remembering the Holocaust? Here it can be noted that, decades later, the Holocaust has shifted from a marginal position to a central one. Around the turn of the millennium, the Holocaust took on a decisive importance for the formation of a European identity on the level of a politically motivated self-image. After protracted and painful discussions, any number of European countries were forced to revise their postwar myths and confront their own collaboration and collusion in the crimes initiated and organized by Germans and Austrians. Together with the Second World War, "Auschwitz" became the negative founding event of modern Europe. Even beyond Europe's borders, the Holocaust has assumed the status of a negative political and cultural norm. In the United States, for reasons of internal and external policy, it was already incorporated into the formation of an American memory and identity in the 1980s and 1990s. Given the character of the United States as a land of immigration with mainly European roots; given the American soldiers' encounter with the violent crimes of the Nazis when liberating the camps; and given America's role in the conduct of war crimes trials, this is hardly surprising. But meanwhile even in Japan, near Hiroshima, there is now a Holocaust Education Center, and South Africa's Capetown has its own Holocaust Museum.

Above all, however, the Task Force for International Cooperation on Holocaust Education, Remembrance and Research (1998 / now the International Holocaust Remembrance Alliance) and the Stockholm International Forum on the Holocaust: a Conference on Education, Remembrance, and Research (2000), the United Nations' Holocaust Outreach Programme (2005), and the establishment of the 27th of January—the day of the liberation of the concentration and extermination camp Auschwitz—as an international day of remembrance for the victims of the Holocaust, attest that the National

Socialist genocide has long since become a matter of transnational historical policy. As early as 1979, UNESCO designated the concentration and extermination camp Auschwitz-Birkenau as a World Heritage Site. Since 1999 the Ringelblum Archive from the Warsaw Ghetto has been listed by UNESCO as a "Witness to the Holocaust" in its Memory of the World Register, as have the *Diary of Anne Frank* since 2009, the International Tracing Service Archives in Bad Arolsen since 2013, and the Frankfurt Auschwitz Trial since 2017.

There has thus been a worldwide attempt, even on a supranational level and far beyond the affected countries, to institutionalize and standardize the memory of the Holocaust. It is perhaps the only historical event ever to be dealt with in such a way. This clearly separates it from other events with a comparable transnational dimension—the First World War, for example—to which no such attention and commemoration are accorded. In the 2000s, recognition of the Holocaust as the ultimate crime against humanity, and of one's own complicity in the Nazis' crimes, if applicable, like championship of human rights or the processing one's own traumatic, conflict-filled past, serves as an entry ticket to the Western world.

In the 1980s, who could have imagined that after all the lies, silence, and suppression, the memory of the Holocaust would one day become hegemonic, state-supporting, and state-supported, and all that on a global scale? In late January 2020, nearly 50 heads of state and government converged on Israel's Holocaust Memorial Yad Vashem to commemorate those historical events.

Transnational relevance was already established by the events themselves, of course, and their geographical extent: during the Second World War, virtually the entire European continent witnessed anti-Jewish discrimination, rape, and mass murder. The European, even global dimension of engagement with the Holocaust is not only the result of emigration and expulsion based on National Socialist policies; it is also a reflection of National Socialism's universal racist, antisemitic ideology, negating all moral restraints, that allowed Germany's mass crimes of the time to become a worldwide ethical challenge.

The universalization of Holocaust commemoration actually appears to have led to the establishment of mass Nazi crimes as a global *lieu de mémoire*. Paradoxically, however, this very universalization has by no means resulted in worldwide recognition of the singularity of the genocide against Jewry. Quite the contrary. Through the symbolic forms of the confession of guilt and apology, and moreover the very practical attempts to compensate for the crimes with restitution and reparation payments, the Holocaust has become a worldwide starting point and model, but also at the same time a competitor for other historical and present mass crimes, in the hope of recognition and "redress," or where appropriate, intervention. In Europe, it is above all the Stalinist crimes and Communist rule in Eastern Europe after 1945 that compete with the Holocaust for public attention and symbolic recognition. Outside of Europe it is the violent history of European colonialism with its exploitation, slavery, genocides, and their long-lasting consequences—a European heritage that in Europe itself, one has to remember, has still not been adequately processed and is, moreover, almost completely ignored in the public consciousness.

So how do things stand now in the year 2020, 75 years after the end of the war, with the present and above all the future of history? Despite the global recognition, it is by no means self-evident that people will continue to gather each year on the 27th of January, invite historians, and confront the story of the Holocaust. For this they deserve gratitude and respect. After all, we would like to see the memory of the Holocaust firmly established and institutionalized, that it be shifted from society's fringes to its heart. But how do we prevent commemoration of the Holocaust from becoming mere ritual and routine, commemoration with no sting, along with institutionalized days of remembrance and official commemorative ceremonies? When everybody mouths a few ready-made phrases: "Never again!," "Never forget!," "Those who cannot remember the past are condemned to repeat it," when people speak of "dark times," and "the unthinkable," only so as to spare our imaginations from the details, even before we have remotely confronted ourselves with what we simply know. Victims' stories are told, and rightly so, because their stories must not be forgotten—not only their suffering, but also their lives before and possibly after. But the naming of perpetrators, beneficiaries, and responsible parties will continue to be avoided in many contexts, as will the mention of continuities beyond the supposed "Zero Hour."

After three decades of truly intensive research and at least two decades of intensive cultivation of memory, we are faced with the fact that people know less and less about the historical events and circumstances. The former concentration and extermination camp Auschwitz has become a mass tourism magnet, with more than two million visitors from around the world each year. Naturally it is a good thing that lots of people see the memorial; that's what we always wanted. Yet I ask myself what the people who take selfies in front of crematoria and gas chambers might be thinking of, or those who have themselves photographed leaping towards the formerly electrified barbed wire fence. Or those who buy the refrigerator magnets picturing the Birkenau gatehouse to take home. Institutionalization has brought with it normalization and banalization. Perhaps that should not surprise us, inasmuch as the global upswing in Holocaust commemoration has been primed by popular culture, by the American TV miniseries *Holocaust* (1979), for example, and Steven Spielberg's *Schindler's List* (1993).

Meanwhile, not only polls, but also election results in Europe and the rest of the world show us that populism, extremism, and authoritarianism are again on the rise. Liberal democracy has largely lost its luster as an ideal. Not only are antisemitism and racism increasingly being voiced; they are increasingly inciting violence. Human rights are being called into question. Have we completely failed, as historians, as teachers, as public intellectuals, as politicians? At least we see in this the lessons from the Holocaust—for example, in the manifesto *For a Vital Memory Culture in Styria* we read: ""Defend democracy and human rights against all attacks; stand up against radicalism, violence, racism, antisemitism, and xenophobia and for an open, liberal, and tolerant society."[4] Of course, what this means in detail is by no means so easy to say, or is today largely disputed. There is virtually no understanding of racism in Europe, in any case, as the annual debates about the Epiphany Singers have once again made clear. The recent attempt to use the memory of the Holocaust for nationalist, racist, and anti-immigrant exclusionary policies is especially disturbing.

If we seriously want to fight the resurgence of antisemitism, we should be clear about the fact that a growing atmosphere of xenophobia, racism, and populism has the potential of turning into antisemitism at any time. It is obscene, and shows a lack of knowledge of history, to talk about Holocaust memory and at the same time to call for borders to be closed against refugees. Two reminders of this from the history of the Holocaust are: the Evian Conference of 1938 and the odyssey of the MS *St. Louis* in 1939.

Of course, there are far too many wholly unsuitable comparisons and too many attempts to use the memory of the Holocaust inappropriately. Evoking the memory of the Holocaust today when people are being marginalized, stigmatized, segregated, displaced, and persecuted, when they are being herded into camps or in flight, should not be rashly branded as an inadmissible trivialization of the historical event and delegitimized—as is frequently the case so as to protect the memory of the Holocaust, as it is said. I feel that here too it is a matter of a misunderstanding: precisely what the Holocaust

4
Für eine lebendige Erinnerungskultur in der Steiermark, Graz 2017, URL: <https://www.erinnern.at/bundeslaender/steiermark/artikel/201elebendige-erinnerungskultur-in-der-steiermarkk201c-3in3-n3u3-gedenkinitiative-in-der-steiermark> (accessed July 31, 2020).

teaches us is to be vigilant. And we should have understood that it ended in Auschwitz, to be sure, but also that it did not begin there. Keeping the memory of the Holocaust alive can only mean solidarity on a global scale, along with championing of human rights and liberal democracies and a standing up against antisemitism, racism, radicalism, and violence. Advocating an open, liberal, and tolerant society can only mean recognizing without reserve the plurality and diversity of present-day society, which is still frequently denied or rejected. And finally, the Holocaust can never be an argument for depreciating or questioning the suffering of others, past or present.

We are now very far removed in time from the historical event, and increasing numbers of people are living among us who have no familial associations with this history, yet many have other experiences of war and violence. Ultimately we must all ask ourselves time and again: "What does that have to do with me?" if we want to keep the memory of the Holocaust alive—in commemorative events, in school classrooms, in university seminars, but also in society in general. No one claims that this is a simple question. There will be different answers, and they will change over time. But whether the memory of the Holocaust plays a role in our society in the future will depend on how seriously we all engage with this question.

Permit me in closing to let a Holocaust survivor, an Auschwitz survivor, have a chance to speak. In his 1975 novel *Fatelessness* the subsequent Nobel Prize winner Imre Kertész describes the archetypal post-Nazi confrontation between those who experienced and survived the horrors of the Holocaust and so-called bystanders, or observers. The narrator, the young György, having returned to Budapest from Auschwitz and Buchenwald, is sitting in the apartment of his former neighbors. The apartment belonging to his father, who has died in a labor camp, has been expropriated. "'Before all else,' [the neighbor, Herr Steiner] declared, 'you must put the horrors behind you.' Increasingly amazed, I asked, 'Why should I?' 'In order,' he replied, 'to be able to live,' at which Uncle Fleischmann nodded and added, 'One cannot start a new life under such a burden,' and I had to admit he did have a point. Except I didn't quite understand how they could wish for something that was impossible, and indeed I made the comment that what had happened had happened, and anyway, when it came down to it, I could not give orders to my memory. I would only be able to start a new life, I ventured, if I were to be reborn or if some affliction, disease, or something of the sort were to affect my mind, which they surely didn't wish on me, I hoped."

The conversation takes its course. Communication between those who were in Auschwitz and those who only observed, but thought of themselves as the "real" victims of the war, is not easy. Finally, György accuses the neighbor of having said goodbye to his father when he was taken off to a work camp, but otherwise having done nothing.

"'What!,' he bawled, his face red as a beetroot and beating his chest with his fist: 'So it's us who're the guilty ones, is it? Us, the victims!' I tried explaining that it wasn't a crime; all that was needed was to admit it, meekly, simply, merely as a matter of reason, a point of honor, if I might put it that way. It was impossible, they must try and understand, impossible to take everything away from me, impossible for me to be neither winner nor loser, for me not to be right and for me not to be mistaken that I was neither the cause nor the effect of anything; they should try to see, I almost pleaded, that I could not swallow that idiotic bitterness, that I should merely be innocent. But I could see that he did not wish to understand anything,…"[5]

Today, 75 years after the liberation of Auschwitz, what we should attempt above all is to understand something, "meekly, simply, merely as a matter of reason." This is not as simple as it sounds, to be sure—quite the contrary. But it continues to be the enduring challenge to a memory culture that does not wish to congeal into routine, ritual, and dismay.

5
Imre Kertész, *Fatelessness*, trans. Tim Wilkinson, New York: Vintage Books 2004, pp. 256f.

Ydessa Hendeles, *The Steeple and The People*, 2018 | Installation view, *Tell me about ~~yesterday~~ tomorrow*

Harald Pickert, *Die Pestbeulen Europas. Naziterror in Konzentrationslagern (The Plague-Spots of Europe. Nazi Terror in Concentration Camps),*
1939–45, n.d. | Installation view, *Tell me about ~~yesterday~~ tomorrow*

Sem
Works

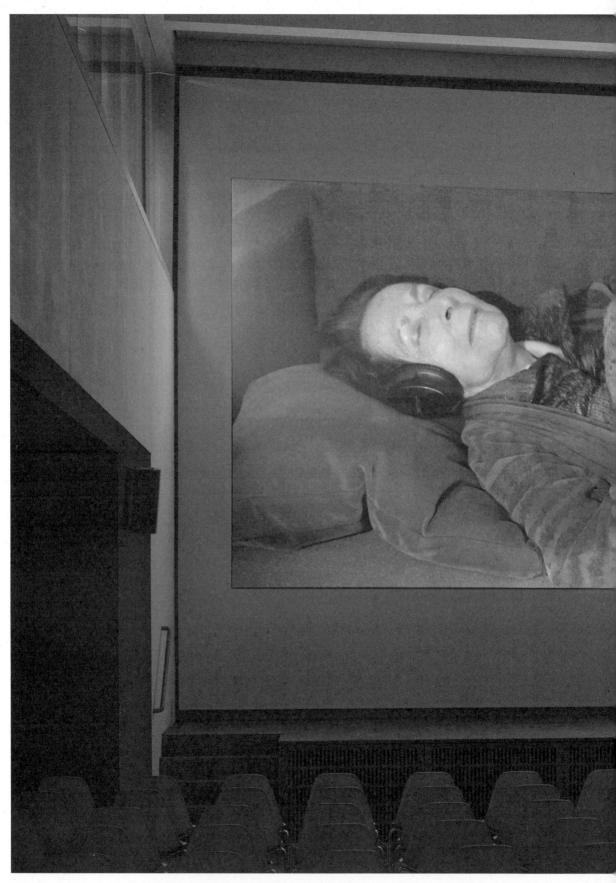

Keren Cytter, *Fashions*, 2019 | Installation view, *Tell me about ~~yesterday~~ tomorrow*

Learning to Learn from History

Until the Second World War, remembering the past in Europe only served to glorify the nation, stir up revanchism, and sanctify heroes. After 1945, the trauma of war, totalitarism, and the Holocaust gave rise to a new ambition: that of learning from history. But has this succeeded?

The 75th anniversary of the end of the Second World War has coincided with a global health crisis that is putting Europe to the test. Reactions to the first wave of the Corona pandemic have demonstrated that we have at least learned a fundamental lesson from the twentieth century : that (?) when man ceases to be humane, he destroys himself.

At a time when people are being reduced to algorithms, consumers, and users and are thought to be identical and interchangeable, the majority of us have affirmed that every person is unique, and irreplaceable, with a basic right to life and a sound body. We have clearly and unambiguously rejected the concepts of natural selection and utilitarianism, which accept that a minority can be sacrificed for the so-called common good. Most of us have agreed that Man does not have the right to decide over life and death, or to compare the value of one life with that of another— even if it is marked by age or illness.

The solidarity of younger generations against older ones and the solidarity—at first somewhat hesitant—between European countries how that in times of crisis we are capable of letting our actions be governed by humanistic ideals. The pandemic has reminded us that our humanity not only lends meaning to life, but that it is prerequisite to our common survival.

This insight had proved to be valid already in the past, but it is nevertheless being threatened. The increasing power of antidemocratic authoritarian figures who propagate lies and conspiracy theories in combination with the development of technological means for mass surveillance threatens to undermine the very promise on which Europe is based: Never again! To preserve and strengthen what we have learned from history, it is not enough to simply mouth these words. We now, in the third generation since the war, need a different way of dealing with the past in order to continue to learn from it.

Now that the last eyewitnesses are dying, how can we pass along a memory that is one no longer?

In order that in future we shall be able to imagine what war, dictatorship, and crimes against humanity mean, it is first of all necessary to preserve the material traces of the past: historical documents, written or recorded testimony, artifacts, sites, buildings, photos, and films.

Fiction and art can also serve this end, although there is a danger of a kind of virtualization of history, so that fiction takes the place of facts, and the war appears only as an exciting Netflix series. Artistic treatment, moreover, runs the risk of simplifying history, or even—more or less willfully—revising it. For example, the neo-realistic Italian cinema of the postwar period, with films like *Roma città aperta* (*Rome, Open City*) or *Paisà* (*Paisan*) by Roberto Rossellini, was guilty of precisely this mistake. It portrayed the Italian populace as mere victims of Fascism, although the majority had supported Mussolini's criminal policies. Perhaps the directors Luchino Visconti, Vittorio De Sica, and Roberto Rossellini were in an unfavorable position from which to judge the situation correctly, inasmuch as they themselves had worked under Fascism with the Duce's son, Vittorio Mussolini, who at the time had a great influence on film production.

Monuments and memorial ceremonies are still an indispensable component of the culture or remembrance. They provide us with the feeling of being part of a whole, of belonging to a community of values based on a similar interpretation of the past. However, this collective memory functions only if all have a common historical background, one that makes it possible for them to understand symbols and references. Otherwise the monuments, sculptures, plaques, and memorials remain only empty shells.

So that citizens can identify with this increasingly distant heritage in future as well, they have to not only understand it, but also feel that it affects them. An emotional tie between them and this past can be established through family memory. An anonymous and generalized history thus becomes something special and private: it becomes part of the family. Life is infused into the abstract past through the history of one's own ancestors, whose faces and names we know. Perhaps many will then ask: What does it mean that my grandparents and great-grandparents made mistakes, or suffered and made sacrifices, if I fail to learn anything from it?

In Germany, the culture of remembrance was borne for a long time by a generation that felt guilty owing to the crimes committed by their parents. This sense of guilt had one positive effect: the anchoring of a deep consciousness of one's own democratic obligations in society. This produced one of the strongest democracies in the world.

In order to preserve and strengthen this achievement, we must continually pass along the memory of our own fallibility, our potential blindness, opportunism and indifference in front of demagogues and manipulators of hatred and lies. But a change in perspective is required: facing up the shadows of history shouldn't be done in a culture of guilt, which is discouraging, but rather in a culture of responsibility. We need a memory that frees us and makes us wiser. Young people seek inspiration. They can draw this from the more recent history of the Federal Republic, from the transformation of a society that questioned itself and managed/ succeeded to create a state of peace and freedom. It took the courage of countless Germans to force society to confront its historical shadows and establish democracy. This change is a part of German history that reminds us that man is not powerless.

* * *

Changing perspectives—and this is also true of other European countries which adopted either the role of victim or that of heroes and martyrs. In countries occupied by the German Reich like Belgium, France, and the Netherlands, memory was distorted by two myths in the decades after the war: first, that the majority of the populace engaged more or less actively in resistance, second, that the authorities had no choice but to submit to the dictates of the National Socialists. The first myth collapsed sooner than the second. Only in 1995 did France apologize for the active and voluntary collaboration of the French state in Nazi crimes, whereas The Dutch State waited until January 2020 before apologizing to the Jewish community for its indifference and fateful misjudgments during the war, which had led to the deportation of 75 percent of the Jews in the Netherlands.

Even such important allies and accomplices of the German Reich as Italy and Austria have taken on the perspective of perpetrators either not at all or only very late. In April 1945, Austria's Second Republic hastily anchored its status as victim of the German Reich in its founding document. It was only in 1991 that the then chancellor Franz Vranitzky recognized Austria's "shared responsibility."

In Italy, the anti-Fascist parties that established the republic in 1946 portrayed the Italian resistance as greater than it was, and minimized the crimes of the Fascists in order to avoid providing a negative image of the country during the peace negotiations. For their part, the allies did not wish for the equivalent of the Nuremberg Trials, for they feared that this would benefit the Communist Party, which was already very powerful in Italy. So the country was given carte blanche to grant mass amnesty. Virtually none of the high-ranking Fascist leaders and criminals were put on trial, and no one was extradited to another country, even though Italy had committed any number of atrocities in the Balkans and in Africa. There are virtually no memorials or museums honoring the victims of those massacres or recalling that Italy built hundreds of concentration camps.

* * *

Eastern Europe is a special case. During the Soviet period, "big brother" Russia forced East European countries to commemorate the "heroism" of the Red Army, which they actually hated. Countries allied to Nazi Germany—Hungary, Slovakia, Romania, Bulgaria, and Croatia—or that had hoped for a German victory over Russia, like the Balkan states and the Ukraine, were forced to identify with the Soviet camp and thus to accept the perspective of heroic martyrdom. Even the German Democratic Republic was founded on the myth that it was the land of Germany's Communists, who had fought against the Nazis on the side of the Soviet Union. While this may have been true of its leaders, the majority of the populace had been "followers" of National Socialism. Constant commemorations were meant to inject the people with anti-Fascism. So whereas the West ultimately accepted its culpability, the East persisted in placing itself on the side of the Communist victims—and allowed the Shoah to disappear under the cloak of silence.

The fall of the Wall and the exposure of countless collaborations from which the National Socialists had profited in Europe made it possible to question the binary notion of "victim countries" versus "perpetrator countries." One after another, almost all the countries in Europe confessed that they were also to blame. This prepared the way for the idea of a common European memory centered on the Holocaust—a crime committed in all of Europe—and was fundamentally responsible for the development of the European Union's canon of values. It was in this sense that the European Union followed the United Nations initiative in 2005 and declared January 27, the day the Auschwitz concentration camp was liberated, to be a European day of commemoration. In a resolution the European Parliament emphatically urged "member states… to intensify their fight against anti-Semitism and racism, so as to raise in young people, especially, an awareness of history and the lessons of the Holocaust."[1] Commitment to this guideline became a condition for entrance in the European Union. In all of Europe, even in the countries of the East, Holocaust memorials and museums followed.

1
European Parliament, resolution of the European Parliament on remembrance of the Holocaust and on ant-Semitism and racism, P6_TA (2005)0018, <https://www.europarl.europa.eu/sides/getDoc.do?pubRef=-//EP//TEXT+TA+20050127+ITEMS+DOC+X<:+V0//DE#sdocta6> (accessed August 17, 2020).

* * *

Fifteen years later, however, we have to recognize that this requirement has not accomplished what was intended. In a number of countries a more intense racism and anti-Semitism is raging, spread by populist parties and conspiracy theories circulating on social networks. In Poland and Hungary it is already completely unchecked, and enjoys virtually institutional status.

For one thing, it is obvious that the enforcement of a culture of remembrance can be counterproductive, especially in the Eastern European countries, which were traumatized by Soviet commemoration decrees. In addition, the imposition of one traumatic memory as an absolute reference runs the risk of destroying another one, for example that of Communism or colonialism.

On the other hand, a state's admission of guilt and the erection of memorials have not often resulted a recognition on the part of its populace of its own historic responsibility. Many have presumably come to feel sympathy for the victims of the Holocaust and loathing for the "monsters" and high-ranking perpetrators, but fail to recognize that such crimes could not have been perpetrated on such a scale without the more or less active complicity of the people. Yet this recognition is of central importance, for it raises the question: What would I have done, and what would I do today? It sends us back to our own present-day responsibilities and our own contradictions; it helps us become aware that each of us can become, or already is, complicit in an injust or criminal system. However, it is altogether more comforting to see oneself as a victim or martyr than as a "perpetrator" or "follower." Populists and extremists have understood this, and they promote the cult of victimhood in order to mislead their voters. By relieving citizens from all suspicion of wrongdoing and all responsibility, they weaken democracy.

A European memory should not lead to an enforced commemoration, but rather make it possible for people to change perspective, to place themselves in both the position of the victim and the perpetrator, to accept a different society's view of their own history—to question themselves and engage in dialogue. As for content, Europe should also make room for other memories in addition to the memory of the Holocaust. A lack of interest in Western Europe for the Communist experience of Eastern Europeans is a major obstacle to East-West rapprochement. And the absence of an objective, not state-run engagement with the Communist past in Eastern Europe weakens democracy there.

Another past, long thrust aside, is now reemerging: colonial history. It is the main link between native Europeans and population groups with a background of migration. If we want to live together in solidarity, this too has to become part of the European memory. If Europe wishes to have a normative influence in the world, if it wishes to assert its model of an open and democratic society as opposed to authoritarian models, the former colonial powers must finally face their historical responsibility.

How many countries in Europe still shy away from coming to terms with the past? It reveals a profound misunderstanding of how important this process is for the democratic maturation of a country and the preservation of peace. Facing up to the shasows of history is not a moral accessory to look good. It helps us to shape the future together and understand the world instead of suffer it. It helps us to identify dangers – those that come from others, but, above all, those that come from ourselves. It helps us to better learn from history.

Ayzit Bostan, *TELL ME EVERYTHING*, 2019 | Installation view, *Tell me about yesterday tomorrow*

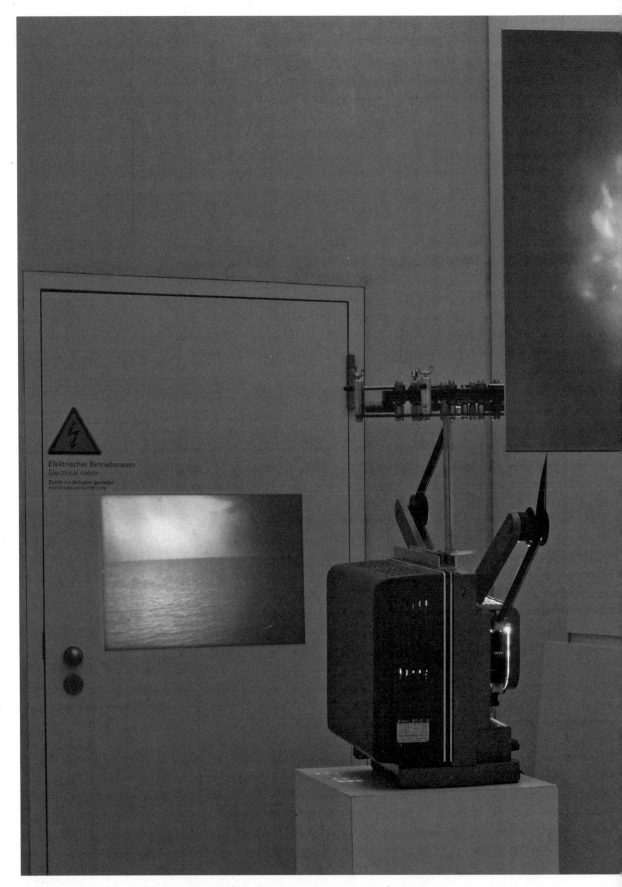

Sirah Foighel Brutman & Eitan Efrat, *Habits*, 2019 | Installation view, *Tell me about ~~yesterday~~ tomorrow*

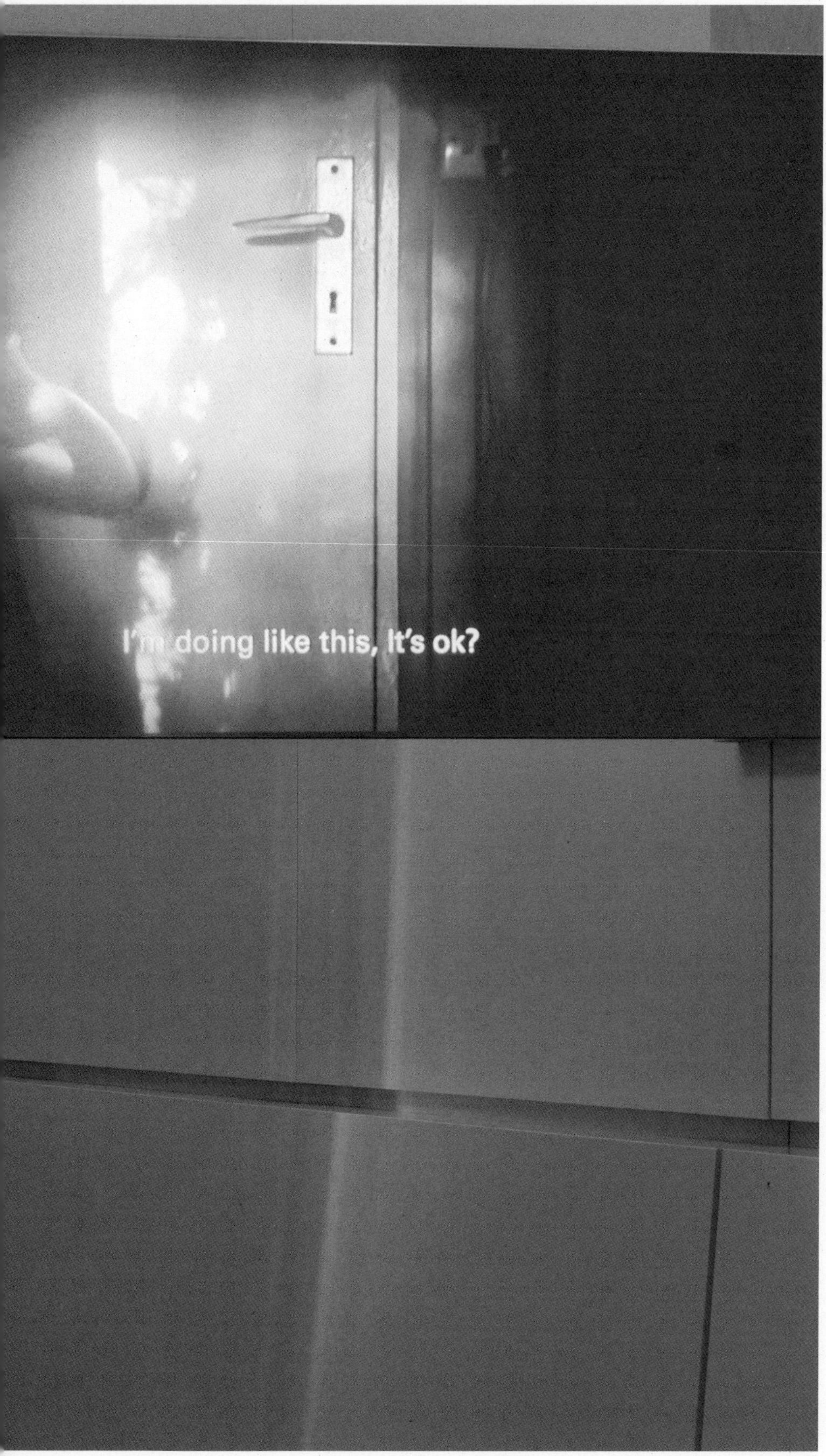
I'm doing like this, It's ok?

Joanna Piotrowska, *Enclosure XLII*, 2019 | Installation view, *Tell me about ~~yesterday~~ tomorrow*

*Tell me
about
yesterday
tomorrow*

of return

Pumbaa, with you, everything's gas.
— THE LION KING

MAX CZOLLEK

I.

kilometers of surface breathed onto the canvas.
you carry the radio through the apartment until
static sets in. suitcase drawn out from beneath the bed,
leaned on the dusty frontier of a beam of light

someone's lived here before. it takes hours
to wipe his outlook off the windows. a sky
lined by airplanes. endless lists of crossed out
things. you hope someone writes along

there are examples for everyone, as many
as fit in your pants pocket. forgotten birthday,
abandoned station. you place the cup at the
window for someone who will wash your hands

you step outside, looking first to find the place where
it burns brightest. sustaining more soldiers in your mind
than a power line. advantage disturbance: you break
into your parents' museum

trees lined in chalk, whispers in the pipes,
brass engraved beneath your feet: are those
organ pedals, stops you walk across,
volume you increase, see what's happening?

take this soap. it can wash everything
except itself. berlin suburbs, end stations
in munich, daily journeys across your skin.
hair you sell for a ticket

do you see the garden gnomes with tiki torches? they've come to betray you. their kidney-stone-sized fists encircle the inner cities. your legs running toward the railway embankment by chance

along the road you stick your hands into the cellars under new-built buildings. your own coat enveloping you from all sides in its shadow, people with their overfilled eye compartments, mouths overgrown tracks

you stand at the platform and the schedules grow like nettle plants. sure that you are breaking an unknown rule. write yourself a warning: the hair, the hand, the soap. wait for the floodlight

II.

one foot still in the track bed, the conductor pulls the whistle. i can say that this is germany. the country falls down right then left of my imagination. don't panic, there's still enough nothing to go around

what follows is the familiar organization of noise. finally my childhood takes center stage: what if i made up six hundred and thirteen questions and what if i simply stopped?

didn't think loudly enough so voices start whispering in the rat-a-tat of wheels and track. doors sliding, familiar faces dropping by. but today i'll leave no glass, no bench seat unoccupied. will greet no delinquent prophets

oh, hey, i wrote you a tune, my shortened muscle
is traveling. you thought they'd announce the stations:
that there was first class, there was second class,
there was the wagon for cow people

in the sick bay, women devouring children, surgeons
acting like they are on frontline duty with heavy artillery.
penetrated route, corrected border line, pronouns
pushing themselves down and around

the thought of the journey's end forces an
undertone from my throat. i seek a smile
in piles of incisor teeth. from the pipes rises
the smell of carrion flowers, flickers our
mothers' love

the garden gnomes rise to their feet shaking themselves off,
illuminate the photos from my suitcase. i was taught
to use gasoline like soap, rules for the rule,
no lighter at the fireplace

this compulsion to turn every journey into an exile.
when it's burning behind the picket fences, i wish i were
under firs. yesterday the woods were still clever enough
to hide in museums. today my new homeland's
called mitropa

when they try to wake me, i pretend to sleep.
when i pretend to sleep, i dream: there were rocks
heavy as dumbbells you removed from my eyes.
it would require sufficient authority to say "love"

III.

yes, love! when we think of germany, the markish sand, think of the moors or cast iron, to hum: *the risen moon is beaming, little golden stars are gleaming, in heavens bright and clear.* stars are yellow and have six points, DAMNIT, the stars are distant clouds of: gas, DAMNIT

we hum: *the woods stand still and hold their silence, and from the meadows rises white mist wonderfully.* the woods, the friendly closemouthed german woods and their unparalleled diversity: birchwald, oakwald, buchenwald, DAMNIT from the meadows rises mist, wonderfully white smoke, DAMNIT

ear to the tracks one time too long, and the fir trees start burning. on the rails before us the forest is consumed by smoke. climbs into the cellars, dusts off cushions, lonely thoughts: what's the deal with the boredom, this german amnesia?

one or two strikes with a metal rod suffice to forget the whole story. what more do our fists know of their fathers than what they destroy? sleeping booby trap beneath a moon with open helm

and so we squat in transit and raise our heads out from among the cargo trucks. actually we still have nothing in our hands but an album of white photographs. reminders of the things we did not live ourselves

so how does one differentiate between
a weapon and a tool? magazines full of
children, supervised areas, overgrowing mouth.
we shoot to kill our unknown ancestors, fold
the day together roughly, dunk hands into
warm cider

that exists, and the seasons exist, say: there
are the burn piles, the witches in children's games,
there's the hunchbacked, hook-nosed rumpelstiltskin.
words like train tracks, *buchen*, soap. messianic
weather out the window

we should console ourselves with that. salvation
leads to the pasture, lord, out upon your sleeping
moors. your lambs hang like discarded dresses
over the baptismal font, drink an ocean from the
map, awaken at the other end

Original text taken from Max Czollek, *Jubeljahre*, Berlin (Verlagshaus Berlin) 2005.
The text is an adaptation of sections of the collectively authored text *Das war Absicht* (G13, SuKuLTuR 2013).

Sebastian Jung, *Besorgte Bürger, Zeichnungen (Worried Citizens, drawings)*, 2018 | Installation view, *Tell me about ~~yesterday~~ tomorrow*

05

1919-1923

Rechtsextremismus:
rassistisch, völkisch,
friedensunfähig
Right-Wing Extremism:
Racist, Ethnic-Chauvinist,
Bellicose

Nationalsozialistische Deutsche Arbeiter-Partei

Heute   Freitag den 20. April 1923   Heute
findet die vierte der großen

Riesenversammlungen
im
Zirkusgebäude auf dem Marsfelde
statt.

Es wird sprechen unser Führer Pg

Adolf Hitler
über:

„Politik u. Rasse"

Warum sind wir
Antisemiten?

Beginn der Versammlung 8 Uhr abds.   Eintritt 100 Mk.   Kriegsbeschädigte frei.   Juden haben keinen Zutritt

Einberufer: Für die Parteileitung. A. Drexler

SIMPLICISSIMUS

Ydessa Hendeles, *The Steeple and The People*, 2018 | Installation view, *Tell me about ~~yesterday~~ tomorrow*

On Memory and Justice:
Why Personal Stories Matter

"I do not want my children to believe that my husband is a war criminal."– Charlotte Wächter, 1977

In the 1960s, my brother and I often visited our grandparents in Paris, near the Gare du Nord. As children, we understood that the past was painful, that we should not ask questions. Their apartment was a place of silences, one haunted by secrets. They only really began to be addressed when I was in my 50s as the consequence of an invitation to deliver a lecture in Lviv, in Ukraine. Come talk about your work on crimes against humanity and genocide, it said. I went to Lviv, and one thing led to another. I found the house where my grandfather Leon was born in 1904. I learned of the terrible events that occurred there, unleashed with a speech delivered by Hans Frank, governor-general of Nazi-occupied Poland, on a warm day in August 1942. His words exterminated my grandfather's family, and hundreds of thousands of other families. Four years later, the speech-giver was hanged in the courtyard of Nuremberg's Palace of Justice, for crimes against humanity. A year after going to Lviv, I met Frank's son Niklas, a fine journalist who despised his father. It was he who introduced me to Horst Arthur Wächter, the son of Otto Wächter, an Austrian, the governor of Krakow and later of Galicia, based in Lviv. Wächter, the father, was indicted for mass murder but never caught. He died in Rome in 1949, in unexpected circumstances. In due course I would learn all about the virus that was said to have killed him. "You will like Horst", Niklas tells me, "although he is different from me: he loves his father." In the spring of 2012 I made the first of many visits to Horst, to the dilapidated twelfth-century castle in the village of Hagenberg, north of Vienna. Horst, who is in his early 70s, is genial and chatty, dressed in a pink shirt and Birkenstocks. We talk, we eat, we drink. He speaks of his parents' Nazi beliefs, his love for his mother Charlotte ("a Nazi until the day she died," Horst's wife, Jacqueline, whispers), and a childhood of plenty ("I was a Nazi child," he says with a smile, named in honor of the *Horst Wessel Song* (the National Socialist Party anthem) and Arthur Seyss-Inquart, who ran Austria after the Anschluss and was Horst's godfather). He can't say he loves Otto, he explains. "I hardly knew him, but it's my duty as a son to find the good in my father."

Horst shares albums filled with black-and-white photos from the 1930s and 40s, images of family holidays on lake or mountain interspersed with the occasional swastika, a picture of Hitler, a haunting photograph of a child in the Warsaw ghetto. The scrapbook tells me that the Wächters sat at the top Nazi table. There is apparently an extensive collection of diaries and letters filled with Charlotte's handwritten reminiscences. These I will only see much later. I leave on that first visit intrigued by Horst and his papers. I like him, as Niklas predicted.

A year passes. I write a profile of Horst and start work on *East West Street*, which catalyzes a commission for a BBC documentary. Filming in the archives of Lviv, Niklas wonders aloud whether Horst is a "new Nazi" (an accusation he later retracts). This upsets Horst, who wants to counter the claim. "Be open," I suggest, making it clear that I do not think of him as a Nazi. I've seen a few pages from his mother's diary, and one or two letters, but nothing more from the family archive. "Give all the materials to a museum, so others can review it." It seems to be a unique collection, tracing the life of a leading Nazi couple from their meeting in 1929 to Otto's death, two decades later. Horst offers the material to the US Holocaust Memorial Museum in Washington DC, where it is digitised and made public. Would I like a set? A few days later, a USB stick drops through my letterbox: 13 gigabytes of digital images, 8,677 pages of letters, postcards, diaries, photographs, news clippings, and official documents.

The collection includes Charlotte's *Erinnerungen* (*Memoir*), written for Horst and the couple's five other children, reminiscences grouped by time: 1938–1942, 1942–1945, etc. There are also *Tonbänder*, sound recordings, 14 old cassette tapes, digitised, allowing me to hear Charlotte's German cadence, methodical and rhythmic, high-pitched, anxious and, I feel, not warm. *Conversation with Melitta Wiedemann*, she labelled a 1977 tape, recorded at the Four Seasons Hotel in Munich. Glasses are clinked, toasts offered, views expressed. A "real personality," Charlotte exclaims of Oswald Mosley. "I was an enthusiastic Nazi," she adds. "So was I," Frau Wiedemann replies. "Still am." "Great times," Charlotte says. "Hitler was our savior." Maybe the material will offer answers to the questions that arise, as I immerse myself in Governor Wächter's nefarious work in Krakow and Lemberg [present-day Lviv], and his apparent role in heaping misery on my grandfather's family, and on so many others. What exactly did he do? Why did he travel to Rome, and what caused him to die there, at just 48 years old? How much did Charlotte know, and what support did she provide? What kind of relationship did they have?

"The Jews are being deported in increasing numbers, and it's hard to get powder for the tennis court."– Otto Wächter, August 1942

The material is voluminous, and mostly handwritten. It lingers for several weeks, until my colleague, the historian Lisa Jardine, intercedes. She has recently delivered an inaugural lecture at University College London, *Temptation in the Archives*. How do you assess archival material of a personal nature? What is the historical value of personal documents?

Brilliant Lisa, who has terminal cancer, nevertheless summons me and a few of my friends to her flat in the shadow of the British Museum. Bring documents, she instructs. Lisa gravitates towards the personal correspondence and diaries. She is struck by the sheer number of letters written in the last months of Otto's life, while he was on the run. "Why would a husband and wife write to each other so often, at such length and detail?" she asks. "Because they loved each other?" I venture.

Lisa is ahead of us. "No, there's more there, sharing things they don't want others to see." Focus on the last year of Otto's life, she advises, and the nature of Charlotte's role. Thus begins a research project over several years, an exploration of what lay between the lines and behind the words. It takes four years, opening unexpected doors. We stumble into a world of escape and espionage, of double dealing and duplicity, of exhumations and reburials, traveling from the Vatican to Syria and South America, into monasteries, over lakes, across mountains, and entering the barely imaginable world of the "ratline"—the escape route used by Nazis to travel from Italy to Argentina and other places. At the heart of the story is a relationship, one that survived, the wife believed, "because our love was without any limits and even went beyond death." Charlotte fascinates and repels. Born into a wealthy family of steelmakers in the small Styrian town of Mürzzuschlag, she was, on her own account, a difficult and rebellious child, intelligent if not intellectual. She enrolled as a student at the Women's Academy and School for Free and Applied Art, developing a fine artistic eye, helped by teachers such as Josef Hoffmann, of the Wiener Werkstätte (a Viennese cooperative of artisans recognised as a pioneer of modern design). A career blossomed, designing fabrics, sold with success in Germany and Britain.

A fine sportswoman, in the spring of 1929 she traveled to the local Schneeberg ski resort, sharing a train compartment with a stranger, a striking young lawyer. "My new 'Baron' was tall, slender, athletic, with delicate features, very beautiful hands," she recorded. "He wore a diamond ring on the little finger of his right hand and had a noble appearance, one that any girl would notice." On April 6 she noted in her diary: "I fell in love with good-looking, cheerful Otto."

They courted for three years before they married. He qualified and became increasingly active in the Austrian chapter of the Nazi party. She supported and encouraged his politics. In the summer of 1934, Otto participated in an unsuccessful coup attempt on the government of Chancellor Engelbert Dollfuß. He fled to Berlin and joined the Sicherheitsdienst, or SD, the intelligence service of the SS, working in the same building as Adolf Eichmann. He entered the orbit of Heinrich Himmler, who became his patron. Charlotte joined him in Berlin in 1936, with Horst's two oldest siblings.

Two years later, in March 1938, Germany seized Austria and they were able to return home. "Every Nazi felt such joy about this miracle," Charlotte recorded. She drove to Vienna to pave the way for her husband's return, a moment of unbridled happiness. "There he was, in the doorway of my parents' flat in Vienna, as a Brigadeführer, in his black SS coat with white lapels and SS uniform," she recalled four decades later. "In spite of the strain and the fatigue, he looked splendid."

They made their way to the Hofburg palace, through crowds overcome with "a spontaneous and heartfelt outburst of joy. Seyss-Inquart and his wife and a number of others came with the Führer, who slowly climbed the stairs of the Hofburg, up to the balcony. He was standing a metre in front of me, and I could see and hear him well." At the bottom of those stairs, after the joy, she told Otto he should accept Seyss-Inquart's offer of a senior job in the new Nazi government, rather than return to the life of a lawyer. The decision changed their lives, as well as those of their children and grandchildren and, it turned out, that of my own family.

Charlotte's diaries pass in silence on the substance of Otto's new position. As a state secretary, his function was to remove Jews and other "undesirables" from public positions, from the federal chancellery to the postal service. He axed thousands of individuals, including his own university teachers. As Otto crossed lines, Charlotte offered unstinting support. She loved the perks, the Mercedes and the cocktail parties, the concerts at the Salzburg Festival and at Bayreuth ("Marvellous," she wrote to Otto, "the Führer is here, eating with H[immler]"). And she appreciated the new homes, freshly emptied and appropriated. In Vienna, they occupied a large villa with its own park (a friend "obtained the Jewess Bettina Mendl's house for us," Charlotte recorded, "along with the china and artworks"). Later, on Lake Zell, they acquired a "small summer house" with 16 hectares, previously owned by Franz Rehrl, the governor of Salzburg, who ended up at Ravensbrück concentration camp.

The arrival of war, in September 1939, propelled Otto's career to even greater heights. Seyss-Inquart procured a new position for Otto, working under Frank as governor of Krakow in western Poland, newly occupied by Germany. Charlotte was fully aware of what he was doing. "There's a lot going on here," Otto wrote in December. "Tomorrow I have to have another 50 Poles publicly shot", a first and notorious act of reprisal killing, on the orders of Hitler. Otto signed off on acts against the city's Jews and Polish intellectuals, then ordered the construction of the Krakow ghetto. I looked for a hint of regret in Charlotte's papers. None was to be found.

Three years later, the Krakow job completed, Charlotte celebrated when Hitler chose her husband to move to Lemberg and "clean up" Distrikt Galicia, recently occupied by Germany. Frank visited in August 1942, lodged with the Wächters, announced the implementation of the "Final Solution," and played and lost a few games of chess with Charlotte. Otto kept her abreast of developments. "There was much to do in Lemberg after you left." The harvest was gathered, Polish workers sent to labor camps ("already 250 000 have been sent from the District!"), and "the current large Jewish operations ("Judenaktionen") implemented. Lots of love, forever," he signed off. "With Hitler – all or nothing." Himmler visited, to check on progress and Otto's commitment to the job. "I was almost embarrassed about how positively he talks about me," Otto reported. On the other hand, manual labor was proving to be difficult to find, as "the Jews are being deported in increasing numbers, and it's hard to get powder for the tennis court." As the deportations and exterminations proceeded, Charlotte spent time with the children on the Schmittenhöhe near Zell am See. There were picnics in solitude, near a pond, with naked dips in the sun. She missed Otto. "We stayed for four hours, on the moss and in the blazing sun, overwhelmed by the sheer extent of nature."

"I hope that the English will be fed up and unite with us."
– Charlotte Wächter, July 1944

Charlotte's papers sometimes refer to a big political event: war, France occupied, Eastern Front difficulties, march of the Red Army, collapse. Throughout, and particularly in her later reminiscences, life with Otto is often presented as an idyll. Lurking below the surface, however, are hints that things are not perfect. In the midst of the tumult and unmentioned mass murder, mundane life continues. Meals are to be cooked, children fed, grandparents tended to. A husband's absence may be a matter of pride (if visiting Herr Himmler) or irritation (if he forgets a daughter's birthday). There is, too, the matter of sex. Otto's looks and power brought ample opportunities, causing Charlotte much unhappiness. Why didn't he take her to Budapest, like lovely

Hans Frank, who took his wife? Charlotte finds ways to get her own back. She terminates a pregnancy. She names their second daughter Traute, after one of her husband's lovers. "That should please you," she tells him.

Digging deeper, Charlotte's diary reveals more. Working as a volunteer nurse at a hospital in Lviv, she records in an English that Otto cannot read that she has lost her heart to a young soldier. And in the spring of 1942, as the Final Solution is being implemented, she falls for Otto's boss, Hans Frank. I send the pages to Niklas. "Sensational!", he responds by mischievous return: perhaps he and Horst are brothers. The letters trace the bitter last weeks of war. At the most acute moments, as the Red Army approaches Lemberg and the end nears, Charlotte and Otto still find time to write to each other, and to hope. Ever the Anglophile, Charlotte imagines a new ally in the struggle against the dreaded Soviets. "I hope that the English will be fed up and unite with us," she writes. There is an impediment, however—the Jews, "always getting involved, contaminating everything." On May 9, 1945, the war is over. Otto is indicted for mass murder and promptly disappears. His name is in the papers, listed as a "wanted war criminal," with Seyss-Inquart, who is caught, put on trial at Nuremberg, convicted and executed. (Seyss-Inquart's photograph hangs near Horst's bed.) To survive, Otto must rely on Charlotte. The tables are turned. A new chapter opens. Evasion and escape require new friends and allies, in the Vatican and beyond. Charlotte's papers provide secret details of Otto's escape: the time spent hiding in the Austrian mountains with a young companion, whom I would come to meet; the manner in which he made his way across the Dolomites from Austria into Italy; the friends and lovers who provided refuge and other forms of assistance and comfort on the way, in Bolzano and other places; and the dramatic arrival and stay in Rome, assisted by senior Vatican figures, including a "very positive… religious gentleman" with connections to the top. There is, too, the matter of what the Americans were doing in the Eternal City, who their new allies were, and what exactly they knew about his whereabouts, and when. The path to the "ratline" comes into view.

"I am so grateful that there are still people today
who … have positive things to say about my husband."
– Charlotte Wächter, 1977

What is it about Horst and his family that captures my imagination? There is no simple answer. I pondered the question a couple of months ago, doing my other job, sitting in the International Court of Justice in The Hague, listening to Aung San Suu Kyi. It could just as easily have been any other leader associated with gross wrongdoing, male or female. She sought to persuade the judges that the Myanmar military's actions against the Rohingya community might be excessive but they were not plausibly genocidal. None of the 17 judges was persuaded. How could she not see the facts as others did? Some who know her believe the reason lies in her relationship with her father, the architect of Burmese independence, founder of the Tatmadaw (Myanmar's armed forces), assassinated six months before independence. As she addressed the court, I thought of Horst and Charlotte.

Love blinds. Over time, it transforms perceptions of reality, and then reality itself. Like me, Horst was born into a family of silences. When the war ended, he—as Charlotte's favorite—was protected, nourished, and loved, and taught that his father was a fine and decent man. "I am so grateful that there are still people today who… have positive things to say about my husband," his mother told Melitta Wiedemann. "I do not want my children to believe that he is a war criminal who murdered hundreds of Jews." Horst doesn't want to believe it either, even if he knows the facts point elsewhere. Together, he and I have stood before a site of mass murder, near Lviv. There, the pain on his face is plain. He does not deny what happened, or his father's connection to the horrors, or his mother's support of them. He just wants to characterize them differently, as Charlotte did. It's a way of being able to live, a means of survival. I cannot share Horst's characterization of the facts, yet I feel an affection for him, and respect his open spirit, his willingness to engage in this project, to respond to suggestions that the looted objects his mother passed on to him should be returned to their rightful owners (we are still working on the china from Villa Mendl, which the owner's daughter, who lives in Australia, has asked for). I feel, too, anxiety for the price he has paid for sharing these personal papers, cutting himself off from much of the rest of his family.

Horst and I are bonded by a sense of dislocation, and to events distant in time and place. Our points of departure were different, opposite sides of a shared story, yet our paths crossed and we arrive at an endpoint. It's a curious waltz, a constant movement, a double act in which each seeks to lead and persuade the other. What emerges are secrets—and questions of lies, justice, and love.

Willem de Rooij, *Proposal towards the Memorialization of 'Asoziale' and 'Berufsverbrecher'*, 2019
Installation view, *Tell me about ~~yesterday~~ tomorrow*

Exterior view of the Munich Documentation Centre for the History of National Socialism, *Tell me about yesterday tomorrow*

Shared Memories

*"How do I integrate myself into a country with an
unresolved history of violence? Is the history never spoken of,
the suppressed history, also my history? Does my new identity
also include the Nazi grandpa next door? What does it mean
for me to visit a Holocaust memorial when, for example,
the reason for my being in a German-speaking country was
a poison gas attack by the regime in my original homeland?"*[1]

After the great influx of refugees in 2015, right-wing and conservative parties in Austria, as elsewhere in Europe, repeatedly demanded
that immigrants and asylum seekers engage with the history of the
Holocaust as a way of proving their "integration willingness" and of
thwarting possible—allegedly specifically Muslim—antisemitic feelings. These demands were often probably not so much the concern
openly expressed as populist self-justification.

But how can proofs of the acceptance of a "foreign history" actually function? Memorials and museums have made sincere efforts
to develop educational programs, tours, and workshops specifically
for visitors with a background of migration. The pedagogues' understanding has broadened in the process: even people without
a history of migration frequently experience the history of National
Socialism as "foreign history," and require bridges connecting their
own experience to the historical one before they are able to grasp
and fully register it.

***

It is difficult to relate historical crimes against humanity committed by
the National Socialists with present-day crimes in various regions of
the world, some of which are currently leading to massive movements
of refugees. Memory of the Holocaust should not be diminished or
altered by comparison to and association with other historical or present-day events. That memory should be preserved in a form associated
as intimately as possible with the first, directly affected generation of
witnesses/survivors. A largely forensic approach to that dark history
has led to the fact that the years of National Socialism and its crimes
have become perhaps the best-documented period in global history.
Thousands of oral history interviews, countless papers belonging to
witnesses to that time are preserved in archives. At the moment it is
still an open question whether the fear that the demise of the last witnesses might lead to a change in the historical record will prove true.
Yet it is clear that there is a desire to inscribe a very specific historical
event indelibly in the world's history—out of respect for the millions

1
These were the opening
questions for a work-
shop in the project
Meine Schwarze Milch
(My Black Milk) by
Alexander Martos and
Niko Wahl, Vienna
2018. The project
concept envisioned
an extensive series of
workshops as well as
a final presentation, in
the framework of which
asylum seekers would
give native Austrians
an introduction to the
Holocaust. The project
was not realized owing
to difficult financial
considerations.

of victims and in the hope of preventing future human catastrophes of such magnitude.

Active engagement with the history of the Holocaust could moreover represent something like a guide to dealing with other crimes against humanity. How does one commemorate the victims of the Armenian genocide, the victims of the Cambodian regime, the genocide in Rwanda, the crimes in Yugoslavia's civil war? How do we talk about historical victims of racism, of colonialism? Can the commemorative tradition in which our social memory of the Holocaust manifests itself, often seemingly sacred, serve as a way to understand and identify with other societies worldwide?

In a global society, "world memory" would at first appear to be a logical construct. On closer consideration, however, memory proves to be primarily a national, regional, local, or otherwise group-specific construct, not a global phenomenon. Memory is frequently seen to be the group's "own," set apart from the historical narratives of other given groups. Access to "others" in one's "own" realm of memory and self-identification is difficult, often avoided, and when accomplished it is frequently met with massive criticism and occasionally even understood as a form of "cultural appropriation."

Fragmented memory is also an indication of a fragmented society. In countless places in Austria, for example, there are warriors' memorials commemorating local men who fell in the Second World War, their deaths explained as "in defense of the fatherland," even though they fell in Russia wearing German uniforms. In immediate proximity to these are commemorative plaques and memorials to concentration camp victims, to resistance fighters, even for deserters from the struggle "for the fatherland." Common to such memorials is that they are limited to clearly defined groups and societies. It is something like a policy of memory coexistence, the paradoxical nature of which is only rarely clearly revealed. A recent exception were two commemorative acts, scarcely registered by the public, by Croatia's ambassador to Austria, who in May 2020 laid wreaths for the victims of fascism at the Mauthausen concentration camp memorial as well as for fallen fascists in Bleiburg. Yet there was no outcry over this form of contradictory commemoration.

***

A special challenge arises when attempts are made to associate different memories, when, for example, spaces dedicated to the memory of the Holocaust are opened up to other memories as well. In 2017/2018 the United States Holocaust Memorial Museum (USHMM) in

Washington presented an exhibition on the Syrian civil war, and the museum also maintains a research division on genocide prevention.

One notable instance of the linkage of present-day instances of persecution with the historical persecutions by the National Socialists is seen in the United Nations High Commission for Refugees (UNHCR), which first formulated its mission under the impression of the fate of people who had survived the Holocaust by escape and/or as displaced persons.[2] The acceptance of people in need of protection in Western nations is therefore a direct result of obligations assumed following the traumatic experience of the Holocaust. The pragmatic need to act on this "legacy"—the practical acceptance of refugees—is as actively disputed as is the implicit linkage of historical events with current ones in the continuing recognition of the rights of refugees.

In a study of Syria's civil war by the division of genocide prevention at the USHMM there is the following sentence: "Seven decades after the Holocaust and despite promises of Never Again, a regime is targeting its own people while the international community stands by."[3] The USHMM here represents a cautious way of dealing with the linkage of Holocaust crimes to events in the Syrian civil war. The exhibition *Tell me about ~~yesterday~~ tomorrow* at the Munich Documentation Centre for the History of National Socialism has taken an important further step. Here, as well, an institution dedicated to National Socialist history has made a cautious attempt to expand its limited subject area historically and geographically, and thereby open up new approaches to the history of National Socialism itself as well as to other incidents of genocide and persecution. The relevance of this exhibition lies not only in its thematic expansion of the center's core subject matter, however, but rather in its invitation to artists from differing contexts to tell their own stories and add their themes to the narrative of the permanent historical exhibition. Artists are thereby allowed to participate with genuine agency in the historiographic process.

Here the fundamental question is: Who is permitted to engage actively with history, to research and compile it, to place it in contexts and ultimately shape it and make it their own? Such expanded access to memory and the writing of history can make one anxious about narrating one's own history, but is at the same time the only way to keep history current and relevant for those to whom one hopes to communicate it.

In the framework of the project *Museum auf der Flucht* (*Museum on the Flight*), which was hosted by Vienna's Volkskundemuseum (Austrian Museum of Folk Life and Folk Art) from 2017 to 2019,

2
<https://www.unhcr.org/admin/hcspeeches/ 3ae68fbc20/preventint-future-genocide-protecting-refugees-adddress-mrs-sadako-ogata.html> (accessed August 29, 2020).

3
<https://www.ushmm.org/genocide-prevention/countries/syria/case-study/introduction/syria> (accessed August 29, 2020).

a team of local curators and others who had come to Europe in 2015 as refugees pursued the question of how memory of the flight and thus the refugees' memories might be preserved in European society. The available material consisted of objects collected along escape routes from the Middle East, across the Balkans, and into Austria—transit objects. The curators discussed each object intensely, what it meant, how well it would display, and whether it would help to foster the desired common European memory. In another part of the project, the curators devoted themselves to the museum's historical collection, and developed perspectives on local history and culture, as well as on the stories the collected objects were meant to tell. Referring to the local collection and to European history writing, one of the curators, a Syrian architect and asylum seeker, asserted: "There are many narrators here. I would like to be one of them."[4]

One of the flight objects had come from the Greek island Lesbos, from a spot known to NGO workers as the "Lifejacket Graveyard," and that can even be found as such on Google Maps. It is a garbage dump in the interior of the island that has been filled with flotsam, things used by refugees in making their way to Europe instead of ordinary rubbish. There are backpacks, inflatable rafts, articles of clothing, foodstuff packages, and water bottles—all the floating objects imaginable as well as the eponymous lifejackets.

Among the objects retrieved from the spot for the Museum auf der Flucht was a child's shoe, which was discussed for possible display in a temporary exhibition and ultimately even in the Volkskundemuseum's permanent exhibition. The shoe itself is perfectly unremarkable: a laced shoe made of plastic, leather, and cloth in pink and white, with tiny decorations and markings probably made by the seawater. Nothing is known about the child that wore it. On reaching the shores of Lesbos the refugees tended to discard their wet clothing immediately and leave it on the beach. In addition, refugees repeatedly tell of the belongings of people who did not survive the crossing from the Turkish coast having been washed up on the shore.

The team of curators debated heatedly whether or not the shoe was worthy of display; they noted that it is a pathetic object, in that it has been so badly damaged by the saltwater; that it is too sad, for it suggests a lost human life; that it is too vague, for it is unclear what may have happened to its one-time wearer. Such were the perspectives of the curators, most of whom had entered Europe by way of these beaches on Lesbos themselves only months before. People outside the group developed a wholly different association with the shoe:

4
Die Küsten Österreichs. Die neue Schausammlung des Volkskundemuseum Wien, Vienna: Österreichisches Museum für Volkskunde 2018, p. 107.

to them the object was reminiscent of the Holocaust, of the mountain of shoes at the Auschwitz memorial, of the shoes of the Jews worked to death that to this day are regularly found in the soil at the site of the former camp at Gunskirchen, or of the bronze shoes on the bank of the Danube in Budapest meant to commemorate the city's deported Jewish population.

A long discussion followed on what public associations the curators would accept, how many levels they would ascribe to the object in the context of an exhibition. One of the curators argued: "If you don't have a shared memory, then it means strangeness."[5] The shoe did not produce the shared memory. The strangeness remained. The curators ultimately decided not to include the shoe in the exhibition.

But the shoe is nevertheless of interest because of its multi-dimensionality; it is at once a historical object and a reminder of a traumatic European moment, a screen onto which a variety of actual stories and experiences can be projected. As a display object, the shoe triggers memories, possibly not shared memories but related ones. It is thus not simply an ambivalent artifact that accommodates arbitrary associations, but a genuine relic that facilitates an integration of parallel memories.

5
Ibid., p. 108.

Ydessa Hendeles, *The Steeple and The People*, 2018 | Installation view, *Tell me about ~~yesterday~~ tomorrow*

Rosemarie Trockel, *Frankfurter Engel (Frankfurt Angel)*, 1994/2019 | Installation view, *Tell me about ~~yesterday~~ tomorrow*

Harald Pickert, *Die Pestbeulen Europas. Naziterror in Konzentrationslagern (The Plague-Spots of Europe. Nazi Terror in Concentration Camps), 1939–45*, n.d. | Installation view, Zentralinstitut für Kunstgeschichte Munich

Gregor Schneider, *Suppe auslöffeln, Geburtshaus Goebbels (Spooning Soup, Birthplace Joseph Goebbels), Odenkirchener Str. 202, Rheydt,* 2014
Installation view, *Tell me about yesterday tomorrow*

*Fragmentos:
Interview with Doris Salcedo*

ANDREAS HUYSSEN

INTRODUCTION

Fragmentos: Espacio de Arte y Memoria is located on a rather ordinary bustling street in Bogotá leading straight to the Presidential Palace, with the mayor's mansion and several ministries just a few blocks away. As you approach, all you see is a whitewashed wall with the letters *F R A G M E N T O S* cut through it, as if to allow the space to breathe.

It is a unique site among the untold memorials, monuments, and museums across the world aiming to nurture collective mourning and accountability in the never-ending struggles of conflict and memories of state terror, civil war, forced disappearances, and genocide. *Fragmentos* is a work of art, an architectural marvel, an exhibition space, and a public "act of memory", a term Salcedo has used to describe her widely exhibited sculptures and installations as well as the public commemorative events she has organized over the years on the Plaza Bolivar in Bogotá.

The space is dedicated to the memory of the Colombian civil war and its victims. It was created as a counter-monument in 2018 by Doris Salcedo and her collaborator, architect Carlos Granada, as part of the Museo Nacional of Bogotá. When the government of President Juan Manuel Santos signed the peace treaty with the armed guerrilla, the FARC, in 2016, it was decided that three monuments to the violent struggles that had torn Colombia apart would be built—one in Havana, Cuba, where the treaty was signed, one in New York at the UN, which had facilitated the negotiations, and one in Bogotá, capital of Colombia. The Minister of Culture Mariana Garcez asked Salcedo if she would design the monument for Bogotá. The government's request did have a logic. Each of Salcedo's previous sculptures and installations, both in galleries and in public urban space, had been a counter-monumental memorial to the pain and suffering of all sides in the conflict. As one of Colombia's premier artists, she seemed predestined for the task.

Salcedo's position as a memory artist is different from that of memory artists, say, in Germany, where a lively public culture of *Vergangenheitsaufarbeitung* (dealing with the past) took root several decades ago. By contrast, in Colombia there has been no national public culture of reckoning with the civil war that has lasted for more than half a century, claiming several hundred thousand lives, untold numbers of raped and tortured victims, and several millions of displaced persons. Shouldering the burden of articulating public mourning against all odds is hard, sometimes overwhelming for any artist who works in the tension between rigorous aesthetic demands and an ethos of compassion and collective responsibility. Every one of Salcedo's works is grounded in collective experience. As a witness of witnesses' accounts of violence, she functions as a medium of specific stories of suffering which the artwork will then transform or transcend in order to avoid voyeurism or sentimentality. The powerful emotions her work triggers in spectators testifies to the success of that strategy of affective abstraction. *Fragmentos* is a case in point.

The new construction, imaginatively embedded in the ruin of a colonial building, consists of a minimalist modernist design supported by steel beams and featuring large glass walls, which permit views onto the residues of the colonial ruin, weathered and crumbling walls surrounded by lush green bushes and vegetation. Visitors walk throughout on a floor consisting of dark grey unevenly sculpted tiles, made from 37 tons of melted weapons the guerrilla had surrendered after signing the 2016 peace treaty with the government. A walkway, the spine of the rectangular building, leads past several exhibition and service spaces and then flows into a large typically modernist white cube intended for art exhibits or large lectures. Here the dark tiled floor assumes its most ominous and powerful effect. You suddenly realize that it is this floor that conveys the ultimate meaning of *Fragmentos*: made from thousands of AK-47s and other guns returned to their material substance and shaped into an aesthetic statement: a monument to violence overcome and to a promise of peace.

The proximity of the sparse modernist architecture of glass, steel, and white walls to the residual walls of the former colonial building speaks volumes. The architectural past, though in a state of ruin, is preserved on this site dedicated to silent remembrance and commemorative art. It is as if the design of *Fragmentos* itself were to embody the very nature of memory: being of the past, but always and inevitably fragmentary and part of a present that remediates and preserves memory according to its own historical logic. Part sculptural installation, part memorial, part art museum, it is a space dedicated to the remembrance of a decades-long civil war in a society that still lacks an official politics of memory. It is intended to provide the ground for future art installations commemorating national suffering, for dialogues and discussions of art and politics in Colombia and elsewhere, and, hopefully, for encounters of artists from the global South who all too often lack their own institutions and public sites for exhibition and debate.

In late February of 2020, I had the chance to visit *Fragmentos* and to speak about art, memory, and politics in the building's large lecture hall. The space had officially opened in December 2018 at a time when the peace process was already going in reverse. The conservative government of President Iván Duque, elected in September 2018 on the promise of revising the controversial peace deal, has turned on former FARC members, many of whom have recently been killed in an extrajudicial campaign. As a result, segments of the FARC have taken up arms again and are now entrenched in Colombia's jungles as before. Others are holding on tenuously to the Peace Treaty's promise of participation in the political process. As the violence continues, the Peace Treaty has itself become fragmentary.

The following interview, conducted with Doris Salcedo in Bogotá and Villa de Leyva in early March 2020, tells the story that led to the making of *Fragmentos*, a process that was both individual and collective, state-supported but created by an artist's intense commitment to an art of mourning against all odds and setbacks. It involved politicians, the army and the police, guerrilla leaders and victims of violence at a tenuous historical moment when peace and reconciliation seemed to be possible. It is this floor on which visitors walk, this collectively created installation artwork, which is the conceptual and visual core of the space. It is a testament to the incredible burden Doris Salcedo has been under throughout her career when trying with her art to articulate a culture of collective grief and mourning in a society that lacks any official commitment to a full recognition, let alone a working through, of a violent past.

INTERVIEW

Andreas Huyssen (AH)

So let's talk about *Fragmentos* and how it came about. How did it all begin?

Doris Salcedo (DS)

The Ministry of Culture called me and asked if I wanted to make a monument, and I said no, because arms should not be monumentalized. I hate guns, they are the source of huge suffering. Actually it was the second time I was offered such an opportunity. When the right-wing paramilitaries were given a fake amnesty in 2004, I was also asked to make a monument. I said no, for the same reason. I don't think there should be a monument made out of arms that have caused so much death and destruction.

AH

This was after the decision was made that there should be three monuments?

DS

Yes, and at first I said no again. But then I thought, I don't want a monument glorifying arms to be erected in Bogotá. I wanted to make sure there would not be a traditional triumphant monument. If I don't do it, somebody for sure will do a typical vertical, hierarchical obelisk. I called the Minister of Culture back and said: I changed my mind. I'll do it. And she said: "great".

But then we had a problem. The FARC would never accept a proposal presented by the government. Therefore, if I wanted to do it, I had to find and contact FARC leaders, talk to them and make sure they would give me their arms to make a monument. These arms belonged to them, not to the Colombian government.

AH

So from the beginning your plan was to avoid the traditional shape of monuments and the way arms would figure in them? But did you know that the guerrilla was committed to give up their arms? They had not even handed their arms in yet, when you contacted their leaders, right?

DS

When the guerrilla signed the peace agreement with the government in Havana, it was agreed that three monuments should be built. Havana, New York and Bogotá. For the guerrilla, it was important to state that they had not been defeated, nor disarmed by the government. They wanted to demonstrate that they voluntarily decommissioned their weaponry.

Once the peace agreement was signed, guerrilla men and women moved into several protected areas they had chosen all around the country. To these sites, the United Nations brought metal containers into which the guerrilla would voluntarily deposit their arms. This was a long process. The containers were open and when the guerrillas felt they were willing and ready to give up their arms, they walked up to the container and left their weapon. At that moment, UN staff disabled and weighed them, counted the exact number and kept them under their supervision, until the containers were delivered to the Colombian police. It was stated in the peace accord that nothing should be done with these arms without the approval of the FARC. I began a conversation with Iván Márquez, one of the FARC leaders, who unfortunately left the agreement to take up arms again; we started a dialogue and a negotiation, but I knew I really had nothing to negotiate. I already had a complete idea for the counter-monument.

I told him exactly what I planned to do, and he didn't like it a bit. He thought my proposal would humiliate them.

AH
Because you were going to walk right over them by creating the monument's floor from their melted-down weapons? Reminds me of Gunter Demnig's controversial *Stumbling Stones* project in Germany, those small square concrete cubes embedded in the sidewalks and covered by a brass plate inscribed with the name and life dates of victims of Nazi extermination and persecution. Officials in Munich refused to participate in the project, arguing similarly that it's a humiliation of the victims to step even accidentally on their names installed on the sidewalk in front of the houses they lived in. But the stumbling stones have been very successful as a memorial intervention honoring individual victims and they are now found in many European countries.

DS
Yes, he thought stepping on their arms implied humiliation. More importantly perhaps, he didn't like the fact that women who were raped by the guerrilla would be involved in the creation of the steel tiles by hammering the material from which the molds would be made. Our discussion focused on sexual violence. He was arguing they did not commit that crime. And I said: "Fine. If you didn't do it, then you shouldn't be afraid of it." And I added: "I know the Colombian army has raped a lot of guerrilla women. We need to show the Colombian public that the guerrilla is not only a perpetrator. It is also a victim of this war. The only way to do it is if you allow some of the guerrilla women to hammer this floor alongside civilian victims. Colombians need to understand that you have suffered as well. This is an opportunity to show you care about the pain felt by victims of war. We are finishing a war in which no one triumphed. We all lost."

AH
Particularly women who were victimized by both sides. But how did the conversation with Iván Márquez end?

DS
It ended well. He recounted extremely painful personal experiences. He was aware of the fact that in order to achieve reconciliation between the FARC and civilian society, they had to show solidarity with the population they had victimized.

I was under huge pressure to get his approval. Finally, when he did agree with my proposal, I began a race against the clock. Not only was I going to undergo surgery the next morning, but we had only six months to find a site, precisely budget the project, design the building and produce the piece, before President Juan Manuel Santos's term in office ended.

After my surgery, I was in pretty bad shape for a few months, but in spite of that I had to work closely with the architect, the victims and a large team gathered to make all this possible.

It was clear at that time that the far right would win the elections. If that happened, I had no chances to build *Fragmentos*, since the right's campaign was based on the destruction of the peace process.

For all the reasons I just mentioned the construction of *Fragmentos* was marked by a desperate urgency.

AH
The government had no problem with the idea of bringing women victimized by the military into the process?

DS
They didn't have a problem. I talked to Santos and presented the proposal. It was clear to him the army had committed brutal acts during the war. He said: "You have my full support.", and I did have his full support. Also that of the Minister of Culture. And some key members of the police were really supportive of the peace process as well. When I did get the weapons, I understood why it was so difficult for the guerrilla to give up their AK-47s. Because most of the arms—especially the ones owned by female soldiers—had flowers painted on them, names were inscribed on them, they had glass beads. The guerrilla had their identity linked to the arms. I was shocked when I realized that. They were decorated to an extent I could not imagine. So, then I understood why it was so hard for them, especially for the female guerrilla, to give them up. These arms represented the only possibility poor peasant women had to have some power and control over their own lives.

When I finally opened the building, some of the female guerrilla attended the opening, but they stood in the entrance and they started crying there. I approached them, embraced them and we walked on the floor together. They understood it was a dignifying, respectful space.

Fragmentos is a space that represents the possibility of uniting divergent aspects of our violent past that were difficult to assemble in a single site: arms given up by 13,000 guerillas, the active presence of victims of sexual violence, and the creation of an art institution. An institution devoted to rethinking our violent past through art must have at its center the experiences of survivors of sexual violence. I had been working with victims of rape for a couple of years prior to the making of *Fragmentos*. I decided to continue working with them because I felt really bad about my slow and late recognition of rape as political violence. They taught me the magnitude of the consequences they endure, and what it means to live in a society that refuses to acknowledge the true meaning of rape.

AH

But you must have known that rape has always been systematically used as a tool of warfare?

DS

Yes, yes, but I didn't understand why in the testimonies of victims of war crimes, this fact was not openly discussed. A terrible formula was commonly applied by the different illegal armies. When there is a farm between an inland coca plantation and the coast of Colombia from where the drugs are shipped North, the guerrilla or paramilitary armies would come to the farm to clear the way for the drugs to get out. Whoever is on this farm needs to be eliminated. Usually they kill the men, burn the farm, kill an older son if there is one, displace the family and rape the women. But when the surviving women gave me their testimony, they mentioned how their sons had been killed, or their husbands had been killed, they talked about the farm being burnt, and how they lost their animals and the crops. Sometimes, the last thing they would say is: and I was raped. I had not really understood the meaning of this narrative before. Finally I understood that rape was really *the* crime that attempted to annihilate these women. I felt a great urgency to invite them to give shape to *Fragmentos*.

AH

And you did so very powerfully, especially in the accompanying documentary screened in the black box of *Fragmentos* that shows these women hammering what was later to become the surface of the dark tiles. But getting back to the earlier stages of the process: You did get the weapons. How much was it? 37 tons?

DS

The guerrilla gave up 69 tons of weapons and ammunition. But I did not want to use the ammunition, because it is made in part from bronze; it has a golden color that I did not find appropriate. For this reason, I just used the weapons.

AH
You just wanted the steel.

DS
Yes. All 37 tons of it. Then I started to think technically. I initiated a conversation with the Colombian army. At the beginning they had no intention of helping me; they were clearly laughing at me. They told me they did not have a foundry capable of melting the arms' steel. And they sent me to foundries all over the country. I was stupid enough to go to other cities in search of a foundry. Everyone kept telling me the Colombian army is the only one that can do this job. Because the kind of steel that is used for arms is very, very hard and it needs up to 1,200 degrees centigrade to melt. I went back to talk with President Santos and a few members of his cabinet. I explained to them that the army was not helping, they were giving me all sorts of excuses. While I was in his office, the Minister of Defense called the head of the army to give the order to do the work with me. From then on, the engineers of the army foundry were entirely devoted to working on *Fragmentos.*

AH
How did you then pick the women to collaborate in the creation of the floor?

DS
I had already interviewed hundreds of victims and a few perpetrators at that time. As I said earlier, it was a crime I had been unable to understand and every day I continued interviewing people, hoping that at some point I would understand something. And of course this is something impossible to comprehend. It is very difficult to grasp what motivates these men to commit rape. I had already initiated a friendly relationship with a victims' organization; we were planning to work together in the construction of a shelter. The women who participated in the making of *Fragmentos* are part of this group.

AH
The building of shelters is still going on now? In Bogotá?

DS
Yes, we continue this project. I also traveled with them. It is a group of women that I adore because they call themselves "victimas y pro-fesionales" ("victims and professionals"). This means that they support other victims of rape in a professional manner. They organize

workshops in which they teach how to deal with the consequences of rape, how to survive, how to get compensation from the government, how to denounce what happened to them. I just have nothing but admiration for the "profesionales". I think they do essential work as they give workshops in tiny towns around the country.

Twenty women from this group decided to help me. I also invited twenty guerrilla women who had been raped by the army. Unfortunately, at the very last minute the guerrilla commanders decided that the guerrilla women could not participate. Therefore, only twenty women took part in the making of the piece.

AH

Was it the steel itself that was hammered into the shapes of the floor tiles?

DS

No, that was the original idea. But I had to change it because it was too dangerous.

AH

There would have been splinters popping up from the hammering, injuring people?

DS

The process was unbelievably dangerous. Both melting the arms and casting the tiles had to be done by the army engineers.

AH

So, what did they hammer on then?

DS

We worked on aluminum plates. And they hammered that softer metal, softer than steel. Out of those plates I made the molds, into which the melted arms were then cast.

AH

And where did you do all of this?

DS

We were working at a warehouse, where we had some privacy. Every time there was a break they started talking about what they were hammering. These were the toughest testimonies I have ever heard in my life, really heartbreaking. It was punishing.

AH

And it was the hammering that brought it all out? That's the way you would read it?

DS

Yes, it was a completely different experience from going to their houses and talking to them in a quiet space. In a way hammering gave them back strength, and their own bodies' capacity to affect a material object. An experience that is the opposite of being raped.

AH

Different, because this was a collective enterprise?

DS

One thing that is important with women who have been sexual slaves for a long time: their body is useless to them. Their body did not belong to them any longer. So, the relationship they have with their bodies is very strange. If they enter into a room where one would normally move to the center, they would gather in the back and remain standing against the wall. It's a completely different relation to space. When I gave them the hammers, it was as if they were too heavy for them, but little by little they understood that their body could be making a mark. They could transform that rage, and everything they had experienced, the pain they had, could somehow be put there. They understood right away that their experience was to be at the center of the Colombian war and Colombian history. They *said* that they were making history.

AH

And the stronger the hammering, the better they could articulate their rage and their anger.

DS

It was really the hardest session I ever had in more than thirty years of listening to testimonies. I never experienced anything like it. Never. They were aware of the meaning and importance of destroying arms, hammering. They were never hammering the rape itself but the consequences of the rape. Terrible things had happened to them. They were trying to get it all out.

AH

These aluminum plates, what did they look like? How did they take on their final shape?

DS
Each woman hammered different plates. I was working a little bit with all of them.

AH
You were taking the hammer from them and participating?

DS
Yes, absolutely, absolutely. And it was beautiful because somebody was hammering a plate and then I gave that one to another woman and it became a collective action. It's not that each person worked on one piece. No. Each piece was worked over twenty times by different women, each plate was charged with all those life's experiences. And that's what I gave the Colombian Army who has amazing technology, at a factory where in times of war they produced guns. Somehow the army engineers got really engaged with the work. And they did a beautiful job.

AH
Let us turn toward Carlos's design of the space and its construction.

DS
Yes, we were working closely. The main element was not to have a monumental building, neither a sculptural nor an architectural monument. So, the building had to be as discrete and as invisible as possible. That was the premise we started working with. An invisible building. Nothing imposing, as discrete as possible. The city and government offered different sites, there was the possibility of having bigger spaces west of the city near the airport. I finally chose a space really close to the center of political power. The Congress is two blocks away, the President's house is a block away. And the office of the Mayor of Bogotá is three blocks away. And the Palace of Justice is four blocks away. It is important that a piece made by victims of sexual violence faces the political heart of the city.

This site had the ruins of a nineteenth-century adobe house. Carlos Granada had the brilliant idea of leaving the ruins untouched as a reminder of the legacy of war.

AH
An act of memory right in the government quarters and built under extreme time pressure. Was it finished when the new government came in after the election in August 2018?

DS

By that time, the Ministry of Culture had entirely paid every single contractor. So, when the new government came in, they could not undo anything. *Fragmentos* opened on Dec. 10, 2018. The President did not attend.

AH

Did he send anybody to represent the state?

DS

He sent the Minister of Culture.

AH

But he is also one of his loyalists? The one who is cutting the budget now?

DS

Yes, of course. *Fragmentos* is defunded, as most of the art institutions are in this government. It is increasingly difficult to run the program as I envisioned it, but somehow we managed to continue presenting important works that address war and our recent traumatic history.

AH

What is your sense of how people react to it? There was a lot of coverage in the press, including a story in the *New York Times*.

DS

Fragmentos was generously and widely commented on all over the press and it was discussed as a memorial to the war and as an art installation. I was amazed by the amount and quality of the press coverage, especially in the opinion sections, there were several columns, the majority welcomed the concept and acknowledged the need for a space that would allow us to reflect on what had happened during more than 50 years of war.

AH

How precisely did they write about it?

DS

Most writers wrote on the need to retrieve the memory of violent events, and on art being the best medium to address a difficult past and an even more challenging present.

AH

Now that the building is finished, what is your vision for its future, the events to be planned in it, its financial stability, its administration? When I visited, the three public exhibition spaces of the building were empty. You told me that *Fragmentos* offers a space for artists to show their work, for lectures and discussions. Can you describe how you envision the future of this site as a memorial site?

DS

I thought of *Fragmentos* as the end point of a long and complex peace process. Unfortunately, now the right-wing government is systematically destroying its most important aspect, and has failed to implement its ultimate goal. For this reason, its role has changed. I see it now as an even more urgent project. It has become the road map that we need to follow in order to find lasting and stable peace in the near future. It is more necessary than it was before. Now we must address not only memory, but our current daily life, in a confusing time where we live neither in peace nor in open war.

I believe this situation is common to many countries of the South, where low-intensity conflicts drag on forever. Our next show will be Francis Alÿs' work on Iraq. His research has taught us that there are many common elements. This type of exchange is essential.

AH

How do visitors react to the floor, as they realize what it's made of and what it represents?

DS

Many people come into the space, often directly off the street, unaware of what they are going to find. And they *cry* as they walk through. Some take their shoes off. Most people need to touch it, I think it is hard for us to believe that thousands of arms that have caused so much death, devastation and misery, are lying there for us to freely walk on them. Thus reversing the power relation arms impose on civilian populations.

AH

I had tears in my eyes when I first entered it.

DS

One day I encountered a man in *Fragmentos*, he was crying, he had his shoes off and then said: "My wife was killed by one of these arms." You see, this war has harmed millions of lives. People are touched directly by this piece. It is not abstract for us at all.

AH
What about former FARC guerrillas visiting?

DS
It was wonderful. Because they understood that even though it was not something they had wanted, their arms are presented in a digni-fied manner. The fact that they reached an agreement, that they signed a peace accord is fully acknowledged with this counter-monument. Many in Colombian society have never acknowledged that the guer-rilla had given up their arms. People were thinking that everything was a lie. That it was like a mirage that didn't really happen. So, this is a testimony to the fact that through dialogue, 13,000 guerrillas were disarmed, without firing a single bullet. The arms are there, in the floor. Every ounce of steel from the 37 tons of arms handed over is accounted for. For this reason, the process of how *Fragmentos* was created has been extensively documented[1]. *Fragmentos* testifies to the success of the peace process. It renders peace as an achievable goal. This is why this piece is important for Colombia.

1
https://www.youtube.
com/watch?v=-
i9jpbludQY

Kent Monkman, *The Deluge*, 2019 | Installation view, *Tell me about ~~yesterday~~ tomorrow*

Želimir Žilnik, *Inventur – Metzstraße 11 (Inventory – Metzstrasse 11)*, 1975 | Installation view, *Tell me about ~~yesterday~~ tomorrow*

Heba Y. Amin, *The Devil's Garden*, 2019; Rosemarie Trockel, *Frankfurter Engel (Frankfurt Angel)*, 1994/2019
Installation view, *Tell me about ~~yesterday~~ tomorrow*

The Missing War Memorials to the Victims of Rape during World War II in Europe

On the 75th anniversary of the end of World War II, when increasing numbers of war memorials are being erected, there is still no memorial commemorating one important historical fact: the rape of women, an event which has been unanimously and continuously surrounded by a conspiracy of silence in all participating countries. This holds especially true where the perpetrators were a country's own soldiers. Propaganda machineries were always happy to talk about the crimes that soldiers of other countries were committing. Caricatures or posters in which the enemy was depicted molesting women were distributed in thousands of copies among soldiers, thus encouraging them to fight relentlessly.

During World War II, millions of civilians suffered from sexual violence. It was only in 2020 that a map was completed of military brothels that were forcibly created and maintained for the soldiers by the local female population after the Japanese occupation of Southeast Asia.[1] Although the Japanese government denies their existence until today, it is shocking to see the number of camps that were holding sex slaves. There is no such comprehensive research or statistics on the European battlefields. This is due to the Cold War divisions and nationally-framed historiographies that still taboo or heroize interpretations of wartime sexual violence against women.[2]

The number of wartime rape victims can only be estimated based on health statistics, the number of abortions, and changes in birth rates. The available data proves that it was a mass phenomenon. We will certainly never have exact numbers, as both the perpetrators and often the victims had an interest in silence. Documents are scattered and unrepresentative, and in the case of the Red Army not even available to research.

VISUAL REPRESENTATION OF SEXUAL VIOLENCE DURING WARTIME

The visual representation of rape has been part of European art since antiquity. Traditional, pathetic images depict war rape as the abduction of the Sabine women or the punishment of Apollo, who follows Daphne against her will, while he turns into a tree to escape. The example of Lucretia, who killed herself after the rape, served as a moral yardstick for women for centuries. The artistic representation does not show the rape but her grief after the event and before the suicide. In the Victorian era, a new genre emerged depicting only the result of the violence, trusting that the dead female body and the viewer's imagination would reconstruct

1
https://wam-peace.org/ianjo/map (accessed August 30, 2020).

2
Andrea Pető, *Das Unsagbare erzählen. Sexuelle Gewalt in Ungarn im Zweiten Weltkrieg*, Wallstein Verlag, forthcoming in September 2021.

the steps leading to her death and the moral lessons learned. Violence against the female body, as an explicit depiction of vulnerability, appears in the German *Lustmord* images, inspired by the visual world of destruction after the First World War.[3]

Consequently one might assume that wartime rape, especially in the context of World War II, has found its pathetic representation, manifesting women's sacrificial role by using romantic visual language dating back to ancient traditions. Nonetheless it was a long time before this monumentalization could take place in Europe.

It was not until 2013 that the artist and sculptor Jerzy Bohdan Szumczyk broke this public silence with a Polish guerrilla memorial in Gdańsk. He erected his monument *Komm, Frau*, in which a Soviet soldier is depicted raping a pregnant woman at gunpoint without permission. The sculpture with its German title suggested that Soviet soldiers collectively punished Germans and Poles, and that rape was motivated by revenge. The artist was arrested briefly by the authorities, and the monument was soon removed due to the absence of any official permit. This monument was conceptualized as a narrative monument: the statue tells what happened to women based on the stories of survivors.

More recently, however, two permanent monuments were completed in Hungary. At first glance, the observer does not exactly know what these monuments stand for. The visitor to the monument needs to know the framework and vocabulary to read the story in the artwork. The monument in itself without this context says nothing specific to the viewer about wartime rape.

The first of these monuments is in Csongrád: on a bronze plaque, a naked young woman with a youthful body and long hair tries to cover herself with a shroud, clasping her hands in front of her well-formed breasts, while threatening hands reach out to her.[4] "God shall wipe away all tears from their eyes", a quote from the Book of Revelation, is engraved on the plaque.[5] It was this coded inscription using non-explicit language that made it possible to erect a plaque in the present political context. The relative invisibility is also due to the fact that only the local press reported the unveiling of the plaque. Perhaps this saved the monument from the expected political battles. In view of the rapprochement of the Orbán government and Putin's Russia, any reference to the crimes committed by the Red Army would have immediate consequences.

This memorial is very similar in its visual narrative to the memorial in Manila to Filipino women held captive by occupying

3
See Otto Dix, *Lustmord*, from series *Tod und Auferstehung* (1922), Rudolf Schlichter, *Lustmord* (1924).

4
https://www.delmagyar.hu/csongrad-es-kornyeke/hadd-legyenek-ok-is-tisztak-hosok-szentek-csongradi-nok-kaptak-emlekmuvet-4443792/ (accessed August 30, 2020).

5
Revelation 21: 3-4.

Japanese forces as sex slaves during World War II, erected in December 2017 on the initiative of local NGOs.[6] This bronze statue depicts a blindfolded woman with a flagged, slightly flawed dress clasping her hands in front of her chest as a sign of suffering. In April 2018 the monument was removed because, according to local officials, an exchange of pipes had to be carried out in that very area. Women's organizations protested in vain. During a visit to Manila in January, the Japanese minister of the interior made it clear that economic ties between the two countries could not be strengthened while this monument was in place. A couple of months earlier President Duterte had stated that he would not ignore the will of the NGOs who initiated the erection of the monument. By April, however, his opinion had changed, and the sculpture had been removed indefinitely.

Not so the memorial plaque of Csongrád, which is still in place. The monument to women victims was initiated and financed by József Botos, created by a male sculptor and inaugurated by a male mayor. As the male journalist reporting about the event mentioned, the only woman who spoke at the inauguration was the initiator's wife, Katalin Botos, Minister without Portfolio of the first government (1990–1994) after the collapse of communism. She then observed: "With this monument, we bow our heads before the women and the general human dignity. Their sacrifice was sacred." The monument did not say why the women's sacrifice would have been sacred and who the perpetrators were, but probably this lack of specificity was the price paid for its erection.

Another similar pathetic-romantic monument was erected in Búcsú, also in Hungary, by the Sonnevend family in 2019 with an inscription "in memory of the victims of the communist dictatorship and the captured refugees 1945–1989".[7] The simple gray marble slab is applied to a side wall of the local Catholic Church. Only from the inaugural speeches reported by the press do we know that the sponsor of the monument, who had been only 11 in 1945, erected it in order to commemorate the "humiliated girls and women whose attics were swept empty, who were robbed, who were incessantly harassed, who were tortured, who were labeled as kulaks".

VISUAL NARRATIVES OF WARTIME RAPE

Is it possible to talk about a historical mass crime or to erect a monument for its victims if there is no visual documentation? After all, the few photos remaining from World War II which depict dead female bodies can only be assumed to show victims of rape.

6
https://www.
japantimes.co.jp/
news/2018/04/28/
national/politics-
diplomacy/new-
comfort-women-
memorial-removed-
thoroughfare-manila-
pressure-japanese-
embassy/accessed
August 30, 2020).

7
A vasfüggöny
áldozatainak állítottak
emléket Bucsuban
April 3, 2019, https://
www.vaol.hu/
kozelet/a-vasfuggony-
aldozatainak-allitottak-
emleket-bucsuban-
2947108/ (accessed
August 30, 2020).

8
The Shoah Visual History Archive contains several testimonies about Jewish survivors being raped without any graphic details.

9
Susan Sontag, *Regarding the Pain of Others*, New York 2003.

10
Andrea Pető, "'Non-Remembering' the Holocaust in Hungary and Poland", in: Polin, Vol. 31, 2019, *Poland and Hungary Jewish Realities Compared*, ed. by Francois Guesnet, Howard Lupovitch, and Antony Polonsky, pp. 471–480.

11
See https://www.youtube.com/watch?v=oZTvTvGwY_4 (accessed August 30, 2020).

12
Zsófia Lóránd, "Megszólaltatott félhangok", in: *Kettős Mérce*, 2014, January 24, http://kettosmerce.blog.hu/2014/01/27/megszolaltatott_felhangok (accessed August 30, 2020).

Those who survived rarely gave testimonies, and these testimonies were not filmed or photographed.[8]

The first answer to this question is that maybe such a monument is not desirable anyway. This is Susan Sontag's reasoning; she argues that looking at a picture or statue depicting violence recreates a visual culture of violence.[9] This is one of the arguments for not erecting a monument at all. The other assertion is that recently erected public statues and monuments in Hungary were commissioned without competitions and juries representing public and professional participation. Consequently there was no public dialogue, and the entire procedure lacked transparency and debate.[10]

A turning point in the discourse about sexual violence during World War II in Hungary was Fruzsina Skrabski's film *Silenced Shame* in 2013, in which I participated with an expert interview.[11] The film was the subject of heated debate, especially for its reenactment of actual rape scenes.[12] After screening this film for students of gender studies at the Central European University in Budapest, I was discussing the film with the director. The first controversial point was the visual depiction of rape in the film. In black-and-white inserts the process of rape was reconstructed and performed by actors and actresses based on a story told by one of the survivors. The director justified this choice by arguing that it made the film more "spectacular". Apart from other issues we also disagreed about the number of victims: My calculation, based on medical records, assumes a number of 250,000, while the film speaks of 800,000 victims of wartime rape: This raises not only methodological but also ethical concerns, most importantly as to whether this war on numbers serves the interest of the victims and their families.

The film was seen by hundreds of thousands on YouTube and was broadcast on state television several times. Every high school received a free copy for their library. Consequently, it was suggested that a monument should be built for Hungarian women raped by Soviet soldiers, but only the monuments in Csongrád and Búcsú were completed as private initiatives in 2019. Both depict women in traditional artistic language, and as victims, and both reflect a number of problems in present-day Hungary. The first is the historical framework of 'double occupation': After the illiberal turn of Hungarian memory politics, the government transferred the responsibility of World War II to the occupiers, the Germans and the Soviets, by canonizing the 'double occupation' theory, making the Hungarian collaboration and perpetrators invisible, and thus fundamentally changing the previous memory policy framework. The erection of the black obelisk of the so-called Gulag Monument in Budapest was proposed by a non-governmental organization called the Organization of Former Hungarian Political Prisoners and Forced Laborers in the Soviet Union (Szorakész). The four sides of the obelisk symbolize the four groups of victims who were deported to the Soviet Union: Hungarian political prisoners, prisoners of war, and civilians, as well as Germans deported after 1945. Victims of rape were deliberately excluded and were not remembered as the framework of remembering is different following traditional historical narrative.

Secondly, there is no historical narrative that would reconcile Hungarian national historiography within a European context, thereby including the memories of diverse groups of victims. Though it was mainly Soviet soldiers who committed mass rapes in Hungary, wartime sexual violence was not confined only to soldiers of the Red Army. The Hungarian soldiers, as allies of Nazi Germany, raped women in Ukraine and Yugoslavia, and occupying German troops committed rape in Hungary. Remembering only the rapes committed by the Red Army would make the overall phenomenon of wartime rape and its structural causes invisible. In this competition women's memories always start at a disadvantage unless they are instrumental as symbols of national suffering. The lack of transnational memories and of a willingness to remember women's suffering beyond national narratives, leads to monuments such as the one in Csongrád. The biblical quote refuses to address either the memories of the victims or the responsibility of the perpetrators directly. Hungarian memorial culture still follows the traditional heroization narrative.

The third problem is due to the lack of active involvement by the public in memory politics in Hungary. In general memory operates at different levels: local, regional, national, and transnational, and together they create the diverse layers of memory culture. However, it is a political process in which some groups and narratives exercise more power, especially with the support of a government. Today many Hungarian NGOs are exploring the long overdue history of those citizens who were deported to the Soviet Union. Yet there are no women's NGOs dealing with the war crime rape history.

The fourth problem is that the memory of World War II recently again became a political battlefield. World War II rape monuments are stirring up political debates. The perpetrators were reluctant to admit responsibility even if wartime rape is acknowledged as a crime against humanity now; they (or those who defend their memory) will do everything they can to prevent the monument from being erected. And Russian media follows the Hungarian discussion on rapes committed by the Red Army with keen interest.

The Yugoslav Wars in the 1990s not only changed the legal status of sexual violence to a war crime but redefined the memorialization process. Since then rape has been reflected by female artists who use the tools and symbols of feminist art. Sanje Ivekovic's installation *Frozen Images* is a memorial to women who were raped during the war in former Yugoslavia. It uses dry ice to create the illusion of a mattress for the sleeping woman as a victim of male violence while Amnesty International reports about wartime rapes are being read out loud.[13] Jenny Holzer's *Lustmord* describes the actual rape and murder of Bosnian women in three voices with three poems written on human skin about women experiencing the torture.

But it is especially art projects in Kosovo that I would like to mention here. They reflect an entirely different strategy of erecting a monument for women raped by the occupying Serbian army. In 2015, a public sculpture was erected in Pristina, entitled *20145*, referring to the number of victims, visualized by mosaic-like coins assembled to form a female face. The inscription dedicates the monument to "the multifaceted contribution and sacrifice made by all Albanian women during the Kosovo war of 1998/99, and as a reminder of the cruel crime of rape committed by Serbian forces against nearly twenty thousand women." The second, more interesting and innovative temporary monument, is Alketa Xhafa Mripa's *Thinking of You* from 2015. The artist exhibited five thousand clothes drying on forty-five ropes in a football stadium, a structure that symbolizes hegemonic militarized masculinity.[14] The clothes were collected from and by female victims and their family members from all over the country, thereby initiating a public involvement and fostering an intense debate. The message of this temporary monument is that what happened to the victims is not their fault. The first monument interprets war rape in an intentionalist framework, i.e. the Serbian army came and raped women to harm the Kosovar nation, and the second in a structuralist framework, that is, linking rape to militarism and masculinity.

CONCLUSION

There is no doubt that women truly were victims: the victims of male domination, militarism, and the collapse of the Hungarian state, which was meant to protect its citizens. Yet, the real question is how

13 https://transmediale.de/content/frozen-images (accessed August 30, 2020).

14 https://www.theguardian.com/world/2015/jun/11/kosovo-sexual-violence-survivors-art-dresses (accessed August 30, 2020).

to depict this victimhood while respecting the women's suffering and at the same time to draw lessons for today. In the case of World War II monuments of rape, both the insensitive iconographic simplicity of the Gdańsk statue and the overly euphemistic emotionality and idealization of the monument in Csongrád reaffirm women as victims. The Búcsú monument fits within the larger framework of the victims of communism.

Maybe there will be a change in this visual narrative before long. A resolution was adopted by the General Assembly of the Budapest Capital with the majority of the opposition to the governing Fidesz party in January 2020 about the erection of the "Monument to Women Raped in War" in 2022 with an international competition.[15] This process will involve broad historical and artistic expertise and promises a transparent process involving a public debate.

The planned monument in Budapest is novel in several ways. Firstly because of its participative character, following the example of the monument *Thinking of You* in Kosovo and Doris Salcedo's memorial *Fragmentos* in Bogotá (see Andreas Huyssens's essay in this volume). Also in Budapest, the time has possibly come for a broad public dialogue about innovative, inclusive and public memorialization of the victims of sexual violence during wartime. The 75th anniversary of the end of the World War II is an excellent opportunity for artists to rethink this process of memorialization creatively and to examine how to use an innovative visual language which still respects the dignity of the victims. Another novel element of the project is that artists will be given the opportunity of an open call to think, create, and exhibit their work in a transparent and professional way. This development is to be cherished in the illiberal cultural politics of the Hungarian state, and Budapest expects nothing less than an innovative piece of art.

15
Decision of the Municipality of Budapest 62/2020 (01-29-2020), see https://www.elhallgatva.hu/wp-content/uploads/2020/07/hatarozat_2020jan.pdf?lang=en (accessed August 30, 2020).

Michal BarOr, *Abandoned Property*, 2016 | Installation view, *Tell me about ~~yesterday~~ tomorrow*

Brian Jungen, *Untitled*, 1997 | Installation view, *Tell me about ~~yesterday~~ tomorrow*

Hito Steyerl, *Die leere Mitte (The Empty Center)*, 1998; *Normalität 1–X (Normality 1–X)*, 1999-2001
Installation view, *Tell me about ~~yesterday~~ tomorrow*

Paweł Kowalewski, *Europeans Only*, 2010 | Installation view, *Tell me about ~~yesterday~~ tomorrow*

*At Present: Biographies, Lived Experience,
and Positioning in Research as Practice*

SIMON DENNY & KARAMIA MÜLLER

This conversation courses the approaches of Berlin-based artist Simon Denny in dialogue with Auckland-based Karamia Müller, an academic working across architecture, race, and indigeneity in the recent research project and exhibition *Violent Legalities* (Pōneke Wellington, 2020). Denny sets recent exhibitions *Secret Power* (Venice, 2015), *The Founder's Paradox* (Auckland, 2017, Christchurch, 2019), *Mine* (Tasmania, 2019, Düsseldorf, 2020) and *Security through Obscurity* (San Francisco, 2020) against longer global narratives that include German colonization, the technology sector, the rise of right-wing extremism and racial violence. Müller discusses *Violent Legalities* a collaboration with Lachlan Kermode, Software Lead at Forensic Architecture, which documents the violence of legal processes in furthering racist colonial social orders. At present differently situated in home-base, disciplinary-practice, and intersectional positioning, Denny and Müller once shared a hometown of Auckland, Aotearoa / New Zealand where both attended the brother-sister Grammar schools of their home suburb, below they reflect on their biographies, experiences, and research as well as their own genealogies that implicate them in longer traces of colonial and imperial categories of power.

Simon Denny (SD)

I'm inspired by your work *Violent Legalities*, as I have been thinking recently not only about geographical and legal histories, but also about my own biography.

Karamia Müller (KM)

How so?

SD

One thing that came up for me when looking at it was that I realized that there are various personal moments that are a part of those histories, from my mother's side. Some members of her family occupied leading positions during violent colonial encounters. Several of my family were killed on November 10, 1868 in conflict relating to the colonial forces' pursuit of Te Kooti Arikirangi Te Tūruki (Te Kooti), a key Māori leader during the New Zealand Wars of the nineteenth century. In family documents I recently reviewed, the violence is described as a massacre, which should be challenged, because obviously colonial opposition to Te Kooti and other people surrounding him was a strategic military operation in retaliation following longer histories of legitimated, colonial violence. I have a primary document—written by a relative who was a witness. The account was for a school project, I think, by an uncle of my grandfather's; it is a pretty comprehensive, if biased account that I did not realize I had. I was thinking about the way that was framed in my own personal family history and the way resonant historical moments are contextualized within your project. On my regular jogging route in Berlin-Mitte, I run past what used to be the Reichskolonialamt or 'Imperial Colonial office' in Berlin. That is just one site in my daily routine with a connection to colonialism in the Pacific. As I teach in Hamburg, there is obviously also the long commercial history in Sāmoa as well. I am often reminded of the way that colonial enterprises supposedly begin as commercial exchanges, but are political by nature, then become increasingly politicized in terms of claiming sovereignty. For example, the legacy of German trader J.C. Godeffroy & Sohn[1] is very present in German ethnographic collections—all of which flowed through Hamburg. German commercial pillaging escalated in Sāmoa before it became a German protectorate between 1900 and 1914. There are spatial resonances where I live and work, which make connections to this dialog. I also went through my notes of our exchanges over the years and was reminded of a proposal you wrote for a project working on your own family history, including narratives like that of your cousin and his businesses, and the relationship between Zug, Switzerland, and the Kingdom of Tonga and these different kinds of commercial activities across generations that share a geography.

1
The Hamburg-based family firm Godeffroy & Sohn arrived in Sāmoa in 1857 with the intention of establishing a plantation economy. By 1880, the firm's successors Deutsche Handels- und Plantagen-Gesellschaft der Südsee-Inseln (D.H.P.G) were to control 90 percent of cultivated Sāmoan land, extending their role as an opportunistic merchant venture firm to become a significant political player in shaping commercial development in the nineteenth- and early twentieth-century Pacific.

KM

I wonder if any of us from this part of this world are untouched by the violence of colonialism? The way my own life negotiates colonialism across time and space in my own actions and outside of my own agency refracts across the tangible and intangible elements of the world. When people encounter my name without my face, or body, there is an expectation that I am white, with German heritage; there are events in my life that bring the specifics of that expectation to me that touch race, gender, and colonization. My name ties me, as much as my skin does, to how these categories are constructed socially, culturally, politically, and economically. As you mentioned, the spatial resonances of it are daily occurrences, like my name, and there are also these more geographically expansive narratives. In that project, I proposed to trace my paternal lineage to discover where my family name, Müller, comes from. My great-grandfather Philipp Gotthard Müller was a Swiss citizen who left Zug for the Pacific. The reasons I understand are that he sought trade and a livelihood, since he was one of the younger sons in his family and unlikely to inherit or be able to rely on an income from the family milling plant. From historical accounts, he had an adventurous spirit too, and was perhaps attracted to unconventional life choices. He traveled around the Pacific in the nineteenth century as a free agent, finding work in German colonial enterprises in Papua New Guinea and Sāmoa, after which he settled in Tonga. There he married a Sāmoan woman, Philomena, and rented land to establish a copra plantation. As a foreigner he was legally excluded from freehold—all land belonged to the Crown, which had lasting socio-economic ramifications for the family that remained in Tonga. Almost all of his children were sent back to Switzerland for their education, my grandfather being one of them. Some chose to live in Switzerland, and some chose to go back to Tonga; those forks in the road have been embodied in different lives. [...]

SD

I learn so much hearing about and reading the way you process your family histories. I've found our conversations really enlightening. I recently read a review that you wrote and shared with me, but never published, of an exhibition I did in the *The Founder's Paradox*-Auckland. It reminded me that there was a gap between what I thought I was doing with that exhibition and what I was actually doing. The more distance I get from this project, the more I recognise how on point you were with your criticism. Your review is a comparative text that contrasts *The Founder's Paradox*-Auckland with *Thor: Ragnarok* by Māori Director Taika Waititi. They are two very different kinds of cultural products by two very different producers obviously, but I agree with your point in the text that that film is amazing in the way that Waititi centres indigenous characters in the middle of this giant story, it was a very successful gesture. In contrast, there were several things in *The Founder's Paradox*-Auckland that could have been more carefully articulated.

KM

What do you think about that? I mean, what are the realities of somebody working with cultural material who is not Black, Indigenous or a Person of Color?

SD

I feel like I could not perform that same gesture in the same way. If I were to center indigenous histories in the middle of geopolitical narratives, it would not be my story to tell. Regrettably, I also don't know enough, even if I had a different relationship to the legitimacy to tell such stories. I think one of the ways that I was preparing for the Tasmania show *Mine* at the Museum of Old and New Art, Australia, highlighted this issue—the question of "Which stories can I tell?" came up a lot. At the beginning, I thought I would tell more stories than I finally did. Ultimately, I decided to tell a story of extractive practices enacted through lineages that could be connected to my own. I felt that I had a legitimacy and desire to critique and push back on industrial models that are used repeatedly by people that look like me.

KM

I think it's worthwhile to talk about legitimacy along several axes. One being lived experience, then another being race, particular to this moment. Because we also know different people who are working along those axes in different ways and are exposed to varying degrees of cultural critique. I have received feedback that there are not enough voices in *Violent Legalities* at present, and that without those narratives, even with the best intention, the project is prone to ethical integrity. I am very interested in whether or not you think those ethics are worthwhile to maintain?

SD

I think it is definitely important who tells what story. Part of what I was working towards in *The Founder's Paradox* by including Michael Parekowhai's work was to engage with my own personal history and involve a conversation, which was foundational for me in terms and my way of working in contemporary art. Michael was influential in my education. He was the first artist that I encountered who was a contemporary artist in the idiom that I wanted to work in. He taught me not only about what contemporary sculpture was at the time, but also about history that had been missed out of my education, in terms of, for example, what being Māori meant to him. We had some explicit and implicit conversations in a longer dialog for a couple of years in my early Fine Arts education at the University of Auckland. Michael at once introduced me to a unique conversation about post-colonialism as well as to practices like Jeff Koons. I think the complications of that are really interesting in retrospect because I also didn't really differentiate that input at the time. I didn't think, this is the Jeff Koons part, this is postcolonial discourse, I just took it as a singular category of practice. I think your critique of my *The Founder's Paradox*-Auckland exhibition still stands. This is something that one could ask of some of my work in general, but of that body of work in particular: is getting into the intricacies of the mythologies that essentially legitimate the continuation of white supremacist empire-building through a technology frame, is mapping that history really enough? From my work? It's interesting that media commentators I was following at the time like Whitney Phillips via Data and Society are also questioning methodologies they used during the 2010s to unpack online subcultures that are linked to white supremacy critically. I was simply not as aware of the implications of the mechanisms of legitimation as I should have been.

KM

Still, the way you talk about your work, its foci, and your process does communicate key actors, moments and developments in the tech-sector geo-politic in that all those pieces start to fall into place in a way that makes sense to me. But also, it's so dense that I personally do get overwhelmed by how involved we are. Not only involved, as in involved because we're interested, and involved because of our particular attitudes to our practices of research, but also involved in that the institutions of our respective industries implicate us in challenging ways.

SD

Right. It is an ongoing assessment of what one can do, which to a certain extent involves iteration as a documentation of learning, even if that's not the ideal. I think you can step back from a project or a research arc or an output arc and ask: What was that? In what ways was that valuable? […]

KM

The current climate is asking for us to be more positional. As are critics of the kind of works that we are both interested in, which is to say the people whose work I am interested in, are all asking for more positioning.

SD

Yes. More accountability, which I agree is important. I think this is especially true for people like me who have often had more affordances than many people. I can understand the ways that making positions like mine clearer will hopefully produce a different environment for production, a better one. I have always thought a lot about the gestures that I've made as an artist, but I also think I've missed important

131

things, resulting in unconsciously biased work. I think identifying that in the reception is fair. And again, the way this relates to my biography, my lived experience. This is a good part to bring up another of our past exchanges. You mentioned in another earlier conversation thoughts about thinking through autobiographical narrative as a discursive window for abstraction, quoting American writer Saidiya Hartman, I'm just going to read the quote: "…[T]he autobiographical example, which is not a personal story that folds onto itself; it's not about navel gazing, it's really about trying to look at historical and social process and one's own formation as a window onto social and historical processes, as an example of them."[2] I thought that resonated with what you and I are currently working on. Can you talk about that in the formulation of the final *Violent Legalities* project? […]

2
Patricia J. Saunders,
"Fugitive Dreams of
Diaspora: Conversations
with Saidiya Hartman",
in: *Anthurium. A Carib-
bean Studies Journal*,
2008, vol. 6, no. 1, p. 7.

KM

I am always trying to gain an understanding of my lived experiences and the study of space. For example, my research into using Building Information Modeling software to capture intangible dimensions of diasporic occupations. What initially did not make sense to me was that these spaces that my community were always in, were so hugely absent from the canons of my architectural education. I found that erasure compelling. I had this project about these invisible-to-the-institution spaces that I had to do. I think I always find things, such as institutional invisibilities, interesting. Particularly spaces between my lived experience and knowledge institutions. I think whenever I sense a disconnect between knowledge institutions and my experience, it calls to me in a way I can't, well maybe more accurately I don't want to ignore. I think in the example of Christchurch, I got that sense of disconnect, the wider socio-political surprise at the scale of violence, the surprise and hesitation around racism, and the reluctance in sitting with racism and white supremacy as an enduring presence in New Zealand. I'm not the only researcher who has said this but the rallying cry of "This is not us" post-Christchurch was deafeningly opposed to my experience, which is that racism has always been part of my life in New Zealand. Forensic Architecture documents human rights violations using architectural media techniques, and adopting that approach felt interesting and justified. They also have developed ways of working with online witness narratives, which I thought could form a part of the project as a counter-focus to the shooter's livestream. It felt that while there was an attitude of experimental research design working across disciplines that with such rightfully sensitive material there would have to be some established methods.

With the kind of white supremacy behind Christchurch, the methods had to allow for its more online life, because it is a specific form of white supremacy for example, it's not the same white supremacy behind the skinhead culture also present in Christchurch.

SD

What I think is really interesting about what you're asking is: what is legible and to whom as white supremacy? When there are subcultures with seemingly less direct relationships to the ideology. For example, skinhead culture in the 80s and 90s versus 4Chan or a Twitch stream nowadays. But there is a relationship between these types of white supremacy and the official history of imperial dominance in New Zealand. That's the kind of relationship that's being mapped, I think as well. Right?

KM

I think those links would be made, but it would still require us to map events that index ideological specifics. I think this is one of the benefits of using mapping of both the geographical and the non-locational aspects of an event, in this instance the legislative: it can unfold the abstract such as ideological differences that support more nuanced understandings to a moment, like Christchurch that resonate with people's sense of place.

SD

I'm also making meanings from my own matrix, which is suggested rather than explicitly articulated at this point, because I think about my own production, vis-à-vis *The Founder's Paradox*-Christchurch which was on display in the city when the Christchurch terrorist attack occurred. Some of the imagery and ideology that I had encountered in the research for that project had suddenly become more locally relevant than I anticipated. Some of the violence is implied in the language and logic that my artworks mapped, but also in the way we curated the show with Michael [Parekowhai]—like how and where he placed his works in relation to mine. To me there were spatial articulations of historical violence, but also had echoes of contemporary tensions. The ideology that is mapped in my work is that of a key architect responsible for contemporary internet business infrastructure—Peter Thiel. Businesses that he has influenced arguably created the platforms that could broadcast and amplify the visibility of these attacks. To have the exhibition be geographically adjacent to the massacre was chilling.

133

The business framework connected to the ideologies and methodologies of Thiel, directly influenced and nurtured the practices of Mark Zuckerberg and the growth of Facebook, enabled the broadcast of the Christchurch massacre. We are having this conversation in the context of a publication which will grapple with Germany's past history and present experience of right-wing extremism and racial violence. The fact that Thiel was born in Germany and has a German heritage is relevant here too, I think. I think making *The Founder's Paradox* and staging it in Christchurch in dialogue with Michael's work was a way for me to visualize contemporary re-articulations of right-wing extremism, related violence and the less visible ideologies and structures that enable their spread and how interconnected those histories are with the colonial past in New Zealand, imperialism in Germany, and business in the United States. To make visible possible fascisms explicitly on the rise. [...]

KM

Some of *Violent Legalities* deals with incidences where the swastika as a symbol of white supremacy has been graffitied in sacred Muslim spaces, or in spaces frequented by Asian diaspora. To me, it is worth pausing to consider when the use of these terms conflates in misplaced interpretations of different movements and motivations. I think that's really something that I'm trying to keep in mind. Even though I do so much work in this space at the moment, it took a moment of reflection to better understand the contextual differences between what motivated the skinheads I was told to steer clear of as a child, and what is currently motivating the attitudes to those we see of online radicalized white supremacists. This is obvious, but I think it's important. The white supremacists of my childhood were reacting to a perceived Asian migration threat. Online radicalized white supremacists have a different focus, specific to the geopolitics of the past twenty years. I'm talking to identifying patterns of human behaviour and the broader socio-politics that create them.

SD

In terms of Asian migration this is relevant to the American Project as well. The history of defining race and defining legality in terms of race, again, from some reading I've done around this kind of space: Chinese-Americans had a very different history than African-Americans, but they both experienced legalized exclusion from the project of building a white nation. In the Pacific region also, I recently started reading more about the colonization of the Pacific and those histories, and also the role of forced labor which included Chinese workers. I have been researching this more as it historically contextualizes my family's history and role in colonial administration. [...]

KM

I agree that these systems enable hierarchies to perpetuate along different ideological lines. Same people, same groups, same communities, it always comes down to the minority life threatened perpetually. Forensic Architecture's attitude to human rights violations resonates with my research interests and perspective on what ought to be prioritized. In New Zealand, human rights can be considered through the lens of the Treaty of Waitangi, while I come to both from the discipline of Architecture—without expertise in either, for the indigenous life placing these frameworks in dialog with one another produces rewarding angles towards identifying solidarities for marginalized peoples and groups. So, there appeared going into the project that there could be worthwhile insights by putting them in contact with each other.

SD

Yes. Can you discuss how you see broader understandings of human rights and the Treaty of Waitangi overlapping? I could imagine that a lot of people who are familiar with Forensic Architecture may not know so much about the Treaty.

KM

That's likely. New Zealand does not have a constitutional document; there is, however, this treaty which is an annexation document between Māori and the Crown. It lays out governing principles between the British and Māori to establish a nation state. There are implications around translation and what was understood by both parties at the time of signing. For some people that is ontologically interesting, then for others it's a monument to what is fundamentally wrong with how the state understands sovereignty and the inclusion of Māori at governance level. With *Violent Legalities*, I have been aware of the Treaty of Waitangi up till now at a citizenry level, which is not having expertise, but an understanding that it is a founding document for contemporary New Zealand. Which is to say, I don't know much about the Treaty, but I know that it shapes the experiences of Māori, and that it is a partnership document From my perspective it ought to shape the experiences of all New Zealanders—hopefully for positive outcomes for Māori, and we ought to be engaged with it, but if my experience is any indicator, then for the majority of New Zealanders are for the most part only laterally aware of how it holds the state to account.

SD

Particularly at legal and narrative levels.

KM

Exactly. I think that the fact that I don't know so much about the Treaty of Waitangi is a state failure embedded in how we fundamentally think about its role as a founding document of the contemporary nation. Which relates to what you mentioned earlier with your experience and Michael. I have been required by my education to learn a lot about everywhere else but here. That I as a researcher, also as a woman of color have never been asked to know about this, is indicative to me of not only what the state prioritizes but also what it requires of its citizens to contribute to the civic. As an architectural researcher, I am engaged with the visual dimensions of how culture, social and economic aspects and politics are ordered and then concretized in the built realm. So, as an explorative thinking exercise, I am interested in considering the events of *Violent Legalities* as violations and/or breaches—there is value, I think, about considering them in these contrasting ways, even if ostensibly there is nothing very obvious to be gained. My perspective is there is value there because I think it is not best practice that I have never been asked to know about the Treaty of Waitangi, and I have been through a lot of education. It is probably one reason why *Violent Legalities* works with the material in the way it does, because I am invested in these understandings.

SD

You broke that down in the project into three themes, right? "Terror Legalities", "Treaty Legalities", and "Moral Drift" form the whole project "Violent Legalities".

KM

Yes. We did; they are about New Zealand legal activity and events, so they have a relationship to the Treaty of Waitangi, but to some extent the way the platforms work together is under the broader category of human rights, and violations of those rights. Thinking historically about human rights violations, as well as breaches of the Treaty of Waitangi. And the potential of this is still revealing itself in ongoing conversations with stakeholders. For example, whenever I present the project to indigenous stakeholders, there is a sense of "The software is really interesting!"—I think it's because, in the context of the tech-world and the sector's rate of innovation more broadly, we by comparison rarely have cutting-edge software that centers on our experience as a means to advocate to non-indigenous groups to see material change. I see being kept out of contemporary institutions that are organizing knowledge and by extension power—through intentional or unintentional bias—, as a human rights violation in a way that is still colonial but not only specific to the New Zealand context. From my perspective, for indigenous people, technology that centers our experiences will command attention because it enables us to talk directly to it, and then also archives so that it can be immediately evidentiary—which is a state tool. *Violent Legalities* is a step towards that, using the language of the state, to advocate for the recognition of rights denied to Māori and Muslim communities, and of course other marginalized groups for reasons of race.

SD

Can you give a couple of examples of the way that picking out certain historical moments for the timeline, that—as you indicate here—centers indigenous experiences as a counter-narrative to other histories?

KM

Yes, the more direct one would be the example of the Tūhoe raids in 2007, which is also the case study film for the project's methodology. Tūhoe refers to the *iwi* (tribe) of the Bay of Plenty, also known as the Te Ureweras here in Aotearoa / New Zealand, and "raids" refers to the armed installed roadblocks, arrests, and home invasions by police in the Rūātoki valley, as well as across New Zealand to find and apprehend alleged terrorists who were in breach of the Terrorism Suppression Act. Seventeen people were arrested from those raids as well the communities of the region terrorized by law-enforcement officers; of those seventeen, only four went to trial. There were reports of officers armed with rifles stepping onto a school bus of children. According to police intelligence at the time, the justification for the raids was that there were terrorism training camps in the Te Urewera forest, which is also a national park. Police had surveillance operations on an indigenous land activist group that was meeting in the forest for a year prior to the raids. This surveillance was later found to be unlawful in 2013 by the Independent Police

Conduct Authority. [...] In *Violent Legalities,* we mapped the events that encompassed the raids, against the more abstract legal activity involved in creating the Terrorism Suppression Act. This then led onto the platform "Treaty Legalities," which looks specifically at the longer history of Tūhoe-Crown relationships beginning in the 1840s. What putting those durations of colonial legal technology in dialog does visually is it uses state rhetoric but highlights the enduring harm of colonialism. You can see how the Crown, and by extension the state, are continually operating along a colonial logic, which is to use law-making as a way to oppress. [...] I find it interesting when you speak about legitimacy, because right now, as I explain, my work involves legitimating indigenous narratives to critique state rhetoric.

SD

Right. Tools and methods that are used to legitimize the other side of the experience. All of this apparatus that is part of the sophisticated, rhetorical, and legal technologies of dominance, that can be flipped.[...]

As I said, I've been researching this family history, partly for fun and partly because I think it's relevant to my work. I've recently focused on my great grandfather, John or 'Jack' Wilson, who was for a short time the Chief Justice of Sāmoa, between 1920 and 21, shortly after the New Zealanders forcibly took the occupation of Sāmoa off the Germans.

KM

A relaxed and peaceful changeover for the colonialists from photographic documentation. Although, not without cost to the Sāmoan people though: these occupations cost lives, which relevant today. The New Zealand Government was responsible for exporting the "Spanish" Flu to Sāmoa in 1918, which was catastrophic: 80–90 percent of the population contracted it and one-fifth of the population died.

SD

Yes, I have been reading more on German colonialism. The ways some German scholars frame these histories that I read accounts of are contestable. But I have gained more insight around narratives from that moment when New Zealand occupied Sāmoa. I did not know that Sāmoa was the very first German territory captured in the First World War. In terms of the agriculture and industry that was present, I was interested to read that German industry set up in Sāmoa before

Bismarck, and during the official moment of colonial dominance, different types of crops, such as copra. I think your great-grandfather was involved in Tonga as well, right? The copra plantations were kept during the New Zealand occupation; however, there were also rubber tree plantations all over Sāmoa, cultivated under the German occupation. When New Zealand arrived in its own bid as a dominant local power, they immediately took command of everything. They destroyed a key radio tower in advance, which disabled communication, so when a telegram arrived from Berlin with instructions on how to react to an occupation, it was apparently unreadable as the cipher was lost, and they couldn't decode the central command from Germany, which I also think is interesting in terms of the histories of ciphers and telecommunications and imperial/colonial directives. Regarding these plantations, the rubber plantations were destroyed by the New Zealand occupation as they only wanted short-term yield which was copra. They strategized should the Germans win the war, and they would have to get the territory back there would be nothing of high value. All of the rubber plantations were destroyed due to this short-term profiteering mindset of the New Zealand occupation. […] For me this territorial history between all kinds of political histories that find convergence in Sāmoa is interesting because the powers of colonial Germany, the United States, Britain and then my own birthplace, New Zealand, converge in an imperial collision in Sāmoa in compelling narratives.

KM

I agree with you in the sense that when I'm doing work located in Sāmoa's geography, I'm struck by how tactical Sāmoa was for the United States, Britain, New Zealand, and Germany. I also found it engaging, to think about the geopolitical implications of World War I and II, as enduring traces of a period where militarization was taking on new mobilities. Connecting the military complex innovations specific to that time to the contemporary economic powers we have now, making connections between then and now and recognizing: "This is still happening in a different scale." Because a lot of those negotiations were happening sort of in the Northern hemisphere, Sāmoa's being smaller and located so far away in the Southern Hemisphere, and the creation of the Global South. Recognizing the power differentials, and the militaristic and imperial motivations for grabbing these land grabs that has very different conceptions for the people who live there of it. For me that again is recognizing a disconnect between my experiences and these larger, powerful, power agendas. Yes, there is intrigue, but I think what sustains that intrigue is recognizing the inequity perpetuated through historiographies.

KM
I think through this conversation I've identified why I do what I do, what about why you do what you do?

SD
When I moved from Auckland to Frankfurt in 2007 to study, I arrived with a suitcase and a laptop. I suddenly found myself spending 24 hours on this laptop—I was learning on it, I was keeping in touch with family and friends I dearly missed using it, I was watching TV on it etc. Everything. The reason I embarked on exhibition making about people that own technology companies, and the ideologies they buy into, was because I realized that this portal had become my core tool, almost my entire interface with the world. My practice at the time was about trying to understand the objects in my life. […] In a certain sense, the way I engaged was through material, so when I moved to Frankfurt and I found myself with this laptop in front of me, I guess I also wanted to know what the rub was on that. Like what the fuck is this thing? How this thing really filters all of my thinking, filters all of my interfaces with everybody I know. I thought as a sculptor, if I'm so interested in stuff and what it does to my perception, and presumably that's what I was interested in at the time, then what is this thing? That felt so powerful. I'm still working to make sense of the things which have power over my life and my lived experience. And increasingly, I looked to include the workings behind objects. I had a period where I looked at businesses and internet hardware. Then politics and the superstructure inherent to those technologies, and the ideologies that animate them. That is how I have arrived at where I am now. I'm trying to understand better what it is that I'm living in, you know? […]

KM
Yes. Would you say that you are always investigating that line, or the case, or picking apart everything in our physical world that impacts our personal politics?

SD
Yes, and as one gets older, one also realizes I guess this is also part of looking into a family history that you only have a certain finite plastic

existence and time spent and moments spent are finite. That's kind of a jump but there's something quite profound about the fact that my material and my mediated experience and my social experience and my political experience are all only lived once, through one moment, and as I have less and less of it: I want to make that overtly more and more careful with the way that that resource is spent.

Jumana Manna, *a Magical Substance Flows Into Me*, 2015 | Installation view, *Tell me about ~~yesterday~~ tomorrow*

Marcel Odenbach, *Das große Fenster – Einblick eines Ausblicks (The Big Window – Insight, Looking Out)*, 2001; *Ordnung muß sein (Order must be)*, 2019; *im Land der Dichter und Denker (in the Land of Poets and Thinkers)*, 2019 | Installation view, *Tell me about ~~yesterday~~ tomorrow*

Engaging with Silences Surrounding
Traumatic Events of the Past

MARINA GRŽINIĆ

INTRODUCTION

This text presents an insight into the research project "Genealogy of Amnesia: Rethinking the Past for a New Future of Conviviality" that I embarked on with a team of researchers from 2018 to 2020.[1] In order to study a genealogy of amnesia surrounding traumatic events in Europe, we built an interdisciplinary platform which focused on current politics of oblivion and strategies of silencing historical experiences in three territories—Belgium, Austria, and former Yugoslavia. We investigated the following relationships that are connected to genocides: The construction of a Belgian identity in the aftermath of its colonial past; the construction of national identity in Austria after the *Anschluss*, the annexation of Austria into Nazi Germany on 12 March 1938; and the attempts to create a new national identity in Serbia and "Republika Srpska" ("Serb Republic"), along with the negation of war crimes after the dissolution of Yugoslavia.

These three territories are embedded with silencing methods of genocidal politics of the past. At a time when Europe is witnessing a rise of authoritarian politics, nationalism and increasing social polarization, which are threatened to be reinforced by the Covid-19-pandemic, the question is how to critically engage with silences surrounding genocides and racialized violence in the past and its enduring presence in society today.

Taking the history of Belgium's colonial past, the annexation of Austria into Nazi Germany in 1938, and the history of the Jasenovac concentration camp during the Second World War in Croatia as well as the Srebrenica genocide during the Balkan wars in 1995, we compiled a digital archive that documents events that have often been suppressed and excluded from national representation.[2]

Taking an online digital archive as my starting point, including 82 interviews and positions as well as a collection of digital and digitized materials that address the subjects and objects, the territories, and events of oblivion and amnesia, I am presenting in this text four excerpts from interviews that illustrate neglected aspects within national historical narratives.

We discuss the representation of Congo in Belgium, the Mauthausen concentration camp—today a memorial site—in Austria, and Jasenovac—a concentration camp run by Nazi collaborators in Croatia (Ustasha) and today a memorial site, and conclude with the most recent genocide on European soil that took place in Srebrenica, Bosnia and Herzegovina (BiH), in 1995, to which it is possible to attach a whole list of genocidal sites spread throughout

1
See Genealogy of Amnesia. https://archiveofamnesia.akbild.ac.at/ (accessed on 1 October 2020). The core team consists of Marina Gržinić, a leading researcher, postdoctoral researchers Sophie Uitz, Jovita Pristovšek, and Šefik Tatić, doctoral researcher Christina Jauernik, and a professional associate Valerija Zabret.

2
See https://archiveofamnesia.akbild.ac.at/?page_id=17 (accessed October 1, 2020).

3
It is important to
stress that in contrast
to Austria, Belgium,
and Serbia, "Republika
Srpska" is not a state
– it is an ethnically
homogeneous territorial
entity within BiH,
with aspirations for
separation.

4
Saidiya Hartman, *Venus
in Two Acts*, *Small Axe*,
vol. 12, no. 2, 2008, pp.
1-14, p. 11.

5
I refer here to Hartman's
formulation in *Venus
in Two Acts* (see note 4),
p. 4.

6
Paul Marie Ghislain
Otlet (1868–1944)
was a Belgian author,
entrepreneur, lawyer,
peace activist, and author
of the Universal Decimal
Classification; he is
considered the father of
information science.

7
The Congolese poli-
tician Patrice Émery
Lumumba (1925–1961)
was an independence
leader and the first
Prime Minister of the
independent Democratic
Republic of the Congo
(at that time Republic
of the Congo), who was
assassinated in 1961
during the Congo civil
war. In 1999, Ludo De
Witte's *The Assassination
of Lumumba* prompted
a parliamentary inquiry
questioning Belgian
involvement in
Lumumba's death.
See Ludo De Witte,
De moord op *Lumumba*,
Leuven 1999.

the country. In our research project, this is connected to the city of Prijedor (today in "Republika Srpska," BiH).[3]

Following a question posed by American scholar Saidiya Hartman as to whether it is possible to exceed or negotiate the constitutive limits of the archive,[4] we embarked on a critical examination of ideas of national identity, silencing genocides, and the construction of history. Hartman developed her theoretical and methodological framework in relation to the history of slavery and its afterlives in present forms of racism. She interrogated the historical archive analytically in order to make productive sense of gaps and silences surrounding the experiences of the enslaved by utilizing personal narratives.

A critical examination of three traumatic events in Europe in different historical times and their relationship to collective memory and national representation today is becoming an urgent task.

THE LIVES OF THE DEAD AND THE HISTORY OF THE PRESENT[5]

1. *Brussels (Belgium): Kalvin Soiresse Njall*
    4 May 2018
    Interviewer: Marina Gržinić

Kalvin Soiresse Njall is a Belgian-Togolese teacher of social sciences, a former journalist and a novelist. He is also a co-founder of the Collectif Mémoire Coloniale et Lutte contre les Discriminations (CMCLD) for which he was also a coordinator from 2012 to 2017. CMCLD—the Collective Colonial Memory and Fight against Discrimination—is a decolonial movement, formed by several African associations in Flanders, Brussels, and Wallonia.

Soiresse Njall

In the public space there are many tributes to the people responsible for colonization, who killed many people, but we do not have tributes to people who fought against colonization, black people and white people. This is so, because they used to tell us, you know, that all people were in favor of colonization at that time, and we used to tell them that is not true.

We do not have tributes like this for people who fought against colonization, like communists who were anti-colonialists, like some liberals, like Paul Otlet,[6] and the government was against them. For example, Paul Otlet lost his job because he was an anti-colonialist. So we want to see some tributes in the public space to Patrice Lumumba,[7] for example, to Simon Kimbangu,[8] for example, to Queen Nzinga[9] who fought against the Portuguese. It is very, very important for us and for Belgian society because now we are in complete denial of this history. In schools, in public spaces, in museums, in institutions, even in politics, there are people who are very ignorant of this history or are very cynical about it. That is why [and what] we are fighting for and that's why we begin here. So, here you have this building, which was the headquarters of the colonial administration. People who wanted to go to Congo used to come here to get their papers. In those times, the propaganda said that going to Congo was a "civilizing mission," to civilize the black people who are "savages." It was propagated that service to the colonial system would make people rich. The propaganda told the poor people here that they would be the masters there and that they would make a lot of money. It is true because after independence, it was very traumatic and many Belgians suffered from psychological problems because they had been there, they were masters served by black people and, one day, it was all gone. They had to go back to Belgium. Some white people did not even know Belgium, because they had been born in Congo, served by black people, so it was especially traumatic for them. So, here [next to the previous building] we can see the constitutional court. There is not a single marking there saying it was a colonial building, and we are fighting to make it visible. In the public space, they want to erase so many traces of colonialism, because of the shame they now feel and because of our struggle today. They do not want to have visible signs in the public space. And therefore the fight to make this visible is very, very important. In 1955, the university professor Jef Van Bilsen[10] made a statement telling the political and economic establishment that all the colonies around us were distancing themselves, Congo Brazzaville, the French colonies, and we were managing things as if nothing was happening in Africa. We had to prepare for the independence of Congo; we had to prepare the cultural, political and economic emancipation of the Congolese.

In parliament and in the political establishment they regarded him as a traitor to his country, because he dared to imagine that one day the Congolese would be free. It was inconceivable for the Belgian political establishment. That is why, after independence, there was denial though the independence was marked by the legendary speech of Patrice Lumumba.[11] So, we will now go to the statue of Godfrey of Bouillon[12] because Godfrey of Bouillon was the inspiration for Leopold II[13]. Here is the Place Royale [Royal Square] and this whole area forms a triangle. It was an area where the colonials came back from the Congo and where

8
Simon Kimbangu (1887–1951) was a Congolese religious leader, a founder of the Kimbanguist church.

9
Nzinga Mbande or Queen Nzinga (1583–1663) was a 17th-century queen of the Ndongo and Matamba Kingdoms of the Mbundu people in what is known as Angola today.

10
In December 1955, a Belgian professor Anton Arnold Jozef "Jef" Van Bilsen (1913–1996) proposed a 30-year plan (called the "Van Bilsen Plan") to prepare the Congo for autonomy in the context of its transition from the Belgian Congo. See Jef Van Bilsen, *Un plan de trente ans pour l'émancipation politique de l'Afrique belge*, Les dossiers de l'action sociale catholique, vol. 33, no. 2, 1956, pp. 83–111.

11
Patrice Lumumba delivered his speech on 30 June 1960; it marked the independence of Congo-Léopoldville (today's DR Congo) from Belgium. See Patrice Lumumba. *Speech at the Ceremony of the Proclamation of the Congo's Independence.* June 30, 1960. Marxist Internet Archive, https:// www. marxists.org/subject/ africa/lumumba/1960 /06/independence.htm (accessed June 5, 2019).

12
Godfrey of Bouillon (1060–1100) was a Frankish knight born in today's Walloon Brabant in Belgium. He was one of the leaders of the First Crusade called by Pope Urban II in 1095 to liberate Jerusalem and help the Byzantine Empire, both under attack from Muslim forces at that time.

13
Leopold II, or Leopold II of Belgium (1835–1909), ruled Belgium from 1865 to 1909. He founded Congo Free State (1885–1908), a private colony that he administered with murders, tortures, atrocities and forced labor to gain enormous wealth with which he funded private as well as public projects in Belgium. See Adam Hochschild, *King Leopold's Ghost: A Story of Greed, Terror, and Heroism in Colonial Africa*, Boston 1998.

14
Matongé is a part of the municipality of Ixelles in Brussels, Belgium, formed in the late 50s and known for its Congolese community. It is named after the marketplace and the commercial district in Kinshasa, Democratic Republic of the Congo.

15
Genealogy of Amnesia, *Collectif Mémoire Coloniale et Lutte contre les Discriminations (K. Soiresse Njall)*, https://archiveofamnesia.akbild.ac.at/?videos =kalvin-soiresse-njall-collectif-memoire-coloniale-et-lutte-contre-les-discriminations&_sft_people=collectif-memoire-coloniale-et-lutte-contre-les-discriminations (accessed October 2, 2020).

16
Mauthausen Memorial. About Us, https://www.mauthausen-memorial.org/en/About-us/Organisation (accessed June 16, 2020).

17
See Gordon J. Horwitz, *In the Shadow of Death: Living Outside the Gates of Mauthausen*, London and New York, 1991.

they spent their holidays during those years. Now it is ironic that Matongé,[14] for example, is a cultural center for the descendants of people who were colonized. So, here we are in front of [the statue of] Godfrey of Bouillon; he was the leader of the First Crusade against the Muslims and Jews in Jerusalem. And he was a great inspiration to Leopold II, because Leopold II said that Godfrey of Bouillon was the one who gave Belgium its first colony. For him, Jerusalem was Belgium's colony[15].

2. *Mauthausen Memorial (Austria): Christian Dürr*
    11 October 2019
    Interviewer: Marina Gržinić

Dr. Christian Dürr studied philosophy, history, and communication theory at the University of Vienna. Since 2001 he has been working as an archivist and historian for the Mauthausen Memorial Archives, currently in the role of chief curator.

The Mauthausen Memorial is a site of remembrance and education, preserving the memory of the victims and examining, documenting, and exhibiting the history of the Mauthausen Concentration Camp. The concentration camp was a central component of the system of more than 40 sub-camps and the central site of political, social, and racial persecution by the National Socialist regime in Austria from 1938 to 1945. From a total of 190,000 people imprisoned here, at least 90,000 were killed.[16]

Marina Gržinić

You said before that the Mauthausen concentration camp was very visible, unlike [many other] concentration camps, specifically extermination camps in other parts of Europe, and I wonder how much the local population, the civilians around [Mauthausen-Gusen] were involved in crimes that were committed here? I am asking this [since] there was an event, known as the "Rabbit Hunt," in which Soviet prisoners in 1945 who tried to escape, were hunted down and killed, not only by the SS but also by the local civilians. So, what was the impact of Mauthausen on the social body not only of these regions but also of Austria?

Christian Dürr

This is a topic that has been underestimated for a long time. For a long time there was not much research about it and still there is not a great deal of research on this subject. There was one book by Gordon Horwitz,[17] [which contains] interviews with people from the

150

surrounding population and, for the first time, the question was posed as to how the population actually reacted [to the camp]. But, as I said before, for a long time there was not a lot of attention attached to this question. I think that this also has something to do with the fact that, as we said before, Mauthausen was not one single place; it was a whole network, which extended throughout the whole of Austrian territory. But, by the end of the war and after 1945, the whole culture of commemoration, the whole remembrance, was centralized very much here at this place, here at Mauthausen. And the stronger this place grew as a site of commemoration, the more all the other places were forgotten. On the other hand, the stronger this place grew, the more this crime was seen as a monstrous crime which was represented by the gas chamber here in Mauthausen; by the crematoriums in Mauthausen [concentration camp], a really monstrous crime. But what were no longer in focus were the everyday aspects of these crimes. As you said before, there were people from the surrounding population who were working together with the concentration camp. So, there was not just this monstrous fact of mass extermination, but the population of the whole region was involved with these crimes on an everyday basis. So, by installing this central commemoration site, the focus was put on the monstrous side of the crime and not so much on the everyday aspect of the crime[18].

3. Jasenovac Memorial Site, Jasenovac (Croatia): Ivo Pejaković 29 May 2019
Interviewers: Marina Gržinić and Šefik Tatlić

Ivo Pejaković graduated from Zagreb University in 2006 with a degree in history. In 2019 he was appointed as the director of the Jasenovac Memorial Site, where he had been employed as a curator of the Memorial Museum since 2009. Since 2018 he has represented Croatia in the International Holocaust Remembrance Alliance (IHRA), in the Museums and Memorials Working Group.

The Jasenovac Memorial Site compiles and researches as well as preserving the museum buildings and exhibiting documents of the Jasenovac camp history. It is located near the former concentration camp, Camp III (Brickworks), in Jasenovac, Croatia.[19] The camp complex was established in August 1941 as a string of five camps on the banks of the Sava River, some 100 kilometers south of Zagreb. It has been named the "Auschwitz of the Balkans." It was run solely by the Ustasha regime, and was the largest concentration and camp complex in the so-called Independent State of Croatia (Nezavisna Država Hrvatska, NDH).

18
Genealogy of Amnesia, *Christian Dürr*, https://archiveofamnesia.akbild.ac.at/?videos=christian-durr&_sft_people=durr (accessed October 2, 2020).

19
Jasenovac Memorial Site. Jasenovac Memorial Site, http://www.jusp-jasenovac.hr/Default.aspx?sid=6468 (accessed October 2, 2020).

Ivo Pejaković

When we come to the issue of the number of victims—this is something that has been disputed and talked about since the time when the camp still existed and after the liberation of the [Jasenovac] camp in 1945.[20] Already in 1946 first assessments were made. The first official assessment was made in 1946 by the commission established by the Yugoslav government that was dealing with war crimes committed in the territory of Yugoslavia, and in 1946 they published a small book and mentioned that somewhere between 500,000 and 600,000 people were killed in Jasenovac. Immediately after that, Yugoslavia demanded reparations from Germany for the crimes committed in the territory of Yugoslavia and in those documents it was assessed that about 1.7 million people altogether in the territory of Yugoslavia were killed, regardless of location, and of that number, 700,000 were killed in the Jasenovac camp. So these numbers became official numbers in the period of Yugoslavia and if you look at the *Encyclopedia of Yugoslavia*[21] you can see these numbers mentioned under the title "Jasenovac." In the 1960s there was an attempt by the Federal Institute of Statistics to compile the names of the victims, the persons who were killed. And they sent their researchers throughout the country and the goal was to establish those numbers and basically to confirm the numbers that were officially published, not only for Jasenovac but for all the victims all over Yugoslavia.

In 1964 this research was completed and, altogether, they found about 600,000 names of victims, regardless of the place where they were killed, and out of that number 59,000 names of victims were those killed in Jasenovac. But since this research did not really match these previous, official numbers, in fact it was never published. It was kept in the archives of this institution, the Federal Bureau of Statistics. Only some historians and politicians were aware of this research and its results. In the 1990s, these documents were somehow smuggled out of the institution, and in 1998 the Bosniak Institute [in Sarajevo] actually published the book with the 59,000 names of those killed in Jasenovac. So, sometime around 2005, we as an institution, the Jasenovac Memorial Site, started working on the list of victims and the goal of that research was to find as many names as possible of the people killed in Jasenovac camp. So, through work in archives, in different national or local archives, through the literature, or some local lists of victims that were published in particular counties or municipalities, through contacts with families of all the victims, we tried to make this list as correct as possible. At the moment, we have about

20
In late April 1945 the Partisan Resistance Movement approached Jasenovac. Several hundred prisoners rose up against the camp guards that murdered most of them before Partisans overran Jasenovac in early May 1945.

21
Jasenovac, in: *Enciklopedija Jugoslavije*, vol. 3, ed. by Jugoslavenski leksikografski zavod, Zagreb 1958, p. 648f.

22
Genealogy of Amnesia, *Ivo Pejaković*, https:// archiveofamnesia. akbild.ac.at/?videos =ivo-pejakovic&_ sft_people=pejakovic (accessed October 2, 2020).

23
International Criminal Tribunal for the former Yugoslavia. Kvočka et al. (IT-98-30/1), Omarska, Keraterm & Trnopolje Camps, http://www.icty.org/x/ cases/kvocka/ cis/en/ cis_kvocka_al_en.pdf, p. 7. (accessed October 2, 2020).

24
International Criminal Tribunal for the former Yugoslavia. *Bridging the Gap in Prijedor, Bosnia and Herzegovina*, https://www.icty. org/en/outreach/ bridging-the-gap-with- local-communities/ prijedor (accessed October 2, 2020).

25

83,000 records of the victims in our database and we always try to emphasize that this is not the total number. It is impossible to find exactly, name by name, how many people were killed because when you go through the archives, when you go through these different documents and the lists of victims sometimes under the section "place of death" stands "unknown". This was when somebody was arrested, deported somewhere, did not return, and did not survive the war, but there is just not enough evidence to establish and claim that these persons were killed in some particular place or a camp. So, we are always clear in emphasizing that this is not the total number, the number is probably higher than that, but for us, it is also difficult to try to guess what that total number might be. We are careful not to go public with any specific numbers[22].

4. *Prijedor (BiH): Goran Zorić & participant in the "White Armband" commemoration day 31 May 2019 Interviewers: Marina Gržinić and Šefik Tatlić*

Prijedor, a town located in north-west Bosnia and Herzegovina, is the site of the second largest genocide committed during the Balkan Wars, while the largest one is the Srebrenica genocide (11–22 July 1995; Bosniak men and boys; 8,372 deaths).

Shortly before the takeover of Prijedor, Serb forces relieved the non-Serbs, Muslims and Bosnian Croats of all their official positions; many were fired and the children prevented from going to school. Radios broadcast anti-Muslim and anti-Croat propaganda.[23] Following the takeover of Prijedor municipality on 30 April 1992, Serb forces confined thousands of non-Serb civilians in the Omarska, Keraterm and Trnopolje camps.[24]

The war crimes in Prijedor were subjected to 13 trials before the International Criminal Tribunal for former Yugoslavia (ICTY) in The Hague.[25]

The "White Armband Day" commemorates the events that took place on 31 May 1992 in the Prijedor municipality. On that day the Serb authorities imposed a forceful directive, instructing the non-Serb population, mainly Bosniaks and Croats, to display white sheets on their homes and to carry white armbands in all public spaces.

This fascist campaign was a prelude to the ethnic cleansing of the non-Serb population and the genocide against Bosniaks in the Prijedor area. White Armband Day is commemorated in numerous cities in Bosnia and Herzegovina, as well as in numerous cities worldwide.

The ICTY reports in its documents: "[O]n 23 May 1992, Serb forces attacked and gained control of the largely Muslim village of Hambarine, eventually resulting in the displacement of approximately 20,000 non-Serbs. The following day, a successful attack was launched on the town of Kozarac, which was again situated in a predominantly Muslim area (approximately 27,000 non-Serbs lived in the wider Kozarac area and of the 4,000 inhabitants of the town itself, 90% were Muslim). A large number of Muslim citizens of these areas who did not succeed in fleeing in the face of the assaults were rounded up, taken into custody and detained in one of the three camps which were the subject of this case. To avert any desire for resistance by the Croats, and especially the Muslims, the Serbs interrogated any non-Serb who might present a threat, and arrested in particular any persons exerting authority, moral or otherwise, or representing some kind of power, in particular economic. At the same time, the men were separated from the women, children and elderly. Men in particular were interrogated. The Serbs assembled the non-Serbs who had not left the region in detention centres. This is when the camps of Omarska, Keraterm and Trnopolje were established." International Criminal Tribunal for the former Yugoslavia. Kvočka et al. (IT-98-30/1), Omarska, Keraterm & Trnopolje Camps, http://www.icty.org/x/cases/kvocka/cis/en/cis_kvocka_al_en.pdf, p. 7.

Taking part in the White Armband Day commemoration of the victims of genocide in Prijedor on 31 May 2019, we talked with Goran Zorić. He is a co-founder of the initiative "Jer me se tiče" (Because I Care) and is committed to work with issues concerning confrontation with the past and human rights.

Goran Zorić

Today's gathering, like the six previous ones, was organized by the initiative "Jer me se tiče" (Because I Care) […] Today's event, as in previous years, is dedicated to the support of the initiative of the parents of murdered children that demand a monument in remembrance of 102 children who were killed, to be constructed in the center of Prijedor. […] In 2012, Emir Hodžić, who was a protagonist, stood alone at the square wearing a white armband. From that point this massive commemorative event started to take shape. It refers to 31 May 1992, when Serb authorities ordered all non-Serb citizens to display white bed-sheets on their homes and wear white armbands when leaving their homes. This gathering clearly outlines the brutality of what happened in Prijedor. This brutality involved systemic crime, which consisted of not only propaganda but also concentration camps, ethnic cleansing etc. Around 3,176 civilians were murdered in Prijedor during the last war, 102 of whom were children[26].

During the course of this event a Bosnian resident of Prijedor also spoke to us. She did not want her name to be publicized but nonetheless asked us to record her statement.

Bosnian woman

[E]verything that happened in the Second World War, what Hitler had been doing against the non-German populations, was the same as everything Serbs have done during the last war in Prijedor. Not only were those children murdered, but around 4,000 citizens were murdered in Prijedor, and not only that, we suffered the same destiny as Srebrenica. They should be afraid and ashamed of everything they did in Prijedor. The whole world should hear about everything that took place here. The world was then turning deaf to everything that happened in Prijedor, but at least now everything that took place here should become known in the name of all the victims from Hambarine, Čarakovo, Kozarac, and all other places. We did not come here to seek justice, but the time has come for the media to be able to disseminate the truth about what happened in Prijedor."[27]

26
Genealogy of Amnesia, *Prijedor*, https://archiveof amnesia.akbild.ac.at/ ?page_id=17&_ sft_people=prijedor (accessed October 2, 2020).

27
https://archive ofamnesia.akbild.ac.at/ ?page_id=17&_sft_ people=prijedor

154

CONCLUSION

The quotes referring to the three territories at the center of the scientific-artistic research project Genealogy of Amnesia (Vienna, 2018-2020) illustrate historical narratives that are not part of a national construction of history. Even though they happened at different times they indicate the troubled relationships between memory, narratives and representation. I have presented this selection of quotes as a result of the research to epitomize the struggle against amnesia. Nevertheless, the possibilities of interpretation of these genocides are to be seen anew as well. Therefore, we have been working on developing counter-histories that Saidiya Hartman connects with the "history of the present," which are "inseparable" as they both touch on an "incomplete project of freedom."[28] a critical examination of the past and its afterlives today is possible through processing the unspoken events in order to become part of the historical archives. Hartman's concept of counter-histories as the intersection of the "lives of the dead" and the "history of the present," and particularly her notion of the present that is "interrupted" by the past, is what the line of apprehending the process we put on work is.

Hartman believes that "a history of the present strives to illuminate the intimacy of our experience with the lives of the dead, to write our present as it is interrupted by this past, and to imagine a free state, not as the time before captivity or slavery, but rather as the anticipated future of this writing."[29] At stake here is not merely past and present but futurity: "this history has engendered me," she writes, "the kinds of stories I have fashioned […] bridge the past and the present."[30] The construction of history is always connected to the conditions of the present time, but can help to understand the past unequal valuation and discrimination of people.

28
Saidiya Hartman,
Venus in Two Acts
(see note 4), p. 4.

29
Ibid.

30
Ibid.

Baseera Khan, *I AM a BODY*, 2018; *iamuslima*, 2018; *Purple Heart*, 2017 | Installation view, *Tell me about ~~yesterday~~ tomorrow*

Baseera Khan, *Nike ID #1*, 2018 | Installation view, *Tell me about ~~yesterday~~ tomorrow*

Leon Kahane, *Pitchipoï*, 2019 | Installation view, *Tell me about ~~yesterday~~ tomorrow*

Mira Schendel, *Livro Obra*, 1971 | Installation view, *Tell me about ~~yesterday~~ tomorrow*

49) Mira Schendel
Livro obra, 1971
Letraset auf pflanzlichem Papier/
on vegetable paper, 18,5 x 31,5 cm

Livro obra, 1973
Letraset auf pflanzlichem Papier/
on vegetable paper, 18,5 x 31,5 cm

Courtesy Marta and Paulo
Kuczynski Collection

*Artworks, Remediation,
and Counter-Conduct*

Performing Remembrance
Contemporary counter-conduct
visible sedition in the air,
subversion under the radar
semiotic guerilla warfare.

Dance to extract a virus,
dance to mitigate history,
dance to de-possess and return,
dance to transition.

Collections are cadavers,
beetles burrowing in peat,
acousmatic echoes,
memories unleashed.

Dance to extract a virus,
dance to mitigate history,
dance to de-possess and return,
dance to transition.

A story within stories
on the failures of humanity,
shackled to its own inventions,
hooked on remembrance.

Dance to extract a virus,
dance to mitigate history,
dance to de-possess and return,
dance to transition.

Anamnesis of the past
ruins ahead of time.
topologies of prediction
vernacular devotion

Dance to extract a virus,
dance to mitigate history,
dance to de-possess and return,
dance to transition.

1
See Romi Crawford, "Theaster Gates and the Centripetal Force of Archives", in: exh. cat. Kunsthaus Bregenz (ed.), *Theaster Gates/ black archive*, Bregenz 2017, p. 83.

2
Paul Rabinow, preface to: Clémentine Deliss (ed.), *Object Atlas, Fieldwork in the Museum*, Bielefeld 2015.

Remediation is one of the most central methodologies of the present day. It partners with twenty-first century debates on reparations and restitution affecting peoples and cultures who have been subjected to violence by European imperialism. To remediate a specific condition, relative to the loss of human dignity and ensuing pain, is to set in motion a dialogue between deeply embedded emotional factors, documents, artworks, and artifacts, and thereby to activate a response that has the potential to *alter-locate*[1] the damaged or dormant residues of meanings transported through archival materiality. Remediation adapts the trope of *metalepsis*, defined by anthropologist Paul Rabinow as a process that "takes up the past or an aspect of the past, or rather the enduring presence of something past, and makes it *operate* within a different narratological milieu—thereby subordinating it to a different function and thus transforming it and making it present."[2] The external channels put into practice by remediation are central to its ability to heal memories and reroute meanings conserved within deep-seated disciplinary regimes. With the shift afforded by the introduction of alternative media, the artefact transitions from singular semantic reification into the polysemic collective interpretations of contemporary diasporic discourse.

3
See Daniele Lorenzini, "From Counter-Conduct to Critical Attitude. Michel Foucault and the Art of Not Being Governed Quite So Much", in: *Foucault Studies*, no. 21, June 2016, p.19.

Remediation resembles semiotic, aesthetic, and affective surgery performed on a metabolic constitution in mnemonic crisis. In the medical context, *anamnesis* is the opening up of the memory of a patient and depends on the skill of the physician to ask appropriate questions that can provide insight into what the afflicted person may be experiencing. Through experimental "practices of freedom"[3], which like rehearsals or exercises help to fine-tune the curator's stance, one begins to move toward the poetics and politics of the decolonial imperative. The original object is accompanied and expanded by engaged commentaries and alternative voices from representatives of the source communities to artists, designers, students, and researchers. However, public exhibition-making can run the danger of becoming a consensus-producing dispositive, steering behavioral and intellectual reception. Alternatively, it can render the environment of this exegetical dramaturgy into a safe space for remembrance work and remediation to take place. State and municipal collections in Europe contain significant masses of objects and archives that necessitate such curative redesign. With ethnographic collections, the custodian determines the visitor's pathway to knowledge through accepted forms of contextualization. This process is insufficient to guarantee equitable exchange with the producers and former owners of these artefacts. Recondite artefacts extracted from their sites of origin, acquired and looted for their mysticism and exoticism, are permeated with ambiguity and contention. Their unfolding requires a plurality of positions to stimulate close readings and deep descriptions capable of provoking new metaphorical and affect-led points of entry. This is where the non-normative methodologies of remediation run up against the narcissism of Eurocentric nineteenth-century classification and can quickly be construed as a form of academic counter-conduct.

Deaccessioning works by museums is another case of cultural-political counter-conduct. Yet hoarding is equally problematic. Ethnographic collections built from colonial expeditions are the results of acts of serial kleptomania performed on the code and form-finding ingenuity of cultures and peoples. The sheer quantity of objects in European ethno-colonial collections throws up the potential for releasing and returning rather than reaping monetary gains from sales. Who has the right to earn from the deaccessioning of artefacts that were acquired illegitimately? The museum and the state? Who are the speakers actively engaged in the discussions around restitution, circulation, and co-ownership? How far do these debates actually address numerous interlocutors on the African continent, for example?

In response, Azu Nwagbogu, director of the African Artists' Foundation in Lagos, and I developed a concept for an online Home Museum intended to animate a more rapid grassroots response to the politics of restitution.[4] In spring 2020, as we were all forced into domestic isolation, the option to visit a museum and learn from exhibitions, artworks, and collections from the past faded fast. Coincidentally, the return of artifacts, held since colonial times in the museums of the Global North, was discussed more than ever before. The Home Museum was born out of the connection between these two conditions: First, staying inside and reflecting on one's immediate environment, family heirlooms, and personal belongings. Second, initiating a visual conversation across continents on the subject of restitution and the possible roles museums might play in the twenty-first century. Photography proved to be the democratic vector for a process of fast shutter retrieval, promoting greater awareness of cultural heritage both absent and present.

Over two hundred individuals from homes around the world responded to an open call sent out through social media in May 2020. Drafted in Yoruba, Igbo, Hausa, Swahili, Wolof, Pidgin, English, French, Russian, and Chinese, this was a letter addressed as if to a friend, an invitation to take part in co-creating a new virtual museum. "As we go about our busy lives," it read, "we often forget the small things worth preserving—objects that are important to each person, family, and home. Some treasures we use every day, some we keep, some we hold close, some we lose, and some are simply forgotten and not

4
"Home Museum" is part of the Lagos Photo Festival 2020. This year's edition is based on the concept of "Rapid Response Restitution". It is co-curated with Nigerian cultural historian Dr. Oluwatoyin Sogbesan and curator Asya Yaghmurian. For more information, see African Artists' Foundation on https://www.africanartists.org/.

preserved at all. All these things bring back memories and tell stories about our culture and history in ways we don't always recognize." The brief was straightforward: to take part all you needed to do was to use your mobile phone to capture your own "Home Museum" and email a maximum of twelve photographs to the African Artists' Foundation, accompanying these images with a short text describing their contents. One common factor to nearly all the images sent from over twenty African countries but equally from Latin America, China, the Middle East and Europe is that they were taken by individuals living in home exile during the first surge of Covid-19. The result is a self-confident, humble set of visual testimonials of home life during the global pandemic that have been indirectly mediated through this project.

Several participants staged their home as if it were a museum, setting up assemblages of objects, capturing the hang of their personal art collection, or gathering together family archives. These artifacts have been photographed against a wide range of domestic backgrounds, often revealing the realities of home life as a space of inhabited meanings that span across generations and technologies. The images evoke ways of living, but also highlight particular "objects of virtue"— artifacts that have been singled out because they resist anachronism, maintain their aura, and personify memories cherished and renewed. These include different domestic appliances from cooking stoves to crockery, vases, clocks, watches, clothing, and money through to objects of vernacular devotion such as hair, vintage photographs, and family memorabilia. Others highlight early image-making technologies such as cameras, televisions, and phones, creating a double take on the artifact and the history of lens-based media. Such "objects of virtue" become carriers of sentiment and energy, marking journeys, and highlighting kindred histories of the twentieth century. People, too, appear within the Home Museum, holding their exhibits like collectors, or standing in their revered space as if they were guards in an exhibition. Subjective interpretations of family, ancestry, identity, gender, migration, time, technology, and healing are reflected in the way objects have been singled out and photographed by each individual, be they in Abuja, Bamako, Bogotá, or Beijing. Put together, these personal assemblages form a collective online museum, crossing space and time, where each visitor can build their own constellation and develop alternative concepts of cultural value. Infused with humility, love, and generosity, each photograph says: "Come into my home, here is my history. This is my museum."

The engineers of this new museum space are Birds of Knowledge, a research cooperative of artists and social designers studying at the Hamburg University of Fine Arts whose immediate origins hail from

Nigeria, Tunisia, Cameroon, Turkey, Finland, Sweden, Norway, China, New Zealand, and Germany. They have devised different ways of engaging with the diversity of the Home Museum's individual entries. One route enables you to vision all the artists' photographs and read their "Kindred Narratives", and another is to curate your own exhibition by assembling photographs according to your own taxonomic imaginary. This turns the Home Museum into a space for collaboration with participants who have not met before, encouraging connections between people and cultures, enabling an exchange of perceptions and research. A further route involves shuffling the different photographs of the Home Museum into constellations you would like to look at and research in detail. Sensing memories and feeling heritage, while moving through the visual atmospheres created by photography, combines to a personal and intimate understanding of our material world during the crisis of Covid-19. It also animates greater discussion on the role of photography in colonial power regimes, and the different perceptions of restitution from a perspective that has little to do with the politics of European ministries of culture.

To find alternative models of infrastructure which are capable of rendering spaces inclusive and sensitive to diversity requires not only rethinking epistemological and aesthetic concepts, but also bureaucratic, administrative, economic, and legal parameters. This equipment needs to be suspended, deconstructed, and redesigned to provide a platform that enables significant shifts to take place in the institutional metabolism of our venues and who we are today and what we wish for in the future. The increasing erection of borders, the building of detention centers, and the violence performed on those who flee persecution or wish to engage existentially with former nodes of colonial power, indicates that the concepts of "local" and "global" are being instrumentalized by political bodies that seek to produce new classificatory systems of division and conflict. In Europe, we continue to work with aesthetic paradigms that have been founded on imperial and colonial notions of racial and cultural hierarchies, and omissions based on binary systems of classification and evaluation. Ethnographic collections constitute the most valuable resource today for art histories that wish to be inclusive and emancipatory. However, without access to these collections, immovable and sequestered in European museums, it is practically impossible to perform a decolonial form of art-historical exegesis. Ethnology—as art history—reveals itself to be a monocultural project, rather like an intellectual plantation, that determines which episteme can flourish and where, what gets exchanged and marketed, and who has access or not to this stored code. In contrast, museums can begin to recognize their civic role as contemporary sites for the expansion of educational models and research directly based on the analysis of existing collections and their subsequent redefinition. The question is whether documents that directly testify to genocide or severe dehumanization require remediation at all? Are they not in and of themselves sufficiently denotative of the crimes of humanity to warrant public attention, without additional interpretations forged by designers or artists? What role does the artwork play in this exhibitionary context?

Working with collections and archives can lead to the conceptualization of an exhibition. My preference lies with this form of recursive inquiry, which I developed during my term as director of the Weltkulturen Museum in Frankfurt am Main[5]. On average, it took one year to move from the first stage of research in the laboratory to the final exhibition. This adaptive process covered a guest's first visits to the museum's stores, their selection of artifacts, books, documents, and photographs, private inquiry in the laboratory, individual studio practice, and a public lecture at the end of the residency. Through this decelerative relationship with the collection, we gradually identified the theme and contents of a future exhibition. The artist's research and the prototype they produced directly influenced the concept and curatorial organization of the forthcoming show. The non-visible activities initially performed in the laboratory were transformed into collaborative parameters for public inquiry. By leaving some threads frayed and obviating a sanitized hermetic presentation, I hoped that visitors to the exhibitions would be animated through what they saw and thereby wish to conduct their own fieldwork in the exhibition.

If museums wish to encourage the flourishing of a democratic intellect, their directors and funders—state, corporate, and private—have to rethink and experiment with new spatial priorities, not to mention decolonial restructuring. The norms that define how museum architecture is demarcated and made operational—with its standardized cafés, shops, and exhibition displays—is not inflexible per se. Paradoxically, Covid-19 has made us more aware of the articulation of curatorial ergonomics. During the highpoint of the virus in spring 2020, museums were empty of walking human beings. They might just as well have become lazarettes for vulnerable bodies, echoing the makeshift hospitals of World War I. With frescoes on the ceiling, the patients could lie gazing at the pursuits of angels in the embrace of flesh and cloud. Paintings would be hung lower than usual to match the bedridden gaze. Visual projections and whispered words would re-energize the ailing condition. No longer controlled by the museum's opening

5
See Clémentine Deliss, *The Metabolic Museum*, Berlin 2020.

hours, curators, now nurses, would tend to the instruction of patients not the public, 24 hours a day. When artworks are introduced as vectors of remediation—in an exhibition for example—they take on a specific responsibility, which the artist may wish to elucidate or not. However, artworks are not there to illustrate anything in particular, nor can they be treated as aesthetic compensations for an overly didactic display. The discourse of history may be a virus, propagating symptoms and shackling resistance, such that the ruin becomes visible before we experience contagion. All carriers that transport remediation help to turn the virus of history onto itself through a critical act of self-negotiation. For archives and collections from the past are like decomposing cadavers into which our common dung beetle or *nicophores investigator* burrows its way. This lover of decomposition introduces the necrophiliac dance of desire, the *caput mortuum* phase of remembrance work helping to rekindle renewal and repair.

Wherever they are located, museums urgently need to transition away from the capitalist imperative toward a contemporary venue for students and researchers from all over the world, a space of complexity where they can perform exercises in multidisciplinary inquiry based directly on the reassessment of existing collections. These can be seen as reservoirs of memories waiting for emancipation, as banks of stored code, as strata of cosmology, symbolism, and ingenuity and therefore as complex sources of energy whose circulation is hampered beyond the stores. To engage with such collections actually requires redefining the former imperial museum beyond its existing cursus toward a more radical understanding of curatorial intentionality and emergence. The ultimate model may require the construction of a new ergonomic space of education within the museum that is indissociable from its exhibitions and collections. Such a hybrid shelter requires all the necessary technical configurations to make possible in-depth inquiry into artifacts and archives. This is what I call a "museum-university", founded on the unmonetized research collections of the past and their potential to inform new alliances that contradict and aggravate the normativity of inherited disciplines and their genealogies. Here the public is welcomed, but not to consume art so much as to spend time in a "foyer d'expérience" (Foucault)[6], sitting, reading, watching, and conversing with one another, in short, all those activities that were central to museums prior to nineteenth-century colonial models. Like the liver in divinatory practices dating back to 1300 BC, artworks can act as trans-temporal passageways that enable remembrance to be performed once more, and in a non-exclusive manner.

6
Quoted by Lorenzini 2016 (see note 3).

Sammy Baloji, *Untitled #21*, From the series *Mémoire*, 2006 | Installation view, *Tell me about ~~yesterday~~ tomorrow*

Emil Nolde, *Meer und Himmel (Sea and Sky)*, 1937 | Installation view, *Tell me about ~~yesterday~~ tomorrow*

Political Conviction and/or Aesthetic Articulation: the Case of Emil Nolde

Works considered to have unusual merit, to be normative or time-less, make up the canon—that ideal corpus of works that a particular group, a linguistic or national culture, for example, finds to be of value or authorized, whose whereabouts it cares about, and which it therefore preserves. But the canon also refers to a corpus of inter-pretations that identify the social norms and ideals associated with the person or the work: how a work is to be interpreted. The idea of a canon is questionable if only owing to its normative tendency, and it becomes more and more problematic in the course of a general rethinking of what we mean by "linguistic and national culture." Nevertheless, one should not underestimate the continuing effec-tiveness of the notion that there are works representative of values, relevance, and a timeless validity, or the extent to which it justifies a selective approach to an artist's oeuvre, a singling out of works that conform to this idea. Lapses or unfortunate inconsistencies are then rhetorically patched over, politics and aesthetics are considered as distinct spheres, and an artist's biography and his or her oeuvre are carefully separated from each other.

The fact that a painting by Emil Nolde hangs in the exhibi-tion *Tell me about ~~yesterday~~ tomorrow* serves as a starting point from which to attempt to sketch how it happens that certain readings of a work are so dominant that other aspects, not necessarily unrecog-nized but deviating from that narrative, are long ignored. That also implies the question of where, in view of Nolde's painting consist-ing mainly of landscapes, seascapes, and still lifes, his thinking in conflict with the canonized interpretation is expressed: in his biog-raphy or in his work? In terms of hermeneutics or intrinsic value? Can these even be separated?

In 2019, the exhibition *Emil Nolde – a German Legend. The Artist During National Socialism* at Berlin's Hamburger Bahnhof compre-hensively reviewed the artist's role during the Nazi regime on the basis of numerous documents, letters, and his works themselves. This led to a change in the public perception of the artist[1] as well as to the fact that Chancellor Angela Merkel had Nolde's 1936 painting *Breakers*, at first only requested as a loan to the show, as well as his 1915 *Flower Garden –Thersen's House*, removed from her office and returned to their owner, the Prussian Cultural Heritage Foundation.[2]

Nolde was long thought to have been an artist who opposed the Nazi regime or at least failed to approve of its policies. He num-bered (and still does) among the most important representatives of Expressionism, and is one of the best-known and most popular artists of Classic Modernism. Many of his works were vilified by

1
After years of intensive research, the historian Bernhard Fulda and the art historian Aya Soika presented in this exhibition and the accompanying catalogue countless new proofs of Nolde's National Socialist sympathies. It was Christian Ring, the new director of the Nolde Stiftung in Seebüll, who first gave researchers full access to its archives. Ring curated the show together with Fulda and Soika. The exhibition catalogue presents extensive material, and clearly exposes the discrepancies between the artist's claims about himself and the historical facts.

2
In the Berlin exhibition the note next to the painting *Breakers* read: "Between 2006 and 2019 this painting, acquired by the State of Berlin in 1949, hung as a loan in the office of Chancellor Angela Merkel."

the National Socialists as "un-German," and shown in the *Degenerate Art* exhibition in Munich in 1937. In fact, more works by Nolde were expropriated and classified as "degenerate" than by any other artist of his time.[3] Even in the years before and after the Second World War, Nolde's painting seemed ideologically unobjectionable, primarily because of its motifs. And because his art had been stigmatized during the period of Nazi rule he seemed virtually predestined for the role of the dissident, living in retirement, who chose the path of inner emigration owing to his fundamental aesthetic stance. In fact, Emil Nolde was anything but an opponent of National Socialist ideology. He avowed National Socialism early on, was an antisemite and anti-Communist, and hoped to establish a "Nordic, racial" art. Thanks to intensive interventions, he was the only artist who managed to get his works removed from the *Degenerate Art* show in its later venues. There is not even any mention of his name in the third edition of the exhibition brochure.

Then, after 1945, Nolde systematically revised his biography, styling himself as an artist persecuted by the regime, one who uncompromisingly upheld his artistic ideals in spite of all the prohibitions imposed on him. He presented himself as an opponent of the regime in particular by way of his so-called *Unpainted Pictures*, watercolors he produced when prevented from painting during the Nazi dictatorship.[4] That he had definite sympathies for Adolf Hitler was not unknown even in the postwar period, but it has only been in recent years that this has become known to a broader public. It has led to that gradual reevaluation of his oeuvre that among other things brought about the removal of his pictures from the Chancellor's office—even though this was never officially explained.[5] *Tell me about ~~yesterday~~ tomorrow* is exhibiting the painting *Sea and Sky* from 1937, which resembles the picture Merkel had chosen for her office. It pictures in a narrow strip at the bottom a stormy North Sea in an intense dark green interrupted by a few whitecaps. Arching above it is a threatening sky in shades of dark blue to violet. The pigment, applied flat, is employed as an independent value, symbolizing the power of nature. Many of Nolde's pictures from these years are characterized by a fluid transition between sea, sky, and land, an abstract rendering of the painter's North German homeland with its dramatic changes in the weather.

It was the pictures in a continuation of this style, detached from time, that were the focus of the Nolde craze of the postwar period. Their coloring is striking, whereas their composition is often relatively conventional, adhering to a foreground, middle

3
A total of 1,102 works by Nolde were confiscated from German museums, and 50 were included in the exhibition *Degenerate Art* in Munich in 1937. Nolde had been enormously successful during the Weimar Republic and was prominently represented in museum collections, which is why so many of his works could be rounded up.

4
See Bernhard Fulda, "'Hinter jedem Busch lauert Verkennung und Neid.' Emil Noldes Reaktion auf den Sieg der Traditionalisten," in: *Künstler im Nationalsozialismus. Die "Deutsche Kunst," die Kunstpolitik und die Berliner Kunsthochschule*, ed. Wolfgang Ruppert, Cologne, Weimar, and Vienna 2015, pp. 261–286.

ground, and background scheme oriented toward the picture's center. In them, Nolde avoided any contemporary references, and adapted his Expressionist style to the modernist aesthetic that characterized the later postwar avant-garde, with its focus on gestural abstraction as a response to the figuration contaminated by National Socialism and its ideology.

As early as 1933, after he was forced to resign from the Prussian Academy of Arts, Nolde's pictures changed. A year later, to demonstrate his patriotism, the artist joined the Danish National Socialist Consortium of North Schleswig. Despite such attempts to present himself to the regime as a devoted follower, he failed to conform to National Socialist taste in art. To be sure, there had been attempts to establish as a state art a "Nordic" Expressionism with references to the Gothic style and Romanticism, but ultimately a conservative Naturalism prevailed.

At this time, religious motifs, frequently featuring Jewish figures from biblical stories, disappear from Emil Nolde's work in favor of increasingly heroic picture subjects. He turned away from his South Seas motifs, particularly offensive to the National Socialists, and instead emphasized "Nordic" ones. Inspired by ancient sagas, he painted helmet-wearing Vikings and young blond women. Mountains and sacrificial altars also became picture subjects—as did repeatedly that menacing dark sky above the wide-open spaces of North Germany that also characterizes the work formerly hanging in the Chancellery.

Nonetheless, this expressionistic, sublimated, painted version of Nazi ideology failed to elevate him into the ranks of official state artists. In August 1941, Nolde was told that his pictures did not meet the requirements expected of all fine artists active in Germany, for which reason he was henceforth forbidden to work in the realm of art either professionally or semi-professionally. Two months later, he was further informed that he was prohibited from selling, exhibiting, or publishing his art. This exclusion from the Reich Chamber of Culture did not amount to a "painting ban" or state oversight of his artistic activities, as Nolde maintained. The "painting ban" was part of the effective myth-making the artist engaged in after the war in order to rehabilitate himself. Between 1941 and 1945 he made few oil paintings, to be sure, but more than 1,300 watercolors, 60 of which he later translated into oil paintings. The *Unpainted Pictures*, stylized as testaments to his resistance, were thus not so much secretly produced and officially forbidden works as small-format sketches of works to be realized but that could never officially exist.

5
In April 2019, Merkel returned both works from her office to the Prussian Cultural Heritage Foundation. There were no explanations, only a reference to the Foundation's request that *Breakers* be loaned to the show at the Hamburger Bahnhof. On August 6, 2019, Jost Müller-Neuhof wrote in the *Tagesspiegel*: "Internal documents show that despite the Foundation's request and new findings about Nolde, they wished to keep the pictures in the office. State Minister of Culture Monika Grütters (CDU), who had been involved, acquiesced. Merkel herself was obviously willing to let the *Breakers* go, but it was to be returned. From the files that the *Tagesspiegel* managed to consult under the Freedom of Information Act, it moreover appears that the Chancellor's office had been informed in early 2014 at the latest about how the view of Nolde had changed and that Merkel's pictures were affected. Apparently, no one cared. It was only when in the spring some of the media elevated the matter from the art scene to the front pages that the previously steadfast veneration come to an end, and Merkel changed her mind."

6
Haftmann, who had been a Nazi Party member himself, deliberately said nothing about the Nazi affinity in his Nolde catalogues, and in doing so helped to promote the myth of the *Unpainted Pictures.*

7
"To be sure, when Schmidt was Chancellor, he was well aware how politically effective art could be. It was no private eccentricity when he had a new plaque placed on his office door in Bonn indicating that it was henceforth to be called the Nolde Room. To him it was a matter of coming to terms with the past, championing long-ostracized artists who had been persecuted as "degenerate" by the Nazis and ridiculed in postwar Germany. Bringing their art into the public gaze, exhibiting them in the Chancellery, was for him a form of reparation, and an appeal to his countrymen to finally deal with the victims of their "Third Reich." Quoted from Hanno Rauterberg, "Die Macht der Schönheit," in: *Helmut Schmidt. Staatsmann – Publizist – Vordenker*, Hamburg 2015 (*Die Zeit* e-book).

8
Meanwhile, the Nolde Stiftung in Seebüll has now distinguished itself with its outstanding reworking of the artist's biography, providing comprehensive information about his role in the Nazi period.

In 1960, some of these watercolors were exhibited in the fourth annual exhibition at the Nolde Museum in Seebüll, where they met with a euphoric response from the press. A year later, the works were shown in the Palais des Beaux-Arts in Brussels and the Kunstverein Hannover. In 1963, Werner Haftmann published his book devoted to them, *Unpainted Pictures*. In 1964, finally, a selection of the watercolors was presented in a room of their own at documenta III in Kassel, curated by Arnold Bode, which focused on abstract art.[6] Haftmann also served as an advisor to the large committees for painting, sculpture, and drawing. The narrative of the maverick artist, who after initial sympathies for National Socialist ideology soon turned away from it and continued to pursue his artistic vision in secret would characterize the reception of Nolde's art from then on. Large numbers of readers adored Siegfried Lenz's 1968 novel *The German Lesson*, whose protagonist Max Ludwig Nansen was obviously based on Nolde. The artist has to bury his pictures, an idea provided by Haftmann's book, in order to save them.

Corresponding to Nolde's reinterpretation from antisemitic artist hoping to win Hitler's favor into dissident always solely interested in aesthetics, there was now open enthusiasm for his art in political circles. In retrospect, this can be seen as a misguided gesture, an attempt to make "reparation" to a supposed victim of National Socialism. Chancellor Helmut Schmidt, who owned several Nolde works himself, hung one of the artist's paintings in his office in Bonn, and as an appeal to engagement with the past had the plaque "Nolde Room" affixed to the door.[7] In 1982, he organized an exhibition of the artist's works in Bonn's Chancellery. Federal President Richard von Weizsäcker was also among the self-proclaimed Nolde admirers. In Emden, the publicist Henri Nannen erected a museum devoted to the painter, one that adopted the revised version of his past, and for decades the Nolde Stiftung Seebüll, established in 1957, after Nolde's death, actively promoted an image of the artist as a victim of National Socialist cultural policy.[8] In 2006, Angela Merkel, who frequently emphasized how greatly she admired the painter's pictures, chose to borrow his *Breakers* from Berlin's National Gallery. Desolate landscapes with no contemporary references lent Nolde's painting a sense of timelessness and a vague yearning for freedom, features that many viewers obviously associate with North Germany's raw natural beauty. These pictures, painted in a progressive modernist style, make no apparent statement, and for precisely that reason are open to conflicting interpretations. Yet it is impossible to separate them from the painter's political convictions or the latter from his aesthetic concerns.[9] As representatives of the past, historical artworks are always part of our present as well, and accordingly involved in our decisions about how (and whether) we wish to continue to present it. History is constantly being rewritten and interpreted from a present-day perspective—and researched by (art) historians.

In future, these works will be placed in museum contexts that at least question the long canonized image of Emil Nolde. It is no longer appropriate for state officials to use them for representative purposes—especially the *Breakers*, so clearly expressive of the ideology of his time. Distancing ourselves from one of Germany's prominent Expressionists as a representative of German identity is a process that requires us to think about art and politics, work and ideology, at the same time. When Frankfurt's Städel Museum mounted a Nolde retrospective in 2014 that prominently questioned his role during National Socialism, the *Breakers* from Angela Merkel's office was not yet available as a loan. By early 2014 at the latest, the Chancellery had been informed that thinking about Nolde had changed, and in what way, and that this affected its display of the borrowed painting—but at the time there was no response. Thanks to the "Nolde case," one assumes that discussion of what sort of art best represents a democratic country will be more rigorous. People will learn to deal with ambivalences and revisions, and be forced to correct the narrative promoted by the artist and eagerly adopted for so long.

Lest it seems as if I am suggesting that Emil Nolde is the only painter to have been subjected to reevaluation, let me briefly note the example of the Expressionist painter Gabriele Münter, who was closely associated with the artists' group "Der Blaue Reiter" and is included in the German modernist canon. For a long time, exhibitions focused on those works "typical" of the artist working beside Wassily Kandinsky—landscape pictures and highly expressive portraits with intensive, bold planes of color. Less well known are works of hers from the 1930s in which she comes closer to the imagery of the New Objectivity. When the rail line to Garmisch-Partenkirchen and the so-called Olympic Highway were being built in front of Münter's house in Murnau in preparation for the 1936 Winter Games, they became subjects for her pictures. Münter's interest in the work is reflected in such paintings as *The Blue Backhoe*, *Earthworks*, and *Battering Ram*, all of them dating from 1935. Two paintings of backhoes were shown in the 1936 exhibition *Adolf Hitler's Roadways in Art*. And as early as 1934, she had painted *Procession in Murnau*, a picture in which red flags with a white circle hang out of the windows. The swastikas may not be visible, but one intuitively supplies them.

9
This view is nevertheless widespread. As an example of the many comments on the occasion of the return of the pictures from the Chancellor's office, Jürgen Kaube wrote in the *Frankfurter Allgemeine Zeitung* for April 4, 2019: "Anyone who could find the painter's socio-political views in his seascapes, landscapes, and flower pictures, most of them with no figures, would have to apply the same suspicion to the landscape pictures of other Expressionists without any National Socialist associations. The abstract assertion that one cannot separate pictures from their painters' political convictions and these from their aesthetic convictions has been refuted hundreds of times throughout art history."

Were works like these meant to curry favor with the art policies of the Nazi period? Unlike works of the core group of the "Blauer Reiter," Münter's were not vilified as "degenerate," and she was not prevented from exhibiting them, which she did at least until 1939. Inspired by her garden, from then on until her death she painted mainly still lifes and landscapes which now form part of the so-called canon. In 2017 the Lenbachhaus presented the exhibition *Gabriele Münter. Painting without Frills*. In it, Münter's entire oeuvre was explored for the first time, including her New Objectivity works, and not only the canonized ones.[10] This was precisely the needed corrective, a presentation of all aspects of an oeuvre instead of only those works that have defined an artist's image for decades. Just how prominent representatives of Expressionism positioned themselves in the period around 1930 does not necessarily affect our aesthetic appreciation of their works, for not everything carries the stamp of National Socialist ideology. Yet selective views of an artist's work that block out what might challenge his or her canonized image negate the very ambivalences, contradictions, or, as in the case of Nolde, deliberate falsifications of history that are part of the oeuvre, and need to be carefully considered. We are now beginning to deal with this aspect of the history of German art.

10
See *Gabriele Münter – Malen ohne Umschweife*, ed. Isabelle Jansen and Matthias Mühling, exh. cat. Lenbachhaus, Kunstbau, Munich/ Museum Ludwig, Cologne/Louisiana Museum of Modern Art, Humlebaek, Munich 2017.

Jon Rafmann, *Disasters Under The Sun*, 2019 | Installation view, *Tell me about yesterday tomorrow*

Kader Attia, *The Body's Legacies*, 2018 | Installation view, *Tell me about ~~yesterday~~ tomorrow*

Harald Pickert, Die *Pestbeulen Europas. Naziterror in Konzentrationslagern (The Plague-Spots of Europe. Nazi Terror in Concentration Camps)*, *1939–45*, n.d. | Installation view, Zentralinstitut für Kunstgeschichte Munich

A German Discipline

In 1998, when more than forty countries approved the Washington Principles on Nazi-Confiscated Art, they promoted—so to speak inadvertently—the rise of a discipline that was previously more of a minor art-history service: provenance research. The signatories' commitment to researching the whereabouts of art extorted or stolen from Jewish victims of National Socialism and returning it to its proper owners led to a new need for studies that helped to elucidate ownership issues and the origins of works of art. The result? In Germany, more than twenty years after the Washington Declaration, along with scholars, institutes, research facilities, and publicly financed posts for provenance researchers, there are even a few professorships in the discipline. Nonetheless, the problem has not been solved; thousands of paintings, sculptures, antiques, and drawings from Jewish collections have still not been restored to their legal owners or have disappeared. Moreover: provenance research is emerging as a specifically German discipline.

Who could have anticipated that in 2006 the few provenance researchers in the Federal Republic of Germany would be invited to the Federal Chancellery? At that time everything was supposed to change—in the first five years Germany's commitment had led to the return of a mere 160 works of art and a thousand books to their owners or their heirs, and the restitution of Ernst Ludwig Kirchner's painting *Berlin Street Scene* (1913), on display in Berlin's Brücke Museum, was the subject of public dispute. Instead of legal uncertainty and indefinite procedures, it was hoped that a basic strategy for further research and coordination could be worked out. At that time the "Bureau for Provenance Research" was established, which was to assist public institutions like museums and collections with expertise in the clarification of suspected cases. Yet contrary to all the declarations and assurances from politicians and cultural workers, no structure was created that made possible a systematic accounting, financed background research, and linked national and international studies.

German museums, public collections, and libraries had the advantage of possession over those who had been robbed and their representatives or victims' associations, and this only became more pronounced in the drawn-out negotiations, in which provenance researchers competed with the contesting parties. Museum people had direct access to archives, documents, and sources. Outsiders had to fight not only for their right, but frequently for access to information. The promised "accounting" remained a more or less random sequence of individual cases. Most provenance researchers held short-term or case-related positions. On the world stage the politicians had nobly committed themselves to an accounting; however, in practice this commitment was undermined by archivists, curators, scholars, and jurists who could count on the fact that this "self-commitment" had not been translated into legally binding practices. For on the one hand, when asked not only for restitution, but also for information, access to records and archives, museums simply stonewalled. And provenance researchers working under contract to museums and public authorities were primarily engaged in fending off queries, or at least working on legal and historical issues.

Twenty years after the Washington Declaration, Ronald S. Lauder, President of the World Jewish Congress, asked in an interview: "What is preventing the Germans from simply investigating what was purchased in the critical years, that is, between 1933 and 1945? And making this completely public. The task is actually quite clear. But instead of making looted art cases public, the same excuses are presented again and again. That it has to do with federalism, which means that there is always someone else who would have to solve the problem; that it is up to the states, the communes, the private foundations. The excuses are always the same."[1]

That interview was occasioned by the scandal over the collection of Cornelius Gurlitt, the son of the Nazi art dealer Hildebrand Gurlitt, who hoarded artworks in Munich's Schwabing district and a single-family house in Salzburg and supported himself by selling a drawing or a painting on the art market from time to time—a way of life that was perhaps not so unusual in Munich. The story was sensationalized as the "Schwabing Art Trove" or the "Gurlitt Case." In the fall of 2013 the public learned that among the exhibits at the Augsburg state prosecutor's office—which had first prosecuted Gurlitt for tax evasion—more than a thousand paintings and drawings worth several million euros were stored, possibly including art confiscated by the Nazis.

In retrospect, the scandal, widely discussed in the media, was of historic significance on the one hand because finally there were reports about art looted by the Nazis, about perpetrators, networks, dealer rings, and above all about the confiscation system. On the other hand, important questions were left open. The blind spot in the debate was the question—first asked mainly abroad—of how it could be that so many years after the Washington Declaration and the Federal Republic of Germany's commitment to the restitution of confiscated art, the son of one of the dealers involved in the thefts was allowed to hoard such a collection and from a legal point of view

1
Catrin Lorch, "Es sind immer die gleichen Ausreden," in: *Süddeutsche Zeitung*, February 12, 2018, URL: <https://www.sueddeutsche.de/kultur/ronald-lauder-ueberns-raubkunst-es-sindimmer-die-gleichenausreden-1.3864201> (accessed October 1, 2020).

even keep it? The real scandal was that Germany, as the country of the perpetrators, has no looted art law that also applies to private collections or art holdings.

What happened then can also be interpreted in retrospect as a political diversionary maneuver and manipulation of public opinion. The Commissioner for Culture and the Media in the Chancellery, Monika Grütters, stepped in, and her colleague, the administrative jurist Ingeborg Berggreen-Merkel ("We are working as quickly as possible"[2]), negotiated with the elderly Gurlitt, who stubbornly refused to be parted from his possessions, announced that there would be an investigation and legal clarification and set up a "task force" intended to swiftly and purposefully—as its name would suggest— resolve the "case." The eccentric living conditions of the sick, lonely old man—who died in the spring of 2014—made it easy for the media to style him as a unique case.

The work of the task force then dragged on for months, however, and after initial restitutions, little confiscated art was found. Instead of working openly, the responsible parties engaged in reassurance: careful, meticulous scholarly research takes time. A lack of transparency and inaccessibility were the result. For victims' representatives, the actual owners and their legal representatives—inasmuch as they were not directly affected—the situation was thus identical to the one they were already familiar with from the past: it was the Germans who controlled access to the documents and the works in question.

Hardly anyone was aware that Gurlitt himself had agreed to the creation of a databank and commissioned an expert to produce it while he was still alive. This project was also discontinued after his death, for it would not only have made the contents of his collection completely public but also all the relevant documents from Hildebrand Gurlitt: letters, business records, and his painstakingly annotated photo archive. The task force, however, met like a secret society until the collection was handed over to Gurlitt's heir—the Kunstmuseum Bern—and pieces for which the provenance could not be clarified were placed in storage.

The capstone of Gurlitt propaganda was the major exhibition *Inventory Gurlitt. Nazi Art Theft and the Consequences*, which ultimately —for all its professionalism—simply focused once again luridly on the story of the Nazi art-dealer dynasty on the Schwabing art trove. The task force's investigation had been unable to prove that a greater percentage of confiscated art had been in that collection than in any German museum. But an exhibition—especially one claiming to be scholarly and historic—is a powerful intervention instrument.

2
Annika Zeitler, "Gurlitt-Taskforce weist Vorwürfe zurück," in: Deutsche Welle, December 13, 2013, URL: <https://www.dw.com/de/gurlitt-taskforce-weist-vorw%C3%BCrfe-zur%C3%BCck/a-17295999> (accessed October 1, 2020).

There seemed to be no doubt about the quality of German provenance research or the Germans' wish for an accounting. Few people were aware that if the state had truly been interested in cases like Hildebrand Gurlitt's, it could have investigated the looted art dealer's networks, his biography, and his connections, years before the accidental discovery in Schwabing. The scholar Katja Terlau had wanted to systematically investigate "essential biographies" and "dealer networks," but her appeals for the public financing of such basic research were all denied. The limited funds were mainly used for the study of specific restitution petitions.

In this sense one can interpret the "Schwabing art trove" as a media offensive that—steered by politics—meandered between legal disputes, scholarship, research, and campaigns; its primary goal simply was not an accounting, but the preservation of the status quo: Germany has no looted art law, no legally binding procedure, no systematic research. Confiscated art in private collections does not have to be returned. Auction houses, galleries, and art dealers are not required to open their files to scholars or researchers.

Even after the prominent "investigation" of the Gurlitt case, the 2016 scandal remained symptomatic, for example, when it became known to the public that the "Bayerische Staatsgemäldesammlungen" refused to collaborate with the London "Commission for Looted Art in Europe" in order to expose the complicity of Bavarian museums in the postwar period. In the 1950s, looted art confiscated from Jewish owners was "restored" by the Allies not to the victims of Nazi persecution but to the families of the perpetrators—among them the families of Hermann Göring and Baldur von Schirach. While the "Bayerische Staatsgemäldesammlungen's" provenance researchers stonewalled and kept their archive closed with the assurance that they were doing their own research, the return of looted paintings was delayed for years.

At the time, Rüdiger Mahlo, Germany's representative to the "Jewish Claims Conference" (JCC), which supports the restitution claims of Jewish Holocaust victims, wrote: "As long as cover-ups and secrecy prevail even in such high-ranking institutions as the Bayerische Staatsgemäldesammlungen, there can hardly be any satisfactory and peaceful solutions, to say nothing of fair and just ones in line with the Washington Principles." "There is a considerable discrepancy between state-sponsored readiness to return looted art and cultural goods from Jewish collections and the implementation of fair and just solutions."[3]

That museums continue in general to employ researchers and experts only when confronted with restitution demands is one of

3
Catrin Lorch and Jörg Häntzschel, "Endlich Taten!," in: *Süddeutsche Zeitung*, June 28, 2016, URL: <https://www.sueddeutsche.de/kultur/ns-kunstraub-endlich-taten-1.3053978> (accessed October 1, 2020).

the reasons why the accounting is sluggish and protracted. Most of the few centers committed to the systematic study of collections or archives are temporary. And instead of opening up material, sources, depots, documents, and records to an international public, single cases are researched and reported as separate issues. In an interview the freelance scholar Vanessa Voigt criticized that in Germany to this day there are no "informative and regularly updated databanks on collectors, art dealers, and people involved in the looting of art," on references to estates and archives. "Symposiums, conferences, and catalogue contributions are no substitute."[4]

4
Catrin Lorch, "Die Fahnderinnen," in: *Süddeutsche Zeitung*, October 27, 2018, URL: <https://www.sueddeutsche.de/kultur/provenienz forschung-die-fahnderinnen-1.4186575> (accessed October 1, 2020).

Who benefits from this? First, the provenance researchers in museums, who can present themselves to the public or at least to the scholarly public with spectacular research results. Many who are familiar with the scene—including museum employees—continue to assume, however, that collections cannot be readily removed from their possession; at least one can assume that they do not behave as proactively in looted art research in their own collections as would be necessary, for each case has to be studied, evaluated, and legally and professionally accounted for and thus consumes funds and resources.

That talking about looted art has meanwhile become popular and can count on genuine public interest can be seen as a change from the postwar period, when debates frequently centered on the so-called *Schlussstrich*, the "cut-off line." The public and above all the younger generation of art historians are of the opinion that restitution must be made. On the other hand, victims' representatives report that the newly developed understanding, also extended to issues of colonial looted art, is considered to be highly dangerous. What if not only the confiscation of art but also of land, villas, factories, and blocks of shares during the Nazi period were similarly accounted for and reversed?

The Gurlitt case cost the Federal Republic of Germany a great deal of money—but despite all the avowals of politicians the discussion has not led to coordinated research, to new laws, or to the unequivocal opening up and study of public—and private—sources. Yet looting and expropriation were not simply collateral damage, but a central feature of the Holocaust. Against this background the dogged, recalcitrant, secretive practice of German provenance research is profoundly embarrassing. It is up to politicians not only to provide sufficient funds, but also to forcefully implement the accounting of museums, archives, libraries, universities, and scholars promised twenty years ago. Until then, an assessment remains true that was made in 2015 by Ann Webber, co-founder and chairman of the "Commission for Looted Art in Europe": "The impression remains that in Germany people see the looted art problem as a purely German affair. In Germany people look inward and undertake provenance research for its own sake."[5]

5
Catrin Lorch and Jörg Häntzschel, "Eine deutsche Angelegenheit," in: *Süddeutsche Zeitung*, December 2, 2015, URL: <https://www.sueddeutsche.de/kultur/raubkunstexpertin-eine-deutsche-angelegenheit-1.2762446> (accessed October 1, 2020).

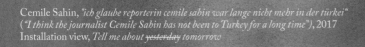

Cemile Sahin, *"ich glaube reporterin cemile sahin war lange nicht mehr in der türkei"*
(*"I think the journalist Cemile Sahin has not been to Turkey for a long time"*), 2017
Installation view, *Tell me about ~~yesterday~~ tomorrow*

Das Exil schafft eine
gemeinsame Daseinsform,

Michaela Melián, *Mann Family House*, 2019 | Installation view, *Tell me about ~~yesterday~~ tomorrow*

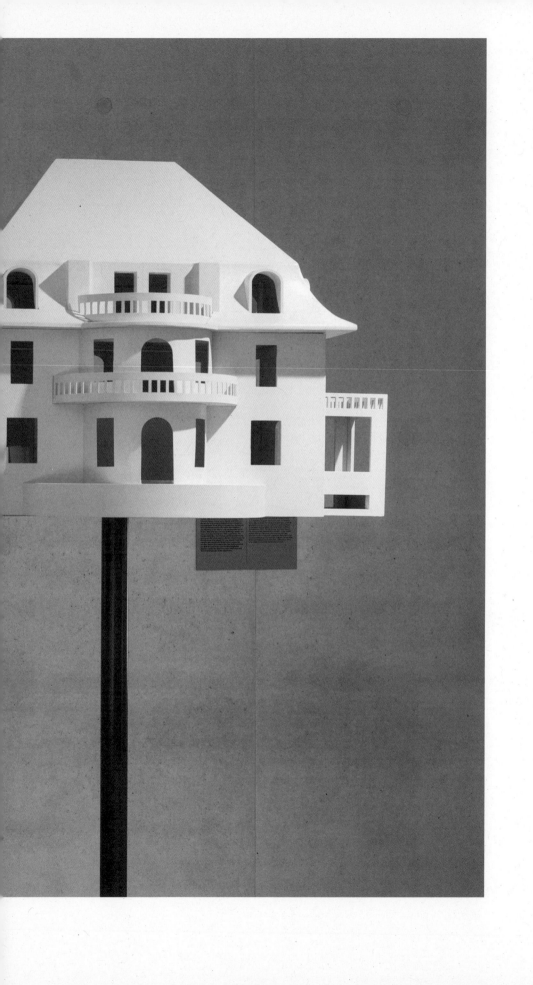

Michal BarOr, *Abandoned Property*, 2016 | Installation view, *Tell me about ~~yesterday~~ tomorrow*

*From "Temple of Art" to Forum for
the Discussion of Issues from Recent
History. The Appreciation, Devaluation
and Revaluation of National Socialist
Showcases for Art*

"The eye does not see things but images of things that mean other things."–Italo Calvino[1]

Urban design and architecture have always been lasting testimony to the social and political makeup of a people. This is particularly true for Germany's urban landscape, with its buildings dating from the time of the National Socialist dictatorship. These wholly or only partially completed building projects are unadulterated documents of the National Socialist tyranny, and stand as admonitions to present and future generations. They impressively convey the megalomania of the rulers and display their racial fanaticism and lust for war; and translate the diminutive impetus of the architecture on the spectator. This effect is undiminished even in art and cultural venues, for the propagandistic ideal of those in power was also meant to find its architectural expression in exhibition spaces.

* * *

In Munich the Haus der Deutschen Kunst (House of German Art) was erected between 1933 and 1937, the first monumental National Socialist structure to be built after the assumption of power. It was designed by Paul Ludwig Troost (1878–1934). In it, neoclassical forms were subjected to a restyling through reduction and elongation. At the laying of the cornerstone, Adolf Hitler lauded the project as the "first beautiful building of the new Reich."[2] At almost the same time, again after designs by Troost, the Führerbau (Führer's Building, Party Headquarters) was erected nearby. After 1945 it was first used as a collection point for evacuated holdings of German museums and looted objects from both inside and outside the country, and soon afterward as an exhibition hall. A few months after the completion of these monumental buildings in Munich, ateliers were erected, first in Baldham, near Munich and then in Berlin, with equally ostentatious intent: they were to serve as work spaces for the sculptors Josef Thorak (1889–1952) and Arno Breker (1900–1991).

As in the exhibition spaces, the importance of these ateliers within their urban setting was reflected in their architecture. Just like fine arts, architecture had been adopted by the regime as a propaganda medium. Building projects were prioritized and a particular style was assigned to each of them, depending on the function of the structure: "The eternally valid forms of antiquity in a version adapted to the present were reserved for representational buildings; schools and youth centers, being rooted in "blood and soil," were to adhere to regional building traditions; and industrial buildings were

1
Italo Calvino, *Le città invisibili*, Turin: Giulio Einaudi Editore 1972 / *Die unsichtbare Städte*, Frankfurt am Main 2013, p. 21. English edition: Italo Calvino, *Invisible Cities*, Orlando: Harcourt Inc., 1974, p. 15.

2
Adolf Hitler, *Reden zur Kunst- und Kulturpolitik, 1933–1939*, ed. Robert Elkmeyer, Frankfurt am Main 2004, p. 59.

3
Winfried Nerdinger,
"Funktion und
Bedeutung von
Architektur im NS-
Staat." in: *Kunst im NS-
Staat. Ideologie, Ästhetik,
Protagonisten*, ed.
Wolfgang Benz, Peter
Eckel, and Andreas
Nachama, Berlin 2015,
p. 279.

4
Ibid., p. 280.

5
Hitler 1933–1939 (see
note 2), p. 168.

to exhibit rational, purpose-based design with an overlay of monumentality."[3] This division according to function indicates at the same time that there is no such thing as a clearly defined National Socialist architecture: "Accordingly, representational buildings stood at the tip of a pyramid of function in the National Socialist system. It is therefore futile to analyze individual buildings or building forms in order to derive from them a 'Nazi style.' Only by considering the objectives and the entirety of functional contexts is it possible to come to any meaningful conclusion about specific elements in this National Socialist architectural pyramid."[4]

While a clear definition of a Nazi building style is accordingly impossible, all the public building projects from this period share one ideological characteristic—they communicate a sense of German superiority over other supposedly "inferior" nations and peoples. Hitler promoted this himself: "Psychologically, the stupendous, gigantic testaments to our society will fill its members with an infinite sense of selfhood, namely that of being Germans."[5]

* * *

All the above-named buildings in Munich and the atelier in Berlin underwent astonishing rededications after the end of the war, reflecting social changes and political interests. In 1949 the exhibitions *Kunstschaffen in Deutschland* (Making Art in Germany) and *Deutschland baut: Architektur seit 1945* (Germany Builds: Architecture since 1945) were presented at the "Central Art Collecting Point" in the former Nazi Party administration building (Führerbau). These were followed in 1950 with a show of the finalists in the well-endowed German Art Prize competition, sponsored by the American Broadway producer Blevin Davis. In 1949 the Haus der Kunst—previously Haus der Deutschen Kunst—presented *Der Blaue Reiter* (The Blue Rider), and in 1950 *Die Maler Am Bauhaus* (The Bauhaus Painters). These structures erected as propaganda for National Socialism and its art thus became exhibition venues for the very Modernism previously proscribed—a reorientation reflecting the interest in a new allocation of such buildings on the part of society and thus expressive of a suppression mechanism controversial to this day. When Okwui Enwezor and David Chipperfield presented their plans for the renovation of Munich's Haus der Kunst in 2017, the *Süddeutsche Zeitung* commented: "One has to admit that this is not the first time that a troubling site is to be rendered harmless by means of ideological rededication. Auto races and concerts serve the same function at the Nazi Party rally grounds in Nuremberg. As Bob Dylan said there in

1978, he felt the need to "deconsecrate" the site. But who is to judge whether such deconsecration has succeeded? Experts? People who live next to the buildings? Tourists? It has never been possible to definitively answer such questions, and as the Haus der Kunst shows, with every passing year they become more complex."[6]

* * *

Kunsthaus Dahlem, opened as an exhibition space a few years ago in the former Breker atelier, was met with the same kind of questioning—which continues unabated. The regime-built atelier for the sculptor Arno Breker was designed by the architect Hans Freese, and erected in Berlin-Dahlem between 1939 and 1942.[7] Freese modeled it after Albert Speer's 1935/36 design for the sculptor Josef Thorak's atelier in Baldham, near Munich.[8]

The Breker studio was the first of a series of structures which were to be placed at the disposal not only of regime-friendly artists and architects but also of high-ranking military men and politicians. The plan was to settle the dictatorship's new worthies in Berlin's Dahlem quarter, traditionally an elite enclave. Breker was to be given a house, an atelier, and a finishing hall as well as a series of studios and smaller workshops for his master pupils. Due to the outbreak of the war; of the planned structures only the atelier was realized. The complex, consisting of a sequence of four spaces, is one of the few artists' studios built by the National Socialist regime. It was handed over to Breker "for the execution of artistic commissions relating to the redesign of the capital of the Reich."[9] The idea had come from Albert Speer (1905–1981), who as General Building Inspector for Berlin was entrusted with the city's redesign as a center of National Socialist power. Once bombs began falling on Berlin, the project in Grunewald was prematurely ended. Breker fled before the approaching front to South Germany, where in 1948 the de-Nazification court in Donauwörth categorized him as a "fellow traveler." In 1949 he settled in the Rhineland, and died in Düsseldorf in 1991.

* * *

In May 1945 the atelier was briefly used by Soviet troops before being taken over by the Americans once the city was divided into occupation zones. For a year their Information Control Division (ICD) was housed there—the military administration's arm responsible for the de-Nazification of cultural institutions and the issuing of operating licenses. Surrounded by Breker statues, the American administrative personnel set up their offices, from which they regulated the range and content of cultural life in the American Sector. In 1946, the American military

6
Sonja Zekri, "Kunst ist stärker als NS-Geschichte," in: *Süddeutsche Zeitung*, February 1, 2017.

7
For the history of the building's construction, see Nikola Doll, *The Arno Breker State Atelier. History of its Construction and Use 1938–1945* (Publication Series Kunsthaus Dahlem Vol. 1), Berlin 2014.

8
See Rudolf Wolters' suggestion to Hans Freese that he visit the Thorak atelier in Baldham, and Speer's autograph corrections to Freese's designs: Bundesarchiv Berlin, R 4606/2816, sheet 89, Dr. Rudolf Wolters, GBI, Aktenvermerk, Berlin, July 4, 1938; Bundesarchiv Berlin, R 4606/2820, Variante a Variante B (ground plan struck through by Albert Speer).

9
Along with Albert Speer, Leni Riefenstahl, and Josef Thorak, Arno Breker was one of the most prominent artists celebrated by the National Socialist state. His development as sculptor and his ascent in the Third Reich to the vice presidency of the Reichskammer der bildendend Künste (1941) were closely linked with the political leaders of National Socialism.

turned the building over to the State of Berlin. Once the ICD moved out, it was then transferred to the city administration. Kurt Reutti, working at the time in the "Zentralstelle zur Erfassung und Pflege von Kunstwerken" (Center for the Acquisition and Maintainance of Works of Art), first offered the studio to the former State Museums and the Hochschule für Angewandte Kunst (College of Applied Art) in Berlin-Weissensee, but both institution declined the offer. Their decision was based in part on the building's unfortunate location in terms of traffic, but above all on the increasing tensions between the occupying powers. Jan Bontjes van Beek, the director of the Hochschule, explained his refusal as follows: "It would seem that this is not an altogether opportune moment for us, situated as we are in the east, to create a branch in the American Sector, for just now the two occupation zones have become somewhat hypersensitive about such matters."[10] Thus the offer was not declined because of the building's problematic history and its use during the Nazi period, but because of concern that his institution might be split into eastern and western branches.

10
Letter from Jan Bontjes van Beek to Kurt Reutti from July 7, 1948, Landesarchiv Berlin, C Rep. 120, no. 507.

After neither the museums nor the Hochschule chose to make use of the atelier, it was placed at the disposal of Berlin's guild of stonecutters. Reutti's plan to let important sculptors use portions of the building for their larger projects could also be realized: on the recommendation of Adolf Jannasch, then director of the Berlin Senate's Office of Fine Arts, in 1949 the sculptor Bernhard Heiliger moved into the building's east wing. Heiliger, a former pupil of Arno Breker's, had recently settled in the American Sector. He had certain reservations about moving into his former teacher's atelier, as he explained in a letter to a friend: "Since Breker's huge state atelier in Dahlem was placed at my disposal I have made a number of new things. I was somewhat reticent at first, as you can surely imagine, but I accepted anyway, for having the use of such an atelier is a unique opportunity. Now I feel quite at home here, in spite of the comfort."[11] Heiliger lived and worked in the building's east wing until his death in 1995.

11
Bernhard Heiliger Stiftung, *Bernhard Heiliger* 1915–1995, Berlin 2005, p. 35.

In 1964/65 Emilio Vedova, as the first international artist to use the building, occupied its middle section. Among other things, the Italian, who been living in Berlin since November 1963 at the invitation of Werner Haftmann and on a stipend from the American Ford Foundation, created there his major work *Absurdes Berliner Tagebuch* (*Absurd Berlin Diary*), a walk-in painting installation consisting of several painted wood panels, either freestanding or hung from the ceiling. The work was exhibited at documenta III in 1964 and at the Haus am Waldsee in Zehlendorf in 1965. In 2002 the artist donated it to the Berlinische Galerie.

A year after Vedova moved out, in 1966/67, the atelier's neighborhood also changed. The architect Werner Düttmann built the Brücke Museum right next to the atelier, on the site previously destined for Breker's house. A few years later, in 1971/72, the large studio Vedova had used was broken up into eight smaller studios by the architect Rolf Nieballa at the behest of the Friends of the Brücke Museum. These were subsequently awarded to artists from around the world by the Deutscher Akademische Austauschdienst (German Academic Exchange Service) and the Berlin Cultural Senate. Such noted representatives of their fields as the artists Armando, Ouki Cha, Jimmie Durham and his wife the photographer Maria Thereza Alves, Dorothy Iannone, Jean Robert Ipoustéguy, Emmett Williams, Zhu Jinshi, and Qin Yufen have worked in these spaces.

For several years in the 1980s, the artist and co-founder of the Fluxus movement Wolf Vostell occupied the large stone atelier in the west wing, and he worked there until his death in 1998. The atelier program ended in the early 2000s. After restoration and redesign in 2014/15, Kunsthaus Dahlem, an exhibition venue for the art of postwar Modernism in East and West Germany, began its operations there in the summer of 2015.

* * *

Even before its official opening, the press response was clear: the building's history, its original designation, and its relatively brief use during the National Socialist dictatorship would define the story of the house far more than its uses after 1945. In 2011 an article in the newspaper *taz* bore the headline "Des Führers Schatten" ("The Führer's Shadow"), and in that same year the *Tagesspiegel* spoke of "Vergangenheitsüberwältigung" ("The Overwhelming of the Past"), and "Traum vom Raum" ("Dream of Space").[12] In view of such an initial situation, which needed to be dealt with and debated with sensitivity, an exclusive focus on what the gallery was meant to feature—postwar Modernism with an emphasis on sculpture—was unthinkable. For one thing, it was necessary to signal clearly that the institution welcomed open and critical discussion of its heritage, and by no means felt that this dark chapter of German history had been fully processed. And moreover, a fundamental issue in art and museum history needed to be taken up and dealt with, one which was especially contentious in view of the fact that thousands of artists were banished and murdered during the Nazi dictatorship—namely the determination of an art-historical canon. Art, exhibition, and museum histories are per se never definitive, inalterable narratives. Changing aesthetics

12
Nina Apin, "Des Führers Schatten," in: *taz*, July 16, 2011; Christina Tilmann, "Vergangenheitsüberwältigung," in: *Der Tagesspiegel*, June 18, 2011; Daniela Martens, "Traum vom Raum," in: ibid., November 21, 2011.

and belated acknowledgement of marginalized groups and stylistic directions quite rightly force exhibition venues to identify and review their omissions.

With respect to postwar German Modernism, such a review had first to recognize that art after 1945, thanks to the Nazi regime's cultural bloodletting, was a mere vestige of what it would or could have been had there not been all the persecution, defamation, and killing. Any exhibition of postwar Modernism therefore has to include forgotten artists along with the already familiar names. And this means admitting that the concept "postwar Modernism" is itself only useful as a vague means of orientation. No epoch comes into being without precursors and after-effects. Today scholars are agreed that May 1945 by no means represented the "zero hour," the completely new beginning so frequently espoused, but that it also saw an attempt to revive pre-Third Reich Modernism and a tacit continuation of artistic traditions that had survived the twelve years of National Socialist dictatorship more or less intact.[13]

Kunsthaus Dahlem's presentation of the work of persecuted artists has by no means been an attempt to obscure the history and propagandistic uses of a structure like the Breker atelier, but rather a way to counter its original function. Precisely because it was erected as a demonstration of National Socialist power and for the purpose of propaganda, it serves as an ideal showcase for those who had to suffer under the regime.

To be sure, the dimensions of the museum's exhibition spaces necessarily place certain limits on this sort of rehabilitation and the creation of any awareness of historical fallibility: when placed under ceilings almost 33 feet high and between doors more than 15 feet tall, and given the axial symmetry of the entrances and sheer volume of the gallery, exhibited objects necessarily take on a new level of meaning and effectiveness. This was especially apparent at the show of Ulrich Wüst's photography, *Die Pracht der Macht* (*The Magnificence of Power*), in 2016. In that series the artist deals with the imagery of totalitarian and authoritarian regimes by presenting architectural and sculptural details, repeatedly decontextualizing them to the point of making their original intended effect and role in an overall ensemble unrecognizable. In the former Breker atelier the structure itself assumed that function, lending the relatively small-format photographs a unique, site-specific relevance. In such a setting, even the title *Pracht der Macht* lost any shred of neutrality.

Since there is no neutral space, no "white cube" as a presumably value-neutral setting, we are constantly confronted with the

13
See Sabine Eckmann, "Historicizing Postwar German Art," in: *Art of Two Germanys. Cold War Cultures*, ed. Stephanie Barron and Sabine Eckmann, exh. cat. Los Angeles County Museum of Art / Germanisches Nationalmuseum, Nuremberg / Deutsches Historisches Museum, Berlin, Cologne 2009, pp. 34–45.

fundamental problem of the architecture and how to deal with it. History and sociology are communicated verbally—that is to say in language and concepts, whereas architecture appears to be essentially only a material artifact. But in the combination of exhibition and structure it becomes apparent that architecture is capable of conveying far more. In addition to its materiality and its immobility, architecture always represents a realized intention. In his *Critique of Pure Reason* Kant noted: "I understand under architectonics the art of the systems that make one system out of a mere aggregate." In an architectonic space the viewer is made aware of himself, a psychological effect and reaction are evoked. But since it cannot and should not be the intention of an exhibition space to provoke preconceived and pre-formulated reactions, an exhibition program can and should at best point to the fallibility of art and history writing and invite reflection on it.

In Dahlem, the curatorial practice focuses on more general issues when dealing with the physical surroundings—architecture as such, the sociology and psychology of space, form, history, spatial harmony, the object in space—thereby fostering discussion of the art itself. As opposed to more classic, more conventional exhibition formats for the sculpture of postwar Modernism—both by artist and by theme—they have thus managed to promote, by way of dialogue, an engagement with the history and uses of Nazi propaganda structures that is not limited to the curator's own response.

The amount of media attention the general issue continues to receive was recently shown when two sculptures were unearthed in the gallery's garden. Public interest was aroused, both nationally and internationally, when one of them was identified as Arno Breker's *Romanmichel*, long thought to have been lost.

Sebastian Jung, *Art intervention on the NSU trial* | Installation view, Criminal Justice Center Munich

Andrea Büttner, *Karmel Dachau*, 2019 | Installation view, *Tell me about ~~yesterday~~ tomorrow*

207

Annette Kelm, *Travertinsäulen, Recyclingpark Neckartal (Sommer, Parkplatz, morgens) (Travertine Columns, Recycling Park Neckartal (Summer, parking lot, in the morning))*, 2019 | Installation view, *Tell me about ~~yesterday~~ tomorrow*

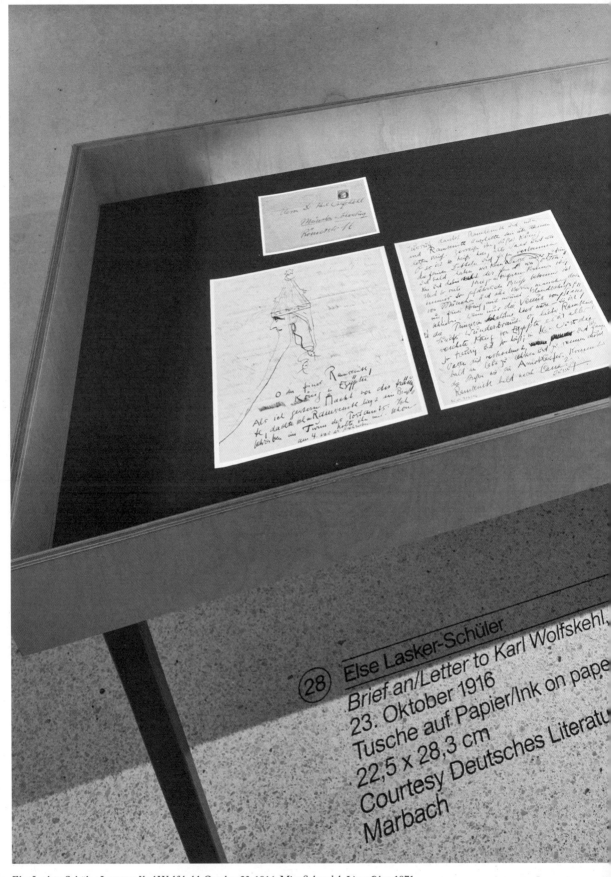

Else Lasker-Schüler, Letter to Karl Wolfskehl, October 23, 1916; Mira Schendel, *Livro Obra*, 1971
Installation view, *Tell me about ~~yesterday~~ tomorrow*

49 Mira Schendel
Livro obra, 1971
Letraset auf pflanzlichem P...
on vegetable paper; 18.5...

Livro obra, 1973
Letraset auf pflan...
on vegetable...

Courtes...
Kucz...

What Is Going On with the Para-Monument? A Review of Okwui Enwezor's Politics of Remembrance at Munich's Haus der Kunst

How does an art institution that wrote perpetrators' history become a space of contested history, present and future? In 2011, Okwui Enwezor assumed the directorship of Munich's Haus der Kunst. He began his work with a critical engagement with the history of the institution, which as the "Haus der Deutschen Kunst" (House of German Art) had been a Nazi showplace. To do so, Enwezor adopted preliminary efforts from the 1990s and 2000s and carried them further.[1] For example, he referred to the work of his predecessor Chris Dercon, who had begun a so-called "critical restoration"—that is to say, a design confrontation with the monumentality of the structure along with a re-historization of the building, an active and critical engagement with the history it was saddled with and that would not be simply left behind. Although work on the building from the 1950s up into the 1990s was intended as "architectural de-Nazification," the creation of small spaces and compartments in the monumental architecture had also failed to obliterate the fact that it was a Nazi structure.

Okwui Enwezor now took up Dercon's approach in order to find his own way of reflecting on the institution's history. Even though he always worked critically and discursively, in dealing with the building he went beyond a merely reflexive position and developed curatorial and institutional reappropriation strategies.[2] He made the Nazi architecture visible, and at the same time used it as an "experimental field and laboratory for international projects." In this, Enwezor to some extent turned the Haus der Kunst into a para-monument, one that incorporated the Nazi structure's massive forms curatorially and turned them against themselves. It is such para-monumental memorial strategies that I wish to discuss here. In the context of the *Tell me about ~~yesterday~~ tomorrow* project, which refers to history with regard to the possibility of a different future, it seems pertinent to remember Okwui Enwezor, for as director of the Haus der Kunst from 2011 to 2018 he developed a number of curatorial and institutional ways of dealing with history with precisely the same thing in mind.

* * *

In May 2012, a year after his appointment as director in Munich, Okwui Enwezor spoke in New York at the Museum of Modern Art about Hans Haacke's work *Germania*, and related it to his own position in Munich.

"Choosing Haacke is also relating to what is becoming my own personal biography, the linkage between Germany, this pavilion and Munich and Haus der Kunst… and I would like to use Haacke as a point of departure to… think through this vision of the crisis of the

1
The Haus der Kunst website in 2012 read: "Critical Restoration. The former 'Hall of Honor,' once ordained to be a display of Nazi power, is now an experimental field and laboratory for international projects. Structural changes, thought of as 'architectural de-Nazification' after the end of the war and meant to disguise its repugnant heritage, were partially reversed in the 1990s and especially since 2003 in the course of the 'critical restoration,' so as to reveal the origins of the onetime Nazi temple of art. Reflection on the complex and complicated historical process that has produced the Haus der Kunst in its present form will continue under the direction of Okwui Enwezor, director of the Haus der Kunst since October 2011"; <https://web.archive.org/web/2012050 4065842/http://www.hausderkunst.de/iindex.php?id=468> (accessed August 16, 2020).

2
Reappropriation as a resistance strategy in dealing with powerful forms and discourses is described in post-colonial theory as "affirmative sabotage of the master's tools"; see Nikita Dhawan, "Affirmative Sabotage of the Master's Tools: The Paradox of Postcolonial Enlightenment," in: idem, *Decolonizing Enlightenment: Transnational Justice, Human Rights and Democracy in a Postcolonial World*, Leverkusen-Opladen 2014. One example of such a strategy of reappropriation in art is Kara Walker, another in painting is Kerry James Marshall: <http://moussemagazine.it/kerry-james-marshall-nav-haq-2013/> (accessed August 16, 2020).

national space.... Haacke's project one can say was really the first time that an artist had taken the National Pavilion as a subject of inquiry. Rather than just simply a space into which things are placed it became a space that was contested. And here the German pavilion and its history and its attachment to its reconstruction in 1938 by the Nazis became the instrument if you will for this inquiry into the instability of the space of the nation."[3]

3
Okwui Enwezor on the origins of Haacke's pavilion, Discussion at MoMA New York, May 29, 2012: <https:// au.phaidon.com/agenda/ art/video/2012/may/29/ okwui-enwezor-on-the-origins-of-haacke-s-pavilion/> (accessed August 16, 2020).

Almost 20 years after his intervention in Venice in 1993, Enwezor succeeded in formulating in his retrospective reference to Haacke's work a curatorial and institutional working program that links the direct and explicit confrontation with Nazi architecture to a transnationalization of the institutional space. From this he developed a spatial and exhibition program, as precise as it was subtle, that was able to focus on colonial history and Nazism, anti-Fascism, and decolonization. Yet the one was never played off against the other, but was based with the greatest care on factual material. In relation to the German "counter-monuments,"[4] which develop a negative form of monumentality between presence and absence, yet are also largely dependent on a certain commemorative pathos, I would describe Enwezor's memory-policy interventions as para-monumental. He did not address the Haus der Kunst admonishingly, but dealt historically in reference to the present. I take para-monuments to be artistic and curatorial strategies for the reappropriation of monuments that do not deny their violent history but also do not bury it. Instead, they allow the entire powerful monumentality of historical relics and violent manifestations to be seen in order to confront them and offset them at the same time.[5] Let us consider this on the basis of a few examples:

4
See James Edward Young, "Counter-Monuments. Memory against Itself in Germany Today," in: *Critical Inquiry* 18, no. 2 (Winter 1992), pp. 267–296.

5
Another example would be Olu Oguibe, *Das Fremdlinge und Flüchtlinge Monument (The Foreigners' and Refugees' Monument)*, Kassel Königsplatz, documenta 14, 2017. See Nora Sternfeld "Münsters Gegen-Monumente," in: *Public Matters. Debatten & Dokumente aus dem Skulptur Projekte Archiv*, ed. Hermann Arnhold, Ursula Frohne, and Marianne Wagner, exh. cat. LWL-Museum für Kunst und Kultur, Münster, Cologne 2019, pp. 233–246.

* * *

June 2012 saw the opening of the exhibition *Geschichten im Konflikt. Das Haus der Kunst und der ideologische Gebrauch von Kunst 1937–1955* (*Histories in Conflict. The Haus der Kunst and the Ideological Use of Art 1937–1955*). The announcement of the show read:

"Reflection on the complex and complicated historical process that has produced the Haus der Kunst in its present form continues to the present day. Thus *Histories in Conflict* in an exemplary way illustrates what Okwui Enwezor, the director of the house since 2011, understands as a 'reflexive museum': being dedicated to contemporary art and investigating and communicating the historical dimension of the present. For *Histories in Conflict*, the Haus der Kunst has invited the Swiss conceptual artist Christian Philipp Müller to develop a dramatic presentation on the building's history."

Engagement with the structure's history culminated in 2014 in its own "Archive Gallery," conceived by the curators Sabine Brantl and Ulrich Wilmes and designed by Martin Schmidl. The institution had already dealt with its history, which begins with the Nazis but does not end with them. To Okwui Enwezor, however, that was too little. A section of the exhibition space was set apart that deliberately had access to the center hall. The history, which did not end in 1945, and engagement with the continuities of Nazism and with their disruptions were to leave their niche-like character and be integrated into the space of the exhibition. Changing projects relating to history and the archives have been presented in the "Archive Gallery" since 2014.

* * *

Thus, even in the first years of his tenure, Enwezor developed a program of critical engagement, one that began with a precise and comprehensive processing and communication of the building's history. And along with that program, from February 15 to May 26, 2013, he presented the exhibition *Aufstieg und Fall der Apartheid. Fotografie und Bürokratie des täglichen Lebens* (*Rise and Fall of Apartheid. Photography and Bureaucracy of Everyday Life*).[6] The show had been previously presented at New York's International Center of Photography, and after Munich it traveled to Milan and Johannesburg. But in the Haus der Kunst it took on a special significance, which I would call "para-monumental". It included an impressive selection of photographs from South Africa's apartheid era. The two most prominent features shared by all the exhibited photos were their outstanding quality as photographs and their resistance perspective. They were anti-Fascist images documenting the history of the struggle against apartheid. In the Haus der Kunst they were mounted larger than life on the vast walls of the "Nazi propaganda architectural showpiece," so that the anti-Fascist struggles of Blacks took over the white Nazi space. At the same time, they made use of its propagandistic power and infiltrated it subtly but radically. The nationalistic view is confronted from two sides. The decentralization of the West[7] did not take place without concrete engagement with the West: the architectural history of the space came up against the global historical dimensions of Fascism, South African resistance against an art space in a former Nazi structure. The deconstructive, para-monumental curatorial strategy brought concretion and displacement together. The precision of the artistic photographs and the audacious appropriation of the monumental space were what gave the show its special impact; it brought to mind the world's racist divisions and their power just as it illustrated the interstices that confront and thwart them.

6
Haus der Kunst, Inteventionen in die Architektur, <https:// hausderkunst.de/ ausstellungen/ aufstieg-und-fall-der-apartheid-fotografie-und-buerokratie-des-taeglichen-lebens> (accessed August 16, 2020).

7
Oliver Marchart, *Hegemonie im Kunstfeld: Die documenta-Aus-stellungen dX, D11, d12 und die Politik der Biennalisierung*, Cologne 2008, p. 11.

During the run of that exhibition, on March 7, 2013, the show *Mel Bochner. Wenn sich die Farbe ändert* (*Mel Bochner: If the Color Changes*) opened. For the opening, the "long-term public sculpture" *The Joys of Yiddish* was installed across the entire length of the Haus der Kunst façade.[8] In yellow letters against a black background, that para-monumental installation pictured a banner inscribed with Yiddish terms of abuse. Mel Bochner, Enwezor explained, was concerned about the disappearance of Yiddish from Germany and with it the disappearance of Jewish culture.[9] Yellow, the color of anti-Semitic stigmatization, was deliberately chosen. To some extent the string of Yiddish words was talking back from the Nazi's building.[10] The words on the banner and their translation read:

> *"KIBBITZER: smart-ass, wise guy KVETCHER: chronic grouch NUDNICK: pain in the neck NEBBISH: half-wit, bungler NUDZH: nuisance, pest MESHUGENER: madman, schmuck ALTER KOCKER: grumpy, crotchety old man PISHER: immature person PLOSHER: braggart, loudmouth PLATKE-MACHER: agitator, troublemaker"*[11]

It was as if the words were shouting at the city in large letters from the façade. The entire Haus der Kunst itself became a para-monument. In this sense, Okwui Enwezor said: "The architecture is our first object. This is not only a building, but a historical object."[12]

* * *

It is significant that both projects—*The Rise and Fall of Apartheid* and *The Joys of Yiddish*—were not only site-specific. They made their point even without the building, but they had been newly developed for the space. As a curatorial gesture of reappropriation of the Nazi building, they both exercised a specifically para-monumental force at the Haus der Kunst, though they were not only produced for that venue. That is remarkable inasmuch as they thereby avoided the classic dialectical problem of intervention, which is always marked by that in which it intervenes. Here we have to do with forms of reappropriation that in their nature as intervention go ahead of and beyond what they intervene in.

From the fall of 2015 to the fall of 2016, Mel Bochner's installation was supplemented by two other works on the façade. For the second presentation in the Haus der Kunst's "Archive Gallery," Okwui Enwezor and Sabine Brantl reinstalled the interventions by Christian Boltanski and Gustav Metzger that had already been developed for the

8
Bochner originally conceived of the monumental banner *The Joys of Yiddish* for the Spertus Museum in Chicago.

9
Haus der Kunst, Interventionen in die Architektur, <https://hausderkunst.de/entdecken/videos/interventionen-in-die-architektur?locale=de> (accessed August 16, 2020); see also the Podium discussion: "Der deutschen Kultur die jiddische Stimme zurückbringen…" in Haus der Kunst on June 17, 2013, <https://www.ikg-m.de/der-deutschen-kultur-die-jiddische-stimme-zuruckbringen/> (accessed August 16, 2020).

10
The term "talking back" was coined by the anti-racist theoretician Bell Hooks in *Talking Back. Thinking Feminist, Thinking Black*, Boston 1989.

11
https://hausderkunst.de/notes/mel-bochner-the-joys-of-yiddish> (accessed August 16, 2020).

12
Haus der Kunst, Interventionen in die Architektur, <https://hausderkunst.de/entdecken/videos/interventionen-in-die-architektur?locale=de> (accessed August 16, 2020).

Haus der Kunst in the 1990s: "With *Résistance* by Christian Boltanski (1993/94) and Gustav Metzger's *Travertin/Judenpech* from 1999, the Haus der Kunst reactivated the first two artistic engagements conceived specifically for the building's façade and portico."[13] *Résistance* shows the pairs of eyes of resistance fighters of the anti-Fascist "Rote Kapelle" movement, which now once again cast their gaze onto the city from the Nazi building. In the installation *Travertin/Judenpech*, in turn, Gustav Metzger paved the entrance with black asphalt, colloquially known since antiquity as "Judenpech" (Jewish tar). Metzger, persecuted as a Jew in Germany himself and forced to flee as a child, was referring to his own history and intervening in the art space that, as Okwui Enwezor put it, "denied his belonging to the German people," also to the "function of the building itself as a showpiece."[14] The re-enactment provided a new perspective on memories that precisely in their repetition point to the need for them and their persistence. As the curator Sabine Brantl said of the Nazi history stamped on the building, it is like a door that never closes: "At times it is more open, and at times more closed, but it never closes completely."[15]

The Mel Bochner installation hung on the façade of the Haus der Kunst from 2013 to 2019. It was then taken down on the occasion of the opening of the exhibition *El Anatsui: Triumphant Scale* and its related façade installation in March 2019. Mel Bochner donated it to the Haus der Kunst; it was placed in storage and according to the institution will be reinstalled in 2021.[16]

* * *

Immediately following the presentation of works on the façade, from October 2016 to March 2017, the Haus der Kunst presented the exhibition *Postwar: Kunst zwischen Pazifik and Atlantik, 1945–1965* (*Postwar: Art between Pacific and Atlantic, 1945–1965*), curated by Okwui Enwezor, Katy Siegel, and Ulrich Wilmes. The show provided an impressive new perspective on and remapping of the postwar period, which it investigated as a global phenomenon. It shifted art-historical assumptions and world regions, and among many other things placed the continuities and breaks in German postwar history in new contexts. In his catalogue essay "Postwar: Denazification and Reeducation"[17] Ulrich Wilmes investigated the role of art in postwar period debates on closure: the restorative function of exhibitions in the 1950s becomes evident. Once again, the exhibition managed to decentralize the West, questioning established interpretations and geographies, and reconsidering German thinking so as to arrive at a different understanding of modernism, one more complex and opposed to the canon.

13
Interventionen in die Architektur – Ausstellung, September 18, 2015–September 18, 2016, <https://hausderkunst.de/ausstellungen/christian-boltanski-resistance-2?locale=de> (accessed August 16, 2020).

14
Haus der Kunst, Interventionen in die Architektur, <https://hausderkunst.de/entdecken/videos/interventionen-in-die-architektur?locale=de> (accessed August 16, 2020).

15
Telephone conversation with the curator Sabine Brantl on August 18, 2020.

16
I am grateful to Sabine Brantl, Markus Müller, and Ulrich Wilmes for their support.

17
Ulrich Wilmes, "Postwar: Denazification and Reeducation," in: *Postwar. Art Between the Pacific and the Atlantic 1945–1965*, exh. cat. Haus der Kunst, Munich, ed. Okwui Enwezor, Katy Siegel, and Ulrich Wilmes, Munich, London, and New York 2016, pp. 58–63.

Again, the national art history was confronted in precise investigations with those it included as well as those it shut out.

At this same time, plans were being made with the architect David Chipperfield for a renovation of the building, plans intended to do justice to the idea of a "critical restoration." Enwezor spoke of them as a way of "thinking historically in the present."[18] To be sure, the design's para-monumental concept was not understood in Munich. One controversy had to do with a row of trees planted in the postwar period, the removal of which would have opened up the view of the building. In the course of the debate there was even talk of a "re-Nazification" of the building. The design could not be realized.

Okwui Enwezor found the controversy, only one of many, painfully incomprehensible, and a public repudiation of his efforts. An interview in *Der Spiegel* in August 2018 bore the title "No longer desired." By that time, Enwezor had left the Haus der Kunst, which he had effectively guided as director since 2011, and he was already very sick.[19] In the interview, he openly spoke of a lack of recognition and encouragement, about political, media, and institutional opposition to his position in Munich.[20]

* * *

On September 16, 2018, soon after Okwui Enwezor had left the directorship, the brief note about the history of the house on the museum's website was changed. To understand present-day disagreements about political history it is instructive to look at the differences between the two entries. Under Enwezor's direction, pressing the website's "History" button brought up the text:

> *"Eventful and in constant change: in more than 75 years the Haus der Kunst has undergone a historic transformation. In 2012 the house marked two important anniversaries: the 75th year since its opening under the Nazis in 1937 and the 20th year since the founding of the private-public Stiftung Haus der Kunst München GmbH in 1992. 'From 1937 to the present day the museum has reflected remarkable historical shifts: from the site of the Great German Art Exhibition (1937–1944) to a U.S. Army officers' club (1945–1955); for years the building housed the most diverse institutions, or served wholly different purposes. From the 1950s to the 1980s it was used as an exhibition space for a mix of formats and*

18
Haus der Kunst, Renovate/Innovate – Gespräch mit David Chipperfield am 16.9.2016, <https:// hausderkunst.de/ entdeckken/videos/ conversation- renovate-innovate- david-chipperfield- and-okwui- enwezor?locale=de> (accessed August 16, 2020).

19
Okwui Enwezor died on March 15, 2019. He was one of the most important curators of the present day. One of the things that made him so, and this is the thrust of my text, is that in all his curatorial work in collaboration with artists he referred to history in order to bring it into the present and question the powerful apparatus of canonization.

20
Okwui Enwezor in the interview "Nicht mehr erwünscht," *Der Spiegel* 34 (2018), p. 116.

*genres. In the 1990s, the Haus der Kunst evolved into
a museum with a structured program for classic modernism,
and since 2003 it has been devoted almost exclusively
to contemporary art. The Haus der Kunst is a work in
progress, embedded in a landscape of constant change—
paradoxically, this is a constant that sets the Haus der
Kunst apart and makes it unique.'* – Okwui Enwezor" [21]

In September 2018 the website's note on the history of the house not only omitted the quote from Enwezor, it also described that history somewhat differently.

* * *

"Haus der Kunst's history is not just any history. More than any other museums, the institution has made its mark on the histories of modern art historiography.

After its opening in 1937 as the "Haus der Deutschen Kunst" [House of German Art], the Neoclassical building served to demonstrate Nazi cultural politics and became the party's leading art institution. After the end of World War II, the museum building was first used by the U.S. Army as an officers' club. Art exhibitions took place as early as 1946. The return of modernism to the very place where the denigration of artists had begun served as part of a larger historical contemplation.

Haus der Kunst became an important venue for featuring avant-garde works—like Picasso's *Guernica* in 1955—and thus a counterbalance to its defamatory stance during the Third Reich. Since then, Haus der Kunst has been transformed radically into an international center of modern art exhibitions, and today into a global museum of contemporary art. The cultural examination and curatorial analysis of this process has become an ongoing, integral part of Haus der Kunst's program." [22]

* * *

Especially interesting in the institution's description of its history since Enwezor's departure is the reference to the 1950s. Modernism, which only 18 months previously, in the same institution's exhibition *Postwar*, had still been considered complicated and contaminated, is now presented as having been simply interrupted. When we read: "The return of modernism to the very place where the denigration of artists had begun served as part of a larger historical contemplation," it would seem as if the continuities of the 1950s, which at that time

21
Website of the Haus der Kunst on February 21, 2017, <https://web.archive.org/web/20117022 21235833/http://www.hausderkunst.de/ueber-uns/geschichte/> (historic URL: <http://www.hausderkunst.de/ueber-uns/geschichte/>) (accessed August 16, 2020).

22
https://hausderkunst.de/en/history (accessed November 8, 2020).

were also tied to efforts to make people forget, to overwrite history with the help of modern art, are being restaged. The suggestion of a "return of modernism" is moreover misleading. Who was allowed to return? Who not? And who, perhaps, did not wish to return? And return to what? To a Nazi building? Here, in the twenty-first century, we have a narration that could have been formulated in the 1950s (one that today is also called "artwashing").[23] a historical narrative whose restorative function Ulrich Wilmes had clearly illustrated in the *Postwar* catalogue was now again admitted into the institution's description of itself.

This accords with the title of an article in the *Frankfurter Allgemeine Zeitung* for July 11, 2020, in which the new dual directors of the Haus der Kunst were introduced: artistic director Andrea Lisson and business manager Wolfgang Orthmayr. It read: "Finally on the Ascent Once Again. Without Old Burdens. New Start in Munich's Haus der Kunst." The references to the Nazi architecture seem correspondingly less complicated: Andrea Lissoni, according to the *Frankfurter Allgemeine*, "has already been on the roof. He recalls that the architect Paul Troost, to whom Hitler had entrusted the design, and Gerdy Troost, who completed it after the death of her husband, were famous for their ship furnishings." Thus he wanted to "make it fly, like a space ship."[24] Here again reference to the past with regard to the future. The question is: which future?

23
This is how I would describe the return-of-modern-art myth in the Federal Republic in the 1950s, which had the function of not having to speak about anti-Semitism and not about the involvement in Nazism and its art and science endeavors, but rather of over-identification with the victims and placing itself in a direct line with "degtnerate art."

24
Brita Sachs, "Endlich wieder einmal Aufwind," in: *Frankfurter Allgemeine Zeitung*, July 11, 2020, p. 11.

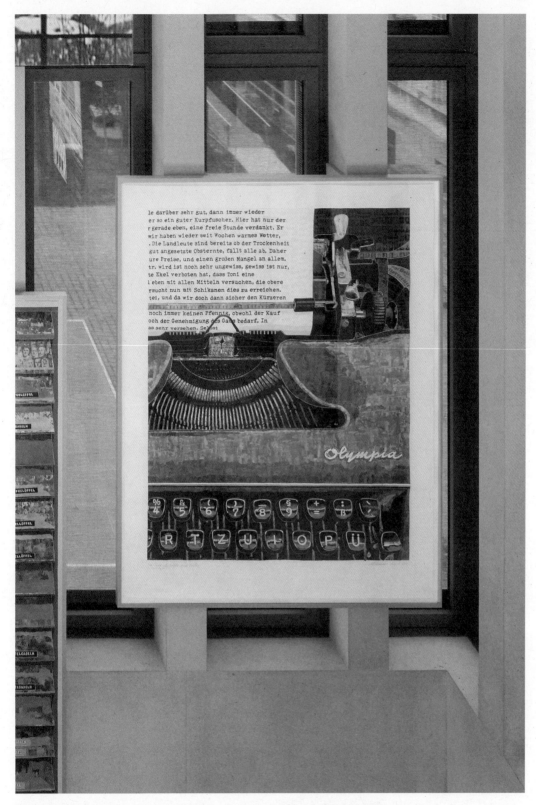

Marcel Odenbach, *im Land der Dichter und Denker (in the Land of Poets and Thinkers)*, 2019
Installation view, *Tell me about ~~yesterday~~ tomorrow*

Paula Markert, *Eine Reise durch Deutschland. Die Mordserie des NSU (A Journey through Germany. The NSU Series of Murders)*, 2014 – 2017
Installation view, *Tell me about ~~yesterday~~ tomorrow*

Ken Lum, *Coming Soon*, 2009 | Installation view, *Tell me about ~~yesterday~~ tomorrow*

For Turkishness and Islam, Against Freemasons, Communists, and Jews

The analysis and criticism of antisemitic statements in literature, culture, and art are frequently made more difficult by the fact that their authors employ implicit allusions, symbols, and codes that first have to be deciphered. Misinterpretation of literature, culture, and art as fundamentally "apolitical" also impedes the exposure of ideological content. This misinterpretation is fostered by the self-identification of writers, artists, and cultural leaders who think of themselves as living in a world of their own, apart from the realms of politics and society. The situation is in fact quite otherwise, as is shown by the case of one such cultural worker discussed here, a prominent figure on the political scene who openly and tirelessly spins antisemitic narratives. In 1975 Recep Tayyip Erdoğan, the present Turkish president, produced the play *Mas-Kom-Yah*, the title of which is composed of the first syllables of the words "Mason" (Freemason), "Komünist" (Communist), and "Yahudi" (Jew). To say that Erdoğan produced this play is somewhat misleading: he simply copied the 1969 play *Kızıl Pençe* (*Red Claw*) by Mustafa Bayburtlu, changed the title, and functioned as director. Both Recep Tayyip Erdoğan and Mustafa Bayburtlu were graduates of a religious Imam-Hatip School, a type of school that is partly responsible for the rise of Islamic conservatism and Islamism in present-day Turkey and one that obviously shaped Erdoğan's worldview. But whereas Erdoğan went on to a highly successful career as a politician, Mustafa Bayburtlu has been virtually forgotten.

FAMILY, FAITH, AND FATHERLAND

The play begins with Bayburtlu's homage to "Islamic soldiers who have fallen in the battle against Communism and Zionism."[1] There then follow two story lines involving the factory owner Ayhan Bey, which play out in different contexts. While the first one turns on Ayhan Bey's son and takes up motifs of Islamic conservatism. It is the second narrative, which describes events in Ayhan Bey's factory and is considerably longer and decidedly political in tone, that conveys features of Islamist ideology. Both stories are characterized by a Turkish nationalist, anti-Western, antisemitic, and anti-Communist stance. It is striking that the belief in a conspiracy on the part of the Freemasons, alluded to at the start of the play's new title, is nowhere mentioned in Bayburtlu's text. But even without any explicit reference, both producers and audiences in the Turkish-Islamist camp could with little effort associate the play's anti-Western narrative with Freemasonry.

1
Mustafa Bayburtlu,
Kızıl Pençe, Çorum
1969.

The story of Orhan, Ayhan Bey's son, is related in a few scenes that take place in Ayhan Bey's home. Orhan's father had sent him to Europe to get a Western and modern education. His grandparents and other older, religious-conservative advisors had criticized that move and urged Ayhan Bey to have his son taught in an Islamic school instead. They feared that Orhan could become an atheist, and abandon his Turkish roots. But Ayhan Bey was convinced that a Western and modern education posed no threats. When Orhan returns from his long years in Europe, however, the worst fears of the Islamist-conservative voices are confirmed: he is disrespectful of his elders, he declines to kiss the hands of his older relatives, and he uses rude language—even in the presence of people deserving of respect. Ayhan Bey is annoyed by his son's behavior from the beginning, but is utterly shocked when it becomes apparent that Orhan no longer believes in God and has no love for Turkey. All involved are distraught, ultimately even Orhan himself, who places the blame for his wayward course on his father, who failed to let him enjoy a proper Turkish, Islamic education.

THE ENEMY: JEWS AND COMMUNISTS

The second story line runs parallel to this one, leaving the family circle to turn to larger political issues. Three young Islamist activists call on Ayhan Bey in his factory and urge him to contribute to the fight against Communism. They maintain that Westernization is weakening religious and national values, allowing for an increasing Communist threat. Ayhan Bey scoffs at the activists, who to his mind are engaged in a senseless cause, since there simply is no Communist danger. Moreover, as a well-to-do factory owner, Ayhan Bey feels insulated from political and social turbulence. In this scene Fazıl Bey, one of his friends, is the warning, Islamist-conservative voice; he supports the young activists and considers Westernization to be the cause of the problem. Throughout this scene, the Communist threat is presented as a product of Westernization. Shortly after his son's return, Ayhan Bey experiences another fateful stroke: the workers seize his factory. They had already managed to secure higher wages by means of a strike, so Ayhan Bey cannot at first understand what the takeover is about. His foreman, Hasan Usta, hesitantly explains that the workers are no longer demanding higher wages; they want to expropriate the factory and operate it themselves. It is then revealed that Mişon, a Jew who poses as a Muslim and calls himself "Memed," has fired up the workers with Communist propaganda. Three workers storm Ayhan Bey's office and declare that the factory is now under the workers' control, and that revolution has spread throughout the country. While the workers are convinced that they have taken over direction of the factory, Ayhan Bey tries to explain that they have been egged on by a Communist Jew, and will soon become victims of this conspiracy as well. A resolution immediately follows, when the Jew enters the office with three subordinate Communist soldiers and has both the factory owner Ayhan Bey and the three workers arrested. Mişon explains to the shocked workers that the workers' revolution had been only an excuse for installing a "Communist regime," and that the country's citizens are slaves of a Communist state. The workers recognize too late that their "Memed" is not a Muslim Turk, in fact, but a Jew. At Mişon's direction one of the Communist soldiers fatally wounds Ayhan Bey, and with his dying breath the industrialist explains that the Islamist struggle is the only true path. This ends the actual play, but there follows a long poem by Mustafa Bayburtlu titled "Defeat the Red Bastards!," in which he exhorts Turkish Muslims to take up the fight against Communism.

RECONCILING NATION WITH FAITH

The play presents in its rather simplistic and explicit language ideological elements of Islamist conservatism and Turkish Islamism, both of them forces of the Turkish Right. It also reveals ties and crossovers between these two currents. Particularly obvious is the presentation of Islamism as an effective agent for Islamic values and traditions, a role featured in several of the central scenes. Equally clearly recognizable and repeated is the link between Westernization and social conflict, which in this narrative necessarily ends in a Jewish, Communist dictatorship. Supposedly the only salvation for Islam and Turkishness is a militant Islamism fighting against "Freemasons" (Westernization), Communism, and Jews. As the play's framing elements, Mustafa Bayburtlu's homage and poem underscore that demand for a militant Islamism. Such an ideologically based idea of the future social order, based on an imaginary past, can be called, to use Zygmunt Bauman's term, "Retrotopia."[2]

Islamist ideology goes hand in hand with Turkish nationalism, which also appears to be militant. So in the play there is repeated explicit reference to the "blood" of nationalist martyrs who have saved Turkey from a non-Muslim occupation. This Turkish blood, which soaks the soil of the entire country, would make Turkey more precious than any other country in the world. At the same time, this reference to nationalist martyrs who gave their lives for their nation and their faith, challenges present generations to be similarly militant

2
Zygmunt Bauman, *Retrotopia, Hoboken*: Wiley 2017.

and willing to make the same sacrifice. Here, too, the past serves as a model for the future, Islamist notions of the future being combined with those of Turkish nationalism. The reconciliation of these right-wing ideologies, previously not without conflict, was cast in a new ideological construct in the 1970s with what Islamist and nationalist intellectuals referred to as a "Turkish-Islamic Synthesis." By the time of the military putsch in 1980 at the latest, and subsequent conservative, nationalist governments, it had been integrated into the state ideology, leading to a state-sponsored re-Islamization of the society. It is notable that Mustafa Bayburtlu had to some extent anticipated this development as early as 1969, and that Recep Tayyip Erdoğan, who is today largely responsible for the implementation of a religious, nationalistic state policy, would have chosen such a script.

There is one feature of the text that is less relevant today than it was at the time. From the Islamist perspective, Communism no longer represents the menace that it did in 1975. By contrast, belief in Jews and the West as enemies has survived to this day. The propagation of a unique, Turkish-Islamist identity, rejection of the West, and a fundamental antiseimitism, now revealed as Islamist anti-Zionism or "criticism of Israel," continue to be effective ideological elements. Erdoğan and other protagonists from the camps of Islamic conservatism and Islamism have been stamped by this narrative, and act accordingly in their politics. Antiseimitism always forms a part of Islamist and nationalist ideology, though it can at times be overshadowed by other currents. In the 1980s, for example, racism and the baiting of the Kurds were clearly more prominent, and took up more space than anti-Jewishness, for debate had shifted to Turkey's war in its Kurdish territories. But this does not mean that antisemitism had disappeared. Even in those years antisemitic elements were woven into anti-Kurdish propaganda, for it was assumed that the Kurdish PKK, which was carrying on an armed struggle against Turkey, was under Jewish control.

WHAT WE DO NOT KNOW

Whereas the ideological aspects of this play can be readily identified, a number of other questions arise that remain unanswered to this day. For example, we know that this play was very frequently performed between 1975 and the military putsch of 1980, but we do not know who organized those country-wide performances and what their motives might have been. Nor is it known what, if any, the public reaction might have been. Moreover, the historical context is obscure: what other plays from this time employed similar narratives and motifs?

And as for the reception of the play itself, it is unclear why to this day there has been virtually no critical examination of its contents. For astonishingly, even Erdoğan's political opponents have refrained from criticizing its obvious antiseimitism and making a scandal out of it. This possibly suggests that in today's Turkey, just as then, hostility toward Jews is no scandal, but rather a widely accepted or partially even desired position. It is also clear that the simultaneity of conservative cultural positions, an anti-modern worldview, and antiseimitism, well-known from German history, can be observed in other states and in other historical epochs.

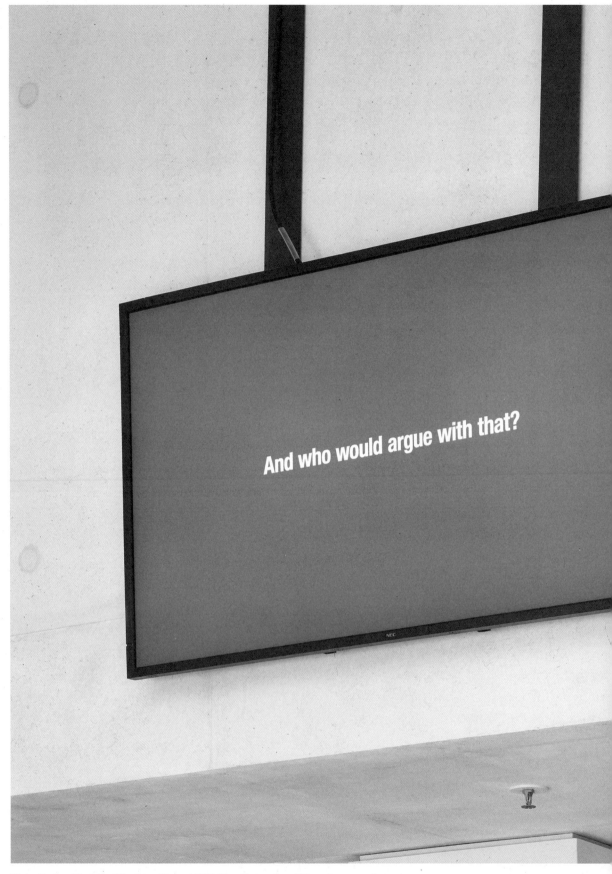

Trevor Paglen, *The Effect Was Almost Magical*, 2009 | Installation view, *Tell me about ~~yesterday~~ tomorrow*

(42) Trevor Paglen
The Effect Was Almost Magical, 2019
Video, 55 min, Loop
Courtesy the artist and PACE
Gallery

Artur (Stefan) Nacht-Samborski, *Martwa Natura z Kwiatami w Wazonie (Still Life with Flowers in a Vase)*, 1950; *Martwa Natura (Dzban Liliowy) (Still Life [Vase of Lilies])*, undated | Installation view, *Tell me about ~~yesterday~~ tomorrow*

Cultural Policy or Culture War?
Poland 2020

When the symposium *Public Art – City. Politics. Memory* opened in Munich in January 2020, the Covid-19 pandemic had already escaped from its point of origin in the Huanan Seafood Wholesale Market in Wuhan, and spread from China to other Asian nations, and would then proceed to the Near East, Australia, Europe, and America. The consequences of the pandemic had—and continue to have—an enormous effect on the symposium's first three designated subjects: public art, city, and politics. However the fourth term,—memory—only took on another, special meaning when George Floyd was murdered by policemen in Minneapolis in May. Just as in other countries, the lockdown in Poland limited the rights of citizens. The pandemic and the communication chaos of the first weeks heightened social tensions, especially during the presidential elections, which the Law and Justice Party candidate, reigning since 2015, was able to decide for himself in July.

The following essay is intended to illuminate the political course Law and Justice and its governing partners are taking in Poland with respect to the cultural realm and its institutions, as well as its attempts to reshape the historical memory—all this with the help of instruments and techniques more reminiscent of a culture war than a cultural policy pursued in the traditional manner. The cultural policy previously practiced for many years, which was defined in democratic terms, was distinguished by a variety of directions, and according to its own definition considered itself pro-European. For the past five years it has been successively supplanted by a campaign whose goal is the creation of an authoritarian, national-Catholic state.

In the 1960s UNESCO defined cultural policy in a general way,[1] and the cultural policy practiced by Polish governments after 1989 roughly conformed to the (Polish) Wikipedia definition. This stated that cultural policy favored "process, institutions, and legal steps that promote the variety and accessibility of culture or contribute to the dissemination of artistic, ethnic, socio-linguistic, and literary forms of expression by exponents of the cultural heritage of the given country."[2] For 30 years, the logic of the changeover begun in 1989 justified the promotion of such values as Europeanization, inclusiveness, diversity, civil society, etc., and liberal governments paid no particular attention to questions of identity or national affiliation, for their program was primarily aimed at urban voters. The globalization of the economy, which at the same time speeds up other global processes (and brought with it a rhetoric of consumer optimism) neglected development in rural areas and smaller towns. EU funds contributed to the improvement of infrastructure there, to be sure, but the new lines of communication only stimulated the mobility of specific groups (especially women), who have moved to the cities or

1
See *Cultural Policy, a preliminary study*. Paris: UNESCO, 1969, <https://unesdoc. unesco.org/ark:/48223/ pf0000001173> (accessed August 28, 2020).

2
<https://pl.wikipedia. org/wiki/Polityka_ kulturalna> (accessed September 15, 2020).

abroad. The upgrading of Internet connections countered this with only a virtual sense of belonging. Opposition parties led by Jarosław Kaczyński successfully exploited these weak spots in the 2015 elections.

His Law and Justice party correctly diagnosed that there was a need for identity-related and patriotic content within groups and conservative circles that had been denied full access to the progress of the last thirty years and saw the changes brought about by globalization with anxiety. In contrast to all the preceding election campaigns, Law and Justice's political offensive in 2015 placed a disproportionate emphasis on culture. This was done on the assumption that in the public life of Poland, culture and history play a special role, and the (actual and exploited) conviction that the cultural elites that had arisen since 1989 were essentially a reprise of their predecessors under the previous system. This led directly to the deliberate, ideology-driven division of the society, and ultimately contributed to the Party's revolutionary stance relating to culture.

DIVIDING LINES IN LAW
AND JUSTICE CULTURAL POLICY

In its platform formulated for the 2015 election, the Party emphasized national and Catholic values. A year before, the Party's chairman Jarosław Kaczyński had said: "Polish culture is… an enormously important realm owing to the policies of the present government. We will concentrate on the preservation of the national heritage, on patriotism, and on everything that contributes to a Polish identity. We do not intend to promote projects that are clearly anti-Polish in nature. Internal anti-Polishness is something extremely dangerous."[3] Tying patriotism to religiosity was in conformity with the pragmatics of the campaign, which relied on the Catholic Church, its structures and media. The rightist, nationalist shift in its own camp was connected with the hope of attracting to its side at least a portion of the radical right electorate, especially young men.

The dividing line was drawn along a few select, symbolic "flash points" that could be ignited at specific moments. Each of these "flash points" permitted the establishment of Manichaean contradictions between "good" and "evil," and their projection onto other problem areas, institutions, and ultimately even individuals.

To the first group numbered historical issues rooted in the catastrophe of the Second World War, which continues to be a central narrative reference point in Poland. Needless to say, such subjects as the Holocaust and the mass wartime killings have not been adequately internalized to this day either in Poland, or in the rest of Europe. At the Party's 2015 convention Jarosław Sellin, then Poland's Deputy Minister for Culture and National Heritage, referred to this as follows:

3
Iwony Kurz, *Powrót centrali, państwowcy, wyklęci I kasa. Raport z "Dobrej Zmiany,"* Warsaw 2019, p. 18.

"One of the state's most important goals is a systematic history policy. Every reputable state proceeds in this way. We have to abandon the notion that history is to be left exclusively to historians, and that we should concentrate solely on the future. We have to break with the prevailing pedagogy of shame and anti-patriotic revisionism in the narration of our history. A wise history policy should uphold pride in our past and our heritage, on which our national and social solidarity is constructed, as well as inform our position with respect to the past in dialogue with other peoples."[4]

One of the most important flash points was the result of historical researches at the beginning of the twenty-first century that revealed that the slaughter of the Jewish population of the village of Jedwabne in July 1941 was committed by the victims' neighbors—Poles. The announcement of this fact in numerous publications and testimonies, especially in the book by Jan Tomasz Gross,[5] unleashed a moral trauma, and led to confusion within a society that had grown up with the cult of its tremendous sacrifices suffered during the war. This provided conservative circles with a motive for declaring war on "anti-Polishness" and the supposed "pedagogy of shame," and after 2015, scholars who studied the Holocaust and Jewish-Polish relations during the occupation and after the war were pilloried by the governmental media. Moreover, in sections of the society this dispute generated anti-Semitic sentiments. And ultimately, complex Polish-Jewish topics would motivate other conflicts.

Another area of conflict proved to be German-Polish relations. Several commentators have pointed out that increased attention of politicians on the right to a possible questioning of the history of the Second World War was caused by the announcement in 2000 of the building of a Center Against Expulsions in Berlin. In this context, after being under construction for eight years, Gdansk's Museum of the Second World War was a successful attempt to universalize the experiences of the war. On its opening it proved to be the spark that ignited conflict on a national and patriotic level. From the start, the museum and its creators were the targets of media and later political attacks. After the completion and opening of the permanent exhibition in 2017, in the first instance the directors were dismissed and subsequently the exhibit itself was revised.

After 2015 the Ministry of Culture and National Heritage, whose budget was significantly increased, undertook intensive steps toward the creation of new history museums intended to keep the memory of Poland's tragic wartime fate and its heroic acts alive. The prototype for the new institutions was the Warsaw Uprising Museum, which at the same time inspired the rise of the "narrative museum" concept in Poland. It had opened during the presidency of Lech Kaczyński with

4
Ibid., p. 22.

5
See Jan Tomasz Gross, *Neighbors: The Destruction of the Jewish Community in Jedwabne*, Princeton, N.J.: Princeton University Press 2001 (original Polish edition Sejny 2000).

6
A Law and Justice campaign slogan in 2015, now a common phrase mostly used ironically.

7
Kurz 2019 (see note 3), p. 23.

a program developed by a group of conservative intellectuals. As Iwona Kurz, the author of the first report on the "good change"[6] in the culture has written, the museum became "a laboratory for a new Polish identity and new history policy. It was a response to societal expectations but simultaneously strengthened them, in that it presented the previously mentioned new myth in an attractive, popular way."[7]

Of the new museums and institutions of "history policy" I would name mainly the following: The Pilecki Institute of Solidarity and Valor (with a branch in Berlin); the Warsaw Ghetto Museum; the Piaśnica Museum in Wejherowo (Pomerania); the Excommunicated Soldiers Museum in Ostrołęka (Masovia); the Westerplatte Museum of the Second World War (Gdansk); and the Inhabitants of the Land of Oświęcim Museum (Oświęcim=Auschwitz). The Ministry has also re-solved to cooperate with local museums already in existence: the Central Prisoner of War Museum in Łambinowice/Opole; the Pilecki Family House Museum in Ostrów Mazowiecka (Masovia); and the Ulma Family Museum of Poles Who Saved Jews in World War II in Markowa (Outer Subcarpathia). The institutional flagship of the new history policy will be the Museum of Polish History in Warsaw, whose opening has already been twice postponed. Of the many new institutions, I would point out the National Institute of Polish Cultural Heritage Abroad, named after Roman Dmowski and Ignacy Jan Paderewski, which takes up the heritage of pre-war nationalistic parties. As Marcin Napiorkowski has written: "If one wishes to understand the present-day museums, one should not only question their motivation, goals, and subject areas, but also "against whom" they were created. Increasingly, a museum is paradoxically based on whom we consider an "adversary" or "foreigner," so as to affirm our own identity."[8] The generous financial support of the government's new history policy as well as forced personnel changes in research facilities (the Institute of National Remembrance, for example) have greatly contributed to the criticism of historians and intellectuals.[9]

8
Marcin Napiórkowski, Sieć pamięci, <http://wiez.com. pl/2020/06/14/siec-pamieci/> (accessed May 20, 2020).

9
See Paweł Machcewicz, "Jak polityka historyczna PiS-u słuzy do produkowania wrogów wewnętrznych," in: *Gazeta Wyborcza*, July 19, 2020. For an example of the countless voices from abroad, see the article by Florian Hassel, Nacht im Museum, *Süddeutsche Zeitung*, September 27, 2018.

Another point of conflict in the cultural landscape was an area I would call (somewhat reductively) the area of critical art. Basically this is not the kind of art presented in galleries and public spaces, but the whole sphere of artists, directors, filmmakers, and activists, as well as the profiles of numerous modern cultural institutions. The list of complaints, dis-missals, judicial proceedings, and political quarrels instigated by radical nationalist organizations and right-wing media with the collaboration of "social forces" is long, and continues to grow. The recent takeover of the directorship of the Warsaw Center for Contemporary Art—a liberal institution with roots in the Solidarity era—by a curator sympathetic to right-wing, radical thinking can be seen as a symbolic victory.

Let me point out here a few mechanisms, by no means new, that are being resorted to in the wholescale attempt to change the face of culture in Poland. Right-wing populist politicians already discovered the first of them in the 1990s (and naturally adopted decades-old patterns): the visual arts were so defenseless that they were an ideal target for ruthless attacks in the spotlight, and on such occasions the scandal-hungry media provided political publicity at no cost.[10]

After many more years, when the Polish cultural sector together with its outstanding directors, well-known artists, and outstanding writers was enjoying worldwide recognition, it allowed itself to be quite simply reduced to a binary formula: cosmopolitanism (under which fall such subjects as moral postures, climate, secularism, gender, women's rights, etc.) versus "our own." As was emphasized in the 2015 Law and Justice platform: "Among the many instances of negligence in past years, culture, this linchpin and core of the national consciousness, which along with tradition forms the basis of society, has been treated in an especially slipshod manner, in a manner, namely, most tellingly reflected in two quotes: 'make what you wish'[11] and 'Polishness is an abnormality.'[12] Accordingly, outrageous or even anti-Polish projects, for example, have been sponsored instead of worthwhile patriotic endeavors in line with our tradition and our justification as a nation."[13]

One further realm of cultural, already revolutionary change has to do with the decentralization of culture and the associated decision-making processes—a model supported by the (liberal and left-wing) governments. Since it stood in opposition to the centralizing efforts of Law and Justice, the programming independence of many cultural institutions and non-governmental organizations as well as advisory rights of a broad circle of experts with respect to cultural financing had to be withdrawn. The latter is closely linked to Law and Justice's fourth, extremely important postulate, namely the enforced replacement of elites in the Polish cultural scene. This was already at the heart of one of the most important national right-wing theories in the late 1990s. Ludwik Dorn, once an influential Kaczyński party ideologue, wrote at that time: "I think that all the people who could form a potential anti-communist government for the restructuring of the republic would find no more… than 400 such persons for this.… They would create the political will to ensure its implementation possibilities, legitimize the work of restructuring in the symbolic realm, but also guarantee the possibility of legal, forced implementation."[14] This process was initiated immediately after the Law and Justice's assumption of power in 2015 and is being consistently pursued; it has served to reshape the cultural landscape and place party figures in director's posts.

10
Art works were physically attacked (Maurizio Cattelan in the curator Harald Szeemann's exhibition in Warsaw's Zachęta Gallery in 2000); the artist Dorota Nieznalska was prosecuted in 2001 (and convicted of offending religious sensibilities); gallery directors were dismissed (Anda Rottenberg from the Zachęta Gallery in 2001); and establishments were completely liquidated (Wyspa Gallery in Gdansk in 2001, Galeria Prowincjonalna in Stubice in 2002).

11
The title of a broadcast in the early 1990s directed by Jerzy Owsiak (chairman of the Poland's largest charitable foundation), a man despised in rightist circles.

12
Donald Tusk as quoted by the magazine *Znak*, 390-391/2011, http://www.miesiecznik.znak.com.pl/6792011donald-tusk-polak-rozlamany/ (accessed January 21, 2021).

13
"Twórcy a polityka kulturalna państwa," in: *Myśląc Polska, Konwencja Programowa Prawa I Sprawiedliwości oraz zjednoczonej prawicy*, Kattowitz 2015, p. 113.

14
Ludwik Dorn, "Reforma państwa dziełem elity przywódczej," in: *Dobry I sprawny rząd*, ed. Kazimierz Michał Ujazdowski, Warsaw 1997, pp. 23f. Dorn would in time become a chief critic of the Kaczynski Party.

Many of the measures named could still be considered part of a cultural policy being implemented by politicians with authoritarian tendencies and a government that strives for a centralist model in the exercise of power. Yet the pressure created by the radically placed dividing line has led to an intensification of measures that one might already rightly define as a culture war, especially since the country's entire justice system is also being subjected to revolutionary changes.

THE LAW AND JUSTICE CULTURE WAR

The term "Kulturkampf", as we know, has long since freed itself from its German etymology dating back to the waning nineteenth century. The battle lines and trenches of modern culture wars run along the lines of social conflict issues. When these are exploited, they can serve populists as a convenient ruling method.[15] Deepening the split and evoking further conflicts, around such issues as homosexuality and abortion, for example, also creating adversarial images such as the foreigner or the enemy of the people, the breaking of religious taboos, or the reinforcing of an arbitrarily established definition of national dignity in cultural works and scholarship, characterize the dynamic of such a war within a society. In Poland this war has already been fought for several years. In the following I shall therefore discuss only a few key battles in the cultural realm (and historical scholarship, or more broadly, the humanities). These battles feature the frequent repetition of the perfidious verbal attacks especially favored by Law and Justice leader Kaczyński and the party apparatus. Whenever they wish to vilify an opponent, they resort to anti-communist rhetoric. Neither the presence in their own ranks of former members of the Communist Party, nor the fact that three decades have already passed since the downfall of communism, prevent Law and Justice politicians from defaming specific social groups, cultural positions, or intellectual circles as "communist" or "Bolshevist."

The most effective weapon in this culture war proves to be the public right-wing media. There have been massive personnel changes at the state television as well as its regional offshoots and at various state radio stations. These have been followed by cutbacks and drastic programming changes as well as the creation of lists of people the media should no longer invite to speak. Censorship and internal directives have led to grotesque situations, as, for example, when public, right-wing television failed to air the awarding of the Nobel Prize to the Polish writer Olga Tokarczuk, and postponed the broadcast to the following days.

A further method is the already mentioned replacement of directors at cultural institutions or the non-appointment of people to directors' posts who might make hiring decisions by themselves. One of

15
See Robert Traba, "Geschichte als Raum des Dialogs," in: *Inter Finitimos* 4 (2006), pp. 68–95.

the first known cases was the non-appointment of the former Minister of Culture, Prof. Małgorzata Omilanowska, as director of Warsaw's Royal Castle in 2015. Another was the dismissal (judged to be illegal) of Paweł Potoroczyn, director of the Adam Mickiewicz Institute. The list of politically motivated staffing decisions is long. One might also recall the most recent, months-long controversy over extending the term of office of Prof. Dariusz Stola, director of the POLIN Museum of the History of Polish Jews. Professor Stola had won the competition announced by the Ministry of Culture, but the minister failed to appoint him to the post in defiance of competition rules. Much the same could be reported from other cultural spheres—film, theater, literary institutions, and the Polish Institutes abroad.

A certain innovation in the waging of the culture war is the establishment of doubles in parallel with cultural establishments, museums, newspapers, and government agencies, a listing of which would exceed this essay's space limitations. The mechanism is simple: the previous establishments slowly cease to function, and their doubles, along with fresh personnel, take over with the help of the necessary financial allocations and media support.

It is striking that the most determined battles in the culture war have taken place around institutions and issues embedded one way or another in an international context. Among these are the above-mentioned Museum of the Second World War (with an international scholarly advisory board as well as an exhibition narrative intended to be universal), the POLIN (with international scholarly advisors, financial supporters, and a long, difficult history of Jewish-Polish relationships), and the European Solidarity Center in Gdansk, which represents an important part of the heritage of the Solidarity Movement, one of Law and Justice's central founding myths.

In the case of the European Solidarity Center—along with the usual chicanery in the form of funding reductions—attempts were also made to remove from the building the famous panels presenting the 21 demands of the 1980 strikers. Thus, as described, a whole series of different steps have been taken—from staffing decisions (including competitions for state's attorneys and other legal steps) to financing cuts, to deceitful dealings of only symbolic importance.

The most spectacular example of the culture war in Poland, and one that caused great waves abroad and led to serious diplomatic crises and loss of face by representatives of the governing apparatus, was the by now well-known 2018 amendment that established fines and prison terms of up to three years for anyone asserting that the Polish nation or Polish state bore responsibility or co-responsibility for crimes of the Third Reich. In essence it aimed at Holocaust research, including research on the collaboration of Polish citizens. Penalizing scholarship and its publications (press reports were also included) in this way led to such violent protests in Poland and around the world that the right-wing nationalist governing apparatus removed the punishments from the law and somewhat moderated it.[16]

VOX POPULI. RETROTOPIA AND PUBLIC ENGAGEMENT

The battle for symbolic values, for "dignity," for a self-identity based on a positive approach to the country's history[17] (an international phenomenon not limited to Poland), as well as the demand to consider the "Polish viewpoint" in museums, scholarly undertakings, etc.—all of these are part of the phenomenon Zygmunt Bauman has described as *Retropia*, a variation on the nostalgia that provides the illusion of a return to a wonderful, safe past romanticized by previous generations.[18] Behind this mindset are the fear of a declining national stature, the perceived "pedagogy of shame" enforced by native and foreign agents, and a revision of history. On top of these there is the added worry about the declining influence of the Catholic Church (to which a number of issues are related, from the fight against pedophilia to sexual preference and minority rights). In this area the culture war has taken an ugly turn in the past year as it set its sights on the LGBT community, starting with municipalities that have declared themselves LGBT-free zones, controversial statements by Andrzej Duda during the presidential election campaign in July, and subsequent political repressions.

To be effective, a culture war requires the engagement of masses, who are offered a role of their own, but with only a simulation of democratic processes. This strategy originated in such early phenomena as the New York Society for the Suppression of Vice (1873–1950) or the Hays Code that was imposed on a distraught Hollywood film industry in the mid-1930s. These examples may have been drawn from the puritanical United States, but they are perfectly well known to us from past culture wars waged by totalitarian organizations.

The ruling Law and Justice party seeks to encourage other foundations, societies, institutes, and movements that it supports with public moneys and that are essentially financed with inexhaustible funds from state-controlled enterprises and banks. Their role is providing social legitimacy to its attacks, in special cases demonstrating opposition (to specific theatrical presentations, exhibitions, publications, or conferences thought to represent an insult to the nation or to religion, tradition, the family, or morality itself). Magnified by

16
<https://www. gazetaprawna.pl/ artykuly/1152438,sejm-zmiana-ustawy-o-ipn-bez-przepisow-karnych. html> (accessed July 5, 2020).

17
"Wstawanie z kolan" ("Get up off your knees") has been a central element of the Law and Order government's foreign policy doctrine since 2015.

18
Zygmunt Bauman, *Retrotopia*, Cambridge: Polity 2017.

the media, this provides an excuse to initiate further measures. A special role in this is played by the Ordo Iuris Institute for Legal Culture, a fundamentalist organization of Catholic jurists that initiates prosecutions and trials with complaints against unyielding opponents. Allied to similarly fundamentalist organizations worldwide, Ordo Iuris appears to be functioning in increasing synergy with the Polish government, and its functionaries have assumed important posts, for example the chairmanship of the state commission for clarifying pedophilic crimes (which was convened after numerous scandals in the Polish Catholic Church were exposed). Another organization that calls itself Reduta Dobrego Imienia (Good Name Redoubt), maintains a website—taking a cue from the Jewish Anti-Defamation League—where people can report incidents from the realms of history or cultural activities that could harm Poland's reputation.

It would be tiresome to list all the other organizations, institutions, and attacks; I here sketch the various fronts in the culture war only in broad strokes. The abundance of organizations listed above and dozens of similar ones, distributed across the entire country and its parishes, are the result of a paradoxical clash between two worlds. The one derives from the past, and was created through processes of life in a post-totalitarian social vacuum. In it a special role is played by the Catholic Church, along with its complex spiritual and secular interests. The second is totally modern and truly universal, defined by new technologies and their algorithms and a whole complex of progress-related anxieties.

The paradox in the whole situation in which we find ourselves is that the politically right-wing groups, many of which arose out of the one-time Solidarity Movement, originally hoped to reform the state, but have now erected a grotesque state model in which real power lies in the hands of the Party leader, who until fall 2020 held no official offices and was a mere delegate. The appropriation of the judiciary, the right-wing public media, the body of public prosecutors, the culture industry, and memory culture have directly led to a hybrid copy of the "real socialism" state toppled in 1989, accused of criminality by the political right.

Aslan Ġoisum, *People of No Consequence*, 2016 | Installation view, *Tell me about ~~yesterday~~ tomorrow*

Loretta Fahrenholz, *Europa II (1–6)*, 2013 | Installation view, *Tell me about ~~yesterday~~ tomorrow*

An Aesthetics of Prolepsis

This Makes Me Want to Predict the Past is a black-and-white film by Cana Bilir-Meier, with a voice-over that includes the titular phrase as well as the line "This makes me want to remember the future," along with many other variants of "This makes me want to…"—taken from the YouTube comments for Childish Gambino's song *Redbone*.[1] Bilir-Meier's short film shows young women in and around the Munich shopping mall where nine people were killed in a racist attack in 2016; in total, more than 200 people have been killed in Germany for racist motives since 1990. There's a monument right outside the center, opposite the Saturn electronics store, dark and grainy images of which can be gleaned in Bilir-Meier's film.

Through photos and performed reenactments, the film also references the 1982 play *Düşler Ülkesi*, about migrant *Gastarbeiter* ("guest workers"), staged with the cooperation of the artist's mother, Zühal Bilir-Meier. While *This Makes Me Want to Predict the Past* is shown as a digital video, it was originally shot on Super 8 film stock—giving it not so much an aura of timelessness as of "out-of-timeness". While the film does not dissolve chronology as such, it instills doubt about the direction of time's arrow. The past has a habit of being all too predictable—or does it? The past has a habit of being all too predictable; or has it? What if there are historical genealogies to be unearthed that disrupt conventional narratives and formatted forms of commemoration? And what if the future, in turn, can already be remembered, and indeed commemorated, as a future of inequality, oppression, murder, and massacres?

Contemporary art is marked by a profound interest in historiography and counter-history, in memory and commemoration—and in the decolonization of institutional memory.[2] I will address these matters in a somewhat indirect manner, by re-reading a set of literary and cinematic practices from the 1960s and 1970s. These are European and (somewhat) German practices, mostly by male and (to some extent) canonical writers and/or filmmakers. From certain angles, then, this might seem a somewhat conservative constellation, but I hope to show that the works in question matter profoundly *now*, if we are attentive to anachronic resonances and disturbances in the canon. In the West Germany of the 1960s and 1970s, artists such as Peter Weiss and Alexander Kluge challenged the Cold War consensus by re-excavating the avant-garde of the 1920s and 1930s and its accompanying debates about artistic autonomy and political activism—debates that had

1
The YouTube comments say "This song makes me want to…"; Bilir-Meier left out "song". https://www.youtube.com/watch?v=Kp7eSUU9oy8 (accessed August 4, 2020).

2
Among the discussions of this "historical turn," see Mark Godfrey, "The Artist as Historian", in: *October*, 2007, no. 120, pp. 140–172; Susanne Leeb, "Flucht nach nicht ganz vorn: Geschichte in der Kunst der Gegenwart", in: *Texte zur Kunst*, 2009, no. 76, pp. 29–45, and Eva Kernbauer's forthcoming book *The Anachronic Here and Now* (Routledge).

intensified as fascism emerged triumphant. Just as these historical practices and discussions echoed in the post-war Federal Republic, haunted by the disavowed memory of Nazism and the Holocaust, so I am interested in the ways in which such post-war artistic production and discourse can disturb the present.

PERMANENT PERGAMON

On October 19, 1965, Peter Weiss's play *Die Ermittlung* (*The Investigation*) premiered simultaneously in a number of West and East German venues, including Erwin Piscator's Freie Volksbühne in West Berlin, and across the Wall in the Volkskammer—the GDR's parliament.[3] Based in Stockholm since 1939, Weiss was present in the cultural and intellectual spheres of both countries, though arguably his most important forum was provided by the West-German Suhrkamp publishing house and the liberal and left-ist media landscape in which it was such an important actor. For *Die Ermittlung*, Weiss condensed the Frankfurt Auschwitz Trials into a spoken "oratorio" in eleven "cantos" in which witnesses present a chilling tableau of life (or of survival, rather) in the extermination camp, including their own implication in the necropolitical system. If the play is documentary in nature, Witness 3 speaks for the author when—in the "Gesang von der Möglichkeit des Überlebens" ("chant of the possibility of survival")—he elaborates on how the guards and inmates were both part of the system: how they shared a cultural heritage and had fought for the same nation—until some of them had been "appointed" inmates instead of guards. *Die Ermittlung* is a carefully composed reenactment of a trial which turns the theatre into a *moralische Anstalt* ("moral institution") à la Schiller, but with a Brechtian political twist. As Witness 3 emphasizes, the camp felt oddly at home as a prolongation of the very society which had created its conditions, and that this can happen again, in even more "efficient" future institutions.[4]

Going beyond a ritualistic "Never Again", Weiss takes aim at the structural antinomies and historical continuities of capitalism, from the Third Reich to the Federal Republic. This made the play perfect for ideological exploitation by the GDR— a state in which Weiss desperately wanted to see a compromised form of social-ism that could yet unfold its potential, as opposed to a sclerotic post-Stalinist regime.[5] While the reception of *Die Ermittlung* got caught up in the Cold War, the play is not reducible to its GDR instrumentalization—as is shown by its equally problematic trans-formation into a pillar of post-1990 German *Erinnerungskultur*

3
On the reception of *Die Ermittlung* in East and West, see the documentation and analysis in Christoph Weiß, *Auschwitz in der geteilten Welt. Peter Weiss und die "Ermittlung" im Kalten Krieg*, St, Ingbert, 2000 (two volumes). In 1966, the play was televized in both East and West Germany.

4
Peter Weiss, *Die Ermittlung. Oratorium in 11 Gesängen*, Frankfurt am Main 1965, pp. 85–86.

5
See Weiß, *Auschwitz in der geteilten Welt*, vol. 1, p. 210.

("culture of remembrance"), with readings in the local parliaments of Lower Saxony (2009) and Bremen (2013) inadvertently recalling the Volkskammer reading of 1965.

During the Cold War, capitalism was stabilized at the cost of neocolonial proxy wars in the "Third World". In 1967, Weiss participated in the Russell Tribunal on the Vietnam War in Stockholm. Whereas *Die Ermittlung* (for which Weiss actually considered the title *Das Tribunal* at one point) was a theatrical re-enactment of the Auschwitz Trials, the Russell Tribunal took aim at American military action and alleged war crimes through the *pre*-enactment of a justice to come, of an "actual" trial with juridical agency.[6] As a trial-by-media, this was a form of *Gegenöffentlichkeit* ("counter-publicness"). In Harun Farocki's 1979 television portrait *Zur Ansicht: Peter Weiss*, the writer recalls his 1968 visit to Vietnam, and the effects of witnessing the Vietnamese struggle on his own conception of art and on the conception of his monumental three-part novel, *Die Ästhetik des Widerstands* (translated into English as *The Aesthetics of Resistance)*. Weiss noted how culture was part of daily life in Vietnam during the war, even during bombings; there would always be some poetry reading or a theatre troupe staging some play. One may scoff at this as a romantic-productivist fantasy, as an avant-garde wish fulfillment by a Western writer—but it is in keeping with a general problematization of an institutionalized "autonomous art", which had become ideologized as a unique selling point of the Free West in the context of the Cold War.

Around 1968–70, many artists and theorists looked back at Brecht, Benjamin, Tretyakov and Heartfield to develop a neo-productivist notion of art as transformative avant-garde practice; art as an engine of a cultural revolution in the context (and in the service) of a social and political revolution. Weiss, who was part of those milieus, was likewise infected with revolutionary fervor.[7] However, by the time the first volume of *The Aesthetics of Resistance* came out, in 1975, it was no longer tenable that the situation in the West was (proto-)revolutionary, or that guerilla tactics from the Global South could be transplanted to Europe. The *Aesthetics* resonated in part because it was anything but sloganesque, and because it was a painstaking inquiry into the failure of the antifascist leftist vanguard of the 1930s. Weiss's novel is certainly partisan, but it sides first and foremost with memory itself, performing a properly materialist *Gedächtnisarbeit* ("memory work") that seeks to keep the dialectic in motion and the future open—all defeats, suicides and genocides notwithstanding.

6
The *Das Tribunal* title is documented by Weiß, *Auschwitz in der geteilten Welt*, vol. 1, p. 123. With Peter Limqueco, Weiss edited the Russell Tribunal's proceedings: *Prevent the Crime of Silence: Reports from the Sessions of the International War Crimes Tribunal Founded by Bertrand Russell*, London/ Stockholm/Roskilde, London 1971.

7
See for instance: "Che Guevara!", in: *Kursbuch*, 1968, No. 11, pp. 1–6.

8
Peter Weiss, *Die Ästhetik des Widerstands*, Berlin 2016, p. 15. My references are all to the first volume, which originally appeared in the Suhrkamp Verlag in 1975; volumes two and three followed 1978 and 1981, respectively. Eventually, a complete edition in one volume was allowed to appear in the GDR, in the Henschel Verlag in 1983. While Weiss's descriptions of Stalinist politics during the 1930s was sensitive matter for the East-German Communist Party (SED), the book was not censored, and shortly before his death, Weiss was able to correct questionable edits made by Suhrkamp, in the third volume in particular. The single-volume 2016 Suhrkamp edition has been compiled based on these two prior versions. English translation from: Peter Weiss, *The Aesthetics of Resistance*, trans. by Joachim Neugroschel, Durham, N.C. 2005, p. 8.

9
For this reception history, see for instance Lionel Gossman, "Imperial Icon: The Pergamon Altar in Wilhelminian Germany", in: *The Journal of Modern History*, 2006, vol. 78,

The novel's narrator is a displacement (in the Freudian sense) of the author. The son of a Hungarian-Jewish factory owner, Weiss had opted for the life of an artist as a young man in the 1930s—becoming precarized, or proletarianized, in the process. By contrast, Weiss's first-person narrator was born a proletarian; he and his comrades are workers who tried to educate themselves, who read voraciously and debate constantly. The famous first "block" of text sees the small group visit the Pergamon Museum in Nazi Berlin, on September 22, 1937, to study and debate the Pergamon Altar with its frieze depicting the battle of the gods against the giants—an allegory of Pergamon's rulers' victories, of "the victory of the aristocrats over an earthbound mix of nations."[8] What this artwork showed the workers, as opposed to what it showed bourgeois or fascist publics, was a perpetual class struggle. Weiss's leftist reading of the frieze was, of course, also an intervention in the monumental work's reception history since its rediscovery and transport to the capital of the new German Empire, where it went on public view in the early 1880s, to be housed in the current Pergamon Museum by 1930. Having been moved to the Soviet Union at the end of World War II, the frieze was transferred to the GDR in 1958-59. It remains on this site in the reunified country—calls for restitution to Turkey notwithstanding.[9]

Later "blocks" of Weiss's novel see an ongoing conversation about Greek mythology and art, about modern art and art's ideological instrumentalization by the powerful and about study ("From the very outset, our studying was rebellion").[10] The *Aesthetics*' content is shaped by its context: the 1930s attempt to forge an anti-fascist Volksfront or Popular Front, which saw the Moscow-led Comintern enter into coalitions and alliances with Social-Democratic and other left-wing parties. Throughout, this endeavor is shown to be fraught with difficulties that have deep historical roots; at one point, the fatal opposition between anarchists and communists in the Spanish Civil War is traced back to the Marx/Bakunin opposition and the split in the First International. Even if this project was politically doomed, however, it is intellectually productive for those workers who refuse to become doctrinaire ideologues: "It was by fighting out conflicts, contradictions that we found what we had in common. There had been rejections, difficulties, and always the striving to pass through thesis and antithesis in order to achieve a condition that was valid for both of us. Just as divergences, disagreements gave rise to new ideas, so too did every action emerge from the clash of antagonisms."[11]

This is also an apt characterization of the discussions about art that run through the *Aesthetics,* with speakers taking different positions on modernism, for example. Was the autonomization of modern art a refusal to take political responsibility?[12] Did modern artists claim artistic independence so that they could remain in the service of the powers that be—even while seemingly keeping their hands clean? Such suspicions notwithstanding, the Nazis' attacks on modern art suggested to some that modern painting ("Max Ernst, Klee, Kandinsky, Schwitters, Dalí, Magritte") could be seen as a "dissolution of visual prejudices," an act of aesthetic sabotage with profound political implications.[13]

Both concerning art and relating to other matters, Weiss's narrator distinguishes between a party line decreed from above and the reality on the ground, where the militants are far less consistent and are prone to doubt and generosity—even if, as the military situation in the Spanish Civil War gets more desperate and as Stalin's Moscow trials unfold, as former heroes of the Revolution and the Soviet avant-garde are sentenced and silenced, a climate of uncertainty and fear takes hold. Mayakovsky's suicide looms large. Even so, with the major capitalist democracies busily appeasing Hitler or staying studiously neutral, the party appears to be the last bulwark against fascism. "We are expecting a world war, so no word that I utter can allow doubts about absolute agreement with our strategy."[14] There is no lack of forebodings, as in a passage about hearing the ominous sounds of the *Anschluss* on the radio: "That night we began to understand what vast temporal expanses the fight would cover." [15] Then, as the Popular Front or People's Front in Spain collapses, there is the half-repressed awareness of the unimaginable: that the war is already lost (or that this episode of the ongoing war is already lost), as the beleaguered Soviet Union is about to withdraw its support.

These are moments of prolepsis; the narrator and other characters see the catastrophe coming because they know they are already in it.[16] The literary device of prolepsis is a foreshadowing of events before their chronological occurrence; a "flash forward". The proleptic temporality of the *Aesthetics of Resistance* also informs its debates about art. As the narrator puts it right in the beginning, discussing the Pergamon Altar: "We looked back at a prehistoric past, and for an instant the prospect of the future likewise filled up with a massacre impenetrable to the thought of liberation."[17]

Towards the end of the first volume the narrator, about to leave Spain, visits the ruins of a Temple of Diana. What could be

no. 3, pp. 551–587; Alina Payne, "Portable Ruins: The Pergamon Altar, Heinrich Wölfflin, and German Art History at the fin de siècle", in *RES: Anthropology and Aesthetics,* 2008, no. 53/54, pp. 168–189; as well as an earlier article by Max Kunze that includes a discussion of Weiss's *Aesthetics*: "Wirkungen des Pergamonaltars auf Kunst und Literatur", in: *Forschungen und Berichte,* 1987, no. 26, pp. 57–74.

10
Weiss, Ästhetik (see note 8), p. 67. English translation from *Aesthetics,* p. 45.

11
Ibid., p. 157. Translation from *Aesthetics,* p. 109.

12
This autonomization is characterized as "Verselbstständigung und Isolierung"; ibid., p. 91.

13
Ibid., p. 71.

14
Ibid., p. 346; English translation from *Aesthetics,* p. 245.

15
Ibid., p. 375. English translation from *Aesthetics,* p. 266, adapted by SL.

16
Robert Buch briefly comments on the proleptic traits of the *Aesthetics of Resistance* in: *The Pathos of the Real: On the Aesthetics of Violence in the Twentieth Century,* Baltimore 2011, p. 115.

17
Weiss, *Ästhetik (Aesthetics)* (see note 8), p. 17. English translation from *Aesthetics,* p. 9.

a standard exercise in cultural tourism becomes a meditation on Ancient Greek colonialism in the Mediterranean, on history as a succession of wars and conquests and the rise of Rome; on the Greek gods surviving only as images on coins, on the ancient origins of capitalism and industrialism.[18] The return to Greek antiquity, then, almost closes the first volume, in a callback to the discussions about Pergamon at the beginning.

Weiss's play *Marat/Sade* (1963) already had a deeply proleptic structure: in 1808, during the Napoleonic Empire, the incarcerated Marquis de Sade and his fellow inmates at the Charenton Asylum stage a play about the assassination of Jean-Paul Marat during the French Revolution, in 1793, with Weiss's Sade gloating at his fictional Marat and his vain hopes of a better future. While *Die Ermittlung* was a seemingly more straightforward documentary work of witness-bearing, here too Weiss inserted brief proleptic statements, and he inserted them into a trial taking place in the audience's present: Witness 3 speaks in the now of the 1960s about a potential future about even more "efficient" future genocides— and perhaps these words are at least as resonant and disturbing today, in the present of 2021.[19]

Weiss's narrator in the *Aesthetics* is entangled in the mess of history and prone to illusions about the party, but he has a clear-eyed sense of the gravity of the situation, of the immanent logic and ultimate program of fascism. Throughout the book, art returns as an ambiguous agent. The two final blocks of Volume I, after the excursion to the Temple of Diana, focus on Picasso's *Guernica* (which the narrator and Ayschmann see as a reproduction in *Cahiers d'Art*), on Goya's *The Third of May 1808*, Delacroix's *Liberty Leading the People* and Géricault's *Raft of the Medusa*, as well Robert Koehler's 1886 canvas *The Strike*. Can modern art—compromised and contradictory, autonomous and *fait social*—be part of the historical process of self-emancipation?[20] Can it help to put an end to the permanence of the Pergamon? Failing that, is its task to bear witness to doomed forms of resistance?

SPACE NAZIS AT THE NEW BAUHAUS

Between January 1969 and April 1970, Alexander Kluge made a number of science-fiction films, largely recording them at the Hochschule für Gestaltung (HfG) in Ulm.[21] In contrast to Weiss, the older exile, Kluge had experienced the collapse of Nazi Germany from the inside as a young teen. In post-war West Germany he became part of several artistic and intellectual

18
Ibid., pp. 396–409.

19
Weiss, *Ermittlung* (see note 4), p. 86.

20
Weiss, *Ästhetik* (see note 8), pp. 409–446.

21
Peter C. Lutze, *Alexander Kluge: The Last Modernist*, Detroit, 1998, p. 225, note 9. Into the 1990s, Kluge continued to tweak the films or make new items for his TV programs based on the material.

networks with links to the pre-Nazi era which had been profoundly marked by the fascist terror. In Frankfurt, during the 1950s, he served as legal counsel for the Institut für Sozialforschung (Institute for Social Research); in some of his later stories, he recalls Adorno and especially Horkheimer's fear of the West-German version of McCarthyism, and their attempts to hide the Marxist roots of Critical Theory. As one of the leading figures of the Neuer Deutscher Film, Kluge became one of the founders of the Institut für Filmgestaltung (Institute for Film Design) at the HfG in Ulm—the so-called "New Bauhaus" founded by survivors from the milieu of the Weiße Rose resistance group who sought to reconnect with Weimar-era modernity.

The historical Bauhaus had exemplified a Western form of Productivism, with painters such as Kandinsky and Klee teaching not new generations of painters but the future designers of the modern world. With Max Bill guaranteeing a genealogical link to the pre-war Bauhaus, the HfG became a temple of precisely the kind of technocratic, instrumental reason that Adorno and Horkheimer criticized: modern design and production methods were regarded as intrinsically good, democratic, and progressive.[22] The Institut für Filmgestaltung, however, had a certain degree of autonomy. Kluge and his colleague Edgar Reitz insisted that film could not be organized along the same formal principles of design. In 1967, the institute became an independent foundation (eingetragener Verein), which allowed it to function after the state of Baden-Württemberg closed the HfG in December of 1968.[23] For a certain period, the building on the Kuhberg subsequently became a commune run by (former) students, and Kluge's institute still used the workshops and facilities.[24] Production on his sci-fi films started in January 1969, in the ex-HfG.

This was the period that saw the first moon landing (July 20, 1969) as well as a thriving production of sci-fi in various media. In Germany, where the *Perry Rhodan* series of pulp novels was virtually synonymous with science fiction, the genre had a profoundly reactionary reputation among the (New) Left.[25] A 1970 episode of the left-wing TV programme *Monitor* attacked the titular character of *Perry Rhodan* as a thinly disguised Hitler, as a space imperialist set on conquering the galaxy. Kluge did not countenance such blunt exercises in ideology critique, delivered with dour-faced self-righteousness.[26] While acknowledging the reactionary tropes in pulp fiction, Kluge insisted on the need to engage with and to re-imagine them. Hence, in the feature-length

22
On Adorno's contacts with the HfG, see Christiane Wachsmann, *Vom Bauhaus beflügelt. Menschen und Ideen an der Hochschule für Gestaltung Ulm*, Stuttgart 2018, pp. 73–74.

23
Ibid., p. 215; see also pp. 218–237 on the HfG's closure and the subsequent use of the buildings.

24
Alexander Kluge, email to the author, March 28, 2019.

25
See for instance the dossier compiled by Jürgen Holtkamp, "Die Eröffnung des rhodesischen Zeitalters oder Einübung in die freie Welt. Science Fiction-Literatur in Deutschland", in: *Kursbuch*, 1968, no. 14, pp. 45–63. A somewhat more ambiguous fascination can be discerned in Hartmut Sander and Ulrich Christians (eds.), *Subkultur Berlin – Selbstdarstellung, Text-Ton- Bilddokumente, Esoterik der Kommunen Rocker subversiven Gruppen*, Berlin 1969, pp. 42–51, 82.

26
Kluge, e-mail to the author (see note 24).

films *Der große Verhau* (The Big Mess) and *Willi Tobler und der Untergang der 6. Flotte* (Willi Tobler and the Demise of the 6th Fleet), as well as in a number of short films and in the slightly later book *Lernprozesse mit tödlichem Ausgang* (Learning Processes with a Deadly Outcome, 1973), he incorporated images from *Perry Rhodan* as well from the *Landserhefte*—hugely popular far-right dime novels that glorified the "heroic sacrifices" of German soldiers in World War II.[27]

Rather than creating an alternative universe, Kluge presents the future as a continuation, an exacerbation; rather than inserting moments of prolepsis, prolepsis becomes the structuring principle. If Ursula Le Guin famously argued that science fiction is not about extrapolating from the present, that it is not about the future but about imagining alternative worlds, Kluge's space opera is practically a parody of extrapolation. After Earth has been blown up in the "Schwarzer Krieg" (The Black War, 2011–15), the military-industrial complex continues doing what it does best in outer space. "The Suez Canal Company survived the Black War only as an idea, since neither documents nor people found refuge in space; in 1956, it had already been dispossessed of its original capital object, the Suez Canal."[28] This colonial corporation has thus made a transition to a galactic financial capitalism with the loss of its original investment; the process of accumulation hops from host to host, from the Isthmus of Suez to the metallic planet Dubna (via Russia), as the value-form colonizes countries and then alien planets. Evoking the Institut für Filmgestaltung's emancipation from its institutional host, the company became a Platonic entity. As a juridico-financial idea, it could go on to extract materials and value from different worlds.

As *Lernprozesse mit tödlichem Ausgang* elaborates, a number of Nazi generals—veterans of Stalingrad with medically prolonged lives—were instrumental in taking the war off-planet. Since they had already lost the *Heimat*, losing planet Earth in the Black War was no big deal.[29] The *Kessel* (or pocket) of Stalingrad is a motif that returns throughout Kluge's oeuvre, to the point where it becomes uncomfortable: it is as though for Adorno's former assistant it is not Auschwitz, but the fate of Germans in Stalingrad that constitutes the haunting event needing to be revisited time and again. However, in the context of Kluge's space opera, the role of the Eastern Front veterans produces a compelling if ambiguous engagement with history as continuity—the continuity of the master-slave dialectic, of exploitation and extermination. The use

27
Ibid.

28
Alexander Kluge, "Lernprozesse mit tödlichem Ausgang (1973)", in: *Chronik der Gefühle*, vol. II. *Lebensläufe*, Frankfurt am Main 2004, p. 876. Translation by Christopher Pavsek, *Learning Processes with a Deadly Outcome*, Durham 1996, p. 55.

29
Ibid., p. 842.

30
Oskar Negt and Alexander Kluge, *Öffentlichkeit und Erfahrung. Zur Organisationanalyse von bürgerlicher und proletarischer Öffentlichkeit*, Frankfurt am Main 1972, p. 59. English translation by Peter Labanyi, Jamie Owen Daniel, and Assenka Oksiloff, *Public Sphere and Experience: Toward and Analysis of the Bourgeois and Proletarian Public Sphere*, Minneapolis 1993, p. 28.

31
Ibid., p. 67; see also pp. 290–294. In the context of the post-war West-German welfare state, Kluge—the

of images from ideologically dodgy schlock suggests the stifling presence of the past, of *Ewiggestrigkeit* as the order of the day.

In the 1972 theoretical volume *Öffentlichkeit und Erfahrung* (Public Sphere and Experience*)*, Kluge and Oskar Negt counter Habermas's idealization of the bourgeois public sphere with an investigation into proletarian forms of publicness, defined in terms of the "autonomous, collective organization of the experience specific to workers".[30] Negt and Kluge put Marx back into the Frankfurt School even while going against the orthodox-Marxist focus on abstract labor-power by foregrounding the libidinal dimensions of labor and the role of fantasy. Under capitalism, fantasy can become a form of false consciousness, as in *Perry Rhodan* dime novels, but fundamentally, fantasy is a "specific means of production" that can never be fully appropriated by capitalism; it pushes to change relations among people and between humans and nature, and to reappropriate history.[31]

In their 1981 follow-up volume *Geschichte und Eigensinn* (History and Obstinacy), Kluge and Negt analyze the human being as a self-regulating "Mangelmutant"—a defective mutant, or mutant of lack, incapable of autonomous being and hence requiring constant social exchange.[32] Like Weiss, they engage with the historical *longue durée* in a manner that goes against the orthodox-Marxist focus on modern capitalism as a specific system of production and exploitation. What ultimately gets reduced to abstract and alienated labor-power ("Arbeitskraft") is capital's always incomplete capture of a volatile aggregate of different labor capacities ("Arbeitsvermögen").[33] Such labor capacities keep emerging and transforming under the impact of social and technological change. In the sci-fi register of Kluge's *Lernprozesse,* one motif is the emergence of such new labor capacities through posthuman mutation: to be able to work on the metal planet Dubna, where gravity is much higher than on earth, women develop 'reinforced lower legs," and their heads and necks are pressed into their shoulders. Customs inspectors develop protruding eyes that see everything. Meanwhile, since it is forbidden to hunt for slaves and to traffic in humans, and since no alien life has been found, mutinying units of the fleet are declared "non-human life-forms," so they can be enslaved—in a galactic repetition of a historical process on earth.[34] Kluge presents pithy speculative comedies in which the "Mangelmutant" keeps branching off and spawning new mutations, from bio-enhanced space Nazis to forced laborers with massive ankles. This is Hegel's (or Kojève's) master-slave dialectic as cosmic comedy.[35]

lawyer—sought to create conditions in which such "Arbeitsvorgänge" could take place, in however compromised and imperfect a form, using public subsidies and legal loopholes, and taking advantage of the situation at the ex-HfG. This was certainly not proletarian publicness in any classical sense, but at times *Geschichte und Eigensinn* appears to theorize such new and precarious "Produktionszusammenhänge".

32
Oskar Negt and Alexander Kluge, *Geschichte und Eigensinn,* Frankfurt am Main 1981, p. 23. For an extensive comparison of *Die Ästhetik des Widerstands* and *Geschichte und Eigensinn,* see Richard Langston, "The Work of Art as Theory of Work: Relationality in the Works of Weiss and Negt & Kluge", in: *The Germanic Review: Literature, Culture, Theory,* 2010, vol. 83, no. 3, pp. 195–216.

33
Negt/Kluge, *Geschichte* (see note 32*)*, pp. 88–114.

34
Kluge, *Lernprozesse* (see note 28), pp. 864–865, 878–881.

35
A related book, *Projekt Groß Weiss-Afrika,* charts an inept last-ditch effort to consolidate white colonial holdings in Africa in what was then the just-future of the mid-1970s. *Projekt Groß Weiss-Afrika* was part of the original publication of *Lernprozesse mit tödlichem Ausgang* (Frankfurt am Main: Suhrkamp, 1973), which, to confuse matters, contained much more than only *Lernprozesse mit tödlichem Ausgang* properly speaking.

In keeping with what Thomas Elsaesser has called the "patchwork *Gesamtkunstwerk*" of Kluge's overall practice, as well as with the Ulm film institute's interest in hybridity, Kluge's space films are jumpy montages of disparate materials.[36] Both the space films and the *Lernprozesse* novel contain appropriated images, which suggests that readers and viewers might be regarded as authors in their own right—as activated and productive spectators who may go on to appropriate Kluge's work in unpredictable ways.[37] Nonetheless, Elsaesser has critiqued Kluge's conception of authorship as being ultimately monological, and as marked by a compulsive repetition of similar plots performed by readymade, schematic characters who are barely more than names.[38] Bad outcomes seem preordained; learning curves end fatally. In Kluge's extrapolatory work, the future has already always happened, which robs it of its proper futural dimension. In keeping with this, *Lernprozesse* is written in the past tense; this is a future that has always already happened.

The intertitles of the films tend to be in the present tense, suggesting that we are eyewitnesses. However, as they are not only composed of intertitles and of cheap and charming special effects (spaceships, alien planets) made in the HfG's workshops, but also largely revolve around improvised scenes featuring a menagerie of bohemian actors, the science-fiction films do introduce a sense of genuine collaboration and improvisation.[39] The traces of the "relatively lively" environment of the "autonomous" ex-HfG are all over the films.[40] In *Der grosse Verhau*, footage of a performance by the band Amon Düül II (a product of the left-wing commune scene) is "integrated" in what passes for the narrative through a title card stating that the band are playing on a spaceship destined for the Planet Krüger 60.

Willi Tobler und der Untergang der 6. Flotte is far superior to *Der große Verhau*, thanks to a stronger narrative and Alfred Edel's magnificent half-bewildered performance as the titular character—a cybernetician caught up in the galactic war. The film is marked throughout by a strong sense of joyful improvisation; Edel and Hark Bohm give the scenes with the leaders of the Sixth Fleet strategizing against the *Geschichtstöterflotte* ("history-killing fleet") a sense of possibly intoxicated chaos while clinging on to clipped snippets of Prussian phraseology. In sending a Krautrock band into space, Kluge's extrapolatory sci-fi patchwork is loyal to a moment of lived utopia, intense and frequently draining as it no doubt often was—suggesting that there may yet be ways of making history otherwise, or of surviving "against the direction of the movement of history."[41]

36
Thomas Elsaesser, "The Stubborn Persistence of Alexander Kluge", in: Tara Forrest (ed.), *Alexander Kluge: Raw Materials for the Imagination*, Amsterdam 2012, p. 28.

37
As Kluge rather wonderfully puts it: "all people relate to their experience like authors—rather than like managers of department stores." Alexander Kluge, "On Film and the Public Sphere", in: Forrest, *ibid.*, p. 34.

38
Elsaesser, *Stubborn Persistence* (see note 36), p. 27.

39
Even if there is no doubt that Kluge is the one trying to manage and structure the production, the very fact that he has kept-re-editing *Willi Tobler* over the decades suggests that these films represent a limiting case.

40
Kluge, e-mail to the author (see note 24).

41
Kluge, *Lernprozesse* (see note 28), p. 829. English translation from Learning *Processes*, p. xiii.

HISTORY LESSONS

Frequently working in Germany during the 1960s and 1970s, Jean-Marie Straub and Danièle Huillet engaged with the German-language avant-garde of the early twentieth century in a number of film projects. Their short film *Einleitung zu Arnold Schoenbergs Begleitmusik zu einer Lichtspielscene* (Introduction to Arnold Schoenberg's Accompaniment to a Cinematographic Scene, 1972) takes its cues both from Schönberg's "autonomous" composition for a hypothetical movie scene, and from the composer's irate letters to Wassily Kandinsky. Schönberg's 1929/30 "movie score" evokes "drohende Gefahr, Angst, Katastrophe" ("the threat of danger, fear and catastrophe") in the tradition of *Programmusik*; Straub-Huillet suggest this mood reflects the composer's awareness of the rising fascist threat, and the extracts from two 1923 letters constitute a highly direct and chilling document of Schönberg's visceral experience with antisemitism, and his sense of where this was leading Germany and Europe. Read out by the filmmaker and writer Günter Peter Straschek as a harangue in a somewhat halting diction, reflecting his and Straub-Huillet's engagement with Brecht's notion of acting not as emoting but as citing or quoting, Schönberg's letters eviscerate Kandinsky. While Kandinsky had invited him to join the Bauhaus, Schönberg could not turn a blind eye to Kandinsky's antisemitic outbursts, which he regarded as legitimizing and announcing pogroms.

Straschek's own 1970 short *Zum Begriff des 'Kritischen Kommunismus' bei Antonio Labriola (1843–1904)* (On the Concept of "Critical Communism" in Antonio Labriola [1843–1904]) was produced with financial and material support from Jean-Marie Straub and Alexander Kluge's Institut für Filmgestaltung; Straschek would go on to produce the five-part TV documentary *Filmemigration aus Nazideutschland* (Film Emigration from Nazi Germany, 1975), on the exodus of (mainly Jewish) filmmakers during the Nazi era. As with Weiss's *Ermittlung*, witnesses speak in a future they were not meant to see, a future thankfully different from what was scripted at the Wannsee Conference—yet hardly devoid of unsettling continuities. In contrast to the official, idealizing narrative about the post-war European unification, the European Union started out as a programmatic attempt to consolidate the various countries' colonial holdings.[42] Continuities with historical fascism came to the surface when the Paris police, led by Vichy collaborator Maurice Papon, massacred protesting Algerians on October 17, 1961, throwing the bodies into the Seine. And of course

42
See Peo Hansen and Stefan Jonsson, *Eurafrica: The Untold Story of European Integration and Colonialism*, London etc. 2014.

the Western European nations had little compunction in supporting any number of American neo-imperialist wars by perfecting the fine art of looking the other way.

Having perfected the art of whataboutism, the GDR exploited such continuities by branding its wall of infamy an "antifaschistischer Schutzwall" ("antifascist bulwark"). In the West, a similar sense of continuity—to the point of identity between the pre-war and the post-war—fueled the Rote Armee Fraktion (RAF). Straschek was a student at the Berlin film academy in 1966/67, together with Harun Farocki, Hartmut Bitomski, and Holger Meins—the latter would later join the RAF and die in Wittlich prison in 1974. In the milieus in which Straschek moved, it was not always clear whether the urgent critique of the capitalist basis of fascism and of the afterlife of Nazism in Germany, as well as the continuing export of violence to the (post-) colonies and minorities, did not lead to a total collapse of distinctions.[43] Straschek, however, went beyond slogans and sought out historical witnesses. The 2018 exhibition *Here and Now: Günter Peter Straschek* at the Museum Ludwig in Cologne dedicated an exhibition to Günter Peter Straschek.[44] In a spatial setting designed by artist Eran Schaerf, the *Filmemigration* series and other films by Straschek were screened at the thin end of wedge-shaped rooms. The scenography was precise and precarious, like unfinished constructivist stage sets foregrounding their temporary nature even while revealing archaeological layers of depth; displays with documents were inserted into some of the walls. Schaerf's thus constituted an ephemeral memorial for memory-work that had been lost to history. Among the films was Straub-Huillet's *Einleitung zu Arnold Schoenberg's Begleitmusik zu einer Lichtspielscene*, which made Straschek's vocal channeling of Schönberg as strong a presence in the exhibition as the (often deeply affecting) elderly talking heads in *Filmemigration*.

As clear-eyed as Schönberg's analysis of antisemitic tropes and *Ressentiment* was, in the *Einleitung* film Danièle Huillet and Peter Nestler pit his refusal to address the capitalist roots of fascism against Brecht's communist analysis. Schönberg *saw it coming,* but in contrast to Brecht he did not arrive at a practical, actionable understanding of the underlying political and economic logic. One can argue that Brecht was all too eager to use "capitalism" as the monocausal magic word that explains everything, while Schönberg may have had a clearer sense of the *longue durée* of antisemitism; nonetheless, a Brechtian analysis could provide

43
Wolfgang Kraushaar has studied the presence of anti-Semitic elements in the anti-imperialism and anti-Zionism that provided justification for German left-wing terrorism in books such as: *Wann endlich beginnt bei Euch der Kampf gegen die heilige Kuh Israel?, Munich 1970: über die antisemitischen Wurzeln des deutschen Terrorismus,* Reinbek 2013.

44
See Julia Friedrich (ed.), *Hier und Jetzt im Museum Ludwig: Günter Peter Straschek,* Cologne 2018.

a basis for accounting for the modern biopolitical or necropolitical operationalization of antisemitism in the framework of "scientific" modern race theory. In any case, for Straub-Huillet—who end their short film by accompanying Schönberg's *Lichtspielszene* music with images of atrocities from the massacring of the Paris Commune via Nazi gas chambers to Vietnam—Brecht's left-wing critique did not in any way negate the composer's achievements, instead serving to bring out the productive problematics of his work.

The duo's 1974 film version of Schönberg's unfinished opera *Moses and Aaron*, shot in a Roman arena in Italy, presents the people of Israel as a small chorus, often compactly grouped rather than arranged in a "cinematic" manner. This Moses is the quintessential rarified intellectual or artist, a Schönberg in Antique drag. He thinks and sees higher truths, but he cannot talk to the people, for which he needs Aaron—and, as the episode of the Golden Calf shows, it can be dangerous to have to rely on translators, on mediators. Gilles Deleuze sought to encapsulate the political dimension of Straub-Huillet (and Resnais) with the phrase "the people are missing".[45] Arguing that "Third world and minorities gave rise to authors who would be in a position, in relation to their nation and their personal situation in that nation to say: the people are what is missing. Kafka and Klee had been the first to state this explicitly".[46] If the reference to Klee—as opposed to Kafka, for instance—may seem surprising, Deleuze refers to a striking comment in a 1924 lecture by Klee: "uns trägt kein Volk"—there is no people to carry us—though Klee added that at the Bauhaus, they were "looking for a people".[47]

"The people" are even more strikingly absent from more explicitly political Straub-Huillet films, among them *Geschichtsunterricht* (History Lessons, 1972), based on the unfinished Brecht novel *Die Geschäfte des Herrn Julius Caesar* (The Business Affairs of Mr. Julius Caesar*).*[48] Here, as in other Straub-Huillet films, speech often consists of *cited* words. While the written sources are usually from the twentieth century, they may refer back to Ancient Rome or the biblical Middle East. The citational speech acts often take place in or against layered landscapes—the result of centuries of (agri) cultural toil, exhibiting the languid clamor of being. As Deleuze noted, Straub-Huillet's films are marked by a stratigraphic, archeological, telluric image.[49] This is thus a *deep time*-image; but who are the actors or non-actors populating these landscapes, and citing those words?

45
Gilles Deleuze, *Cinema 2: The Time-Image*, trans. Hugh Tomlinson and Robert Galeta, London 1989, p. 216.

46
Ibid, p. 217.

47
This January 26, 1924 Jena lecture was posthumously published as: Über die moderne Kunst, Bern-Bümpliz 1945, see p. 53. Using an imperfect translation, the English edition of Deleuze's *Cinema 2* (p. 215, note 41) renders the phrase as "the people are not with us," whereas the French translation used by Deleuze says "Faute d'un people qui nous porte." See Gilles Deleuze, *Cinéma 2: L'image-temps*, Paris 1985, p. 283. In 2009, ExtraCity in Antwerp organized a Straub/Huillet exhibition under the Deleuzian title *Of a People Who Are Missing*.

48
Brecht's incomplete *Die Geschäfte des Julius Caesar* (1938-39) has a complex structure; in the *Rahmenhandlung*, a young lawyer seeks out witnesses of Caesar's rise. In "Geschichtsunterricht", this Roman lawyer has been turned into the young man in contemporary dress who anachronistically interviews ancient Romans.

49
Deleuze, *Cinema 2* (see note 45), p. 243.

"Uns trägt kein Volk": this equally chilling and liberating diagnosis evokes the autonomous modern artist's isolation and possible descent into a minoritarian bohemianism from which the Party (which has History on its side) may offer temporary and dubious respite at best. To be sure, even in its negative mode, Klee's dictum still evokes the nineteenth-century reactionary, essentializing discourse on *das Volk,* as emblazoned in the Reichstag motto: "Dem deutschen Volke" (To the German People), which Hans Haacke, for his installation in the Bundestag, replaced with the more inclusive "Der Bevölkerung" ("population", rather than unified "people"). To little avail: the toxic discourse on *Volk* that was unleashed in 1989–90 has propelled a rise of identitarian and neo-fascist movements. Constantly updated new normals legitimize daily violence. In this situation, we might blend Klee's dictum with a famous 1989 slogan to assert that *Wir sind kein Volk—We are not a people,* but rather a population intent on unlearning the myths of national identity that have long been misused in history lessons.

CODA

For the "NSU-Komplex Auflösen" Tribunal, Cana Bilir-Meier produced the short film *Best court/En iyi mahkeme/Bestes Gericht.* NSU-Komplex Auflösen was a "people's tribunal" in the tradition of the Russell Tribunals, taking issue with the way in which the German state apparatus tried to reduce the Neo-Nazi terrorist NSU—responsible for a racist killing spree that took 10 lives—to a tiny cell, disavowing the role played by a support network and by the secret service. For a long time, the police had refused to consider the possibility that these were racist murders, as they fitted a narrative about immigrant clans and gangs killing each other. In the video, Bilir-Meier watches episodes from the courtroom TV show *Richter Alexander Hold* with an actress who played stereotypical 'migrant woman' roles in these fictionalized courtroom dramas. If people's tribunals are pre-enactments of a future justice that is as yet unattainable in the legal system, TV shows such as Hold's prepare the ground for violence to come. The present is a continuous rehearsal of the future.

Several catastrophic accelerations ago, way back in 2009, Isabelle Stengers acerbically noted that those who insist that fighting capitalism is pointless are effectively saying that barbarism is our destiny.[50] As the social contract that underpinned the post-war "social market economy" collapses under the neoliberal onslaught, with no new narratives after "permanent growth and wealth for all"

50
Isabelle Stengers, *Au temps des catastrophes. Résister à la barbarie qui vient,* Paris 2009, pp. 61–62.

in sight and the chickens of permanent war on the planet and subaltern populations are coming home to roost, it is once again fascist movements and parties—now with accompanying social media filter bubbles, fake news and conspiracy theories—that seem to offer the most successful ideological product. In 2020, the vegan-chef-turned-QAnon-conspiracy-theorist Attila Hildmann bombarded his more than 100,000 followers on Telegram with messages about the Pergamon Altar: according to Hildmann, it is in fact the Throne of Satan, and Rothschild-trained Zionist Satanists such as Angela Merkel and other members of the elite gather in the Pergamon Museum for nocturnal rituals involving human sacrifice and child abuse.[51] As the site of Weiss's workers' self-education becomes a screen for delusional projections, historical consciousness is overrun by weaponized paranoia.

The point is not, as the GDR and the RAF had it in their self-serving propaganda, that the capitalist Bundesrepublik was just a thinly veiled continuation of the Third Reich, and that capitalism always and everywhere equals fascism. However, capitalism's crises tend to reroute its systemic, necropolitical violence from the periphery to the center, putting more groups in the line of fire. Twenty-first century neofascism—which we must *of course* always refer to with euphemisms such as "right-wing populism"— proffers the alluring promise of saving privilege, however relative that privilege may be. Its too-good-to-be-true offer: Others can be made to pay so that you can stay on the right side of the divide between masters and slaves. Remembering the coming barbarism may yet help us to rehearse differently, to introduce deviations that fork into different futures.[52]

51
See screenshot of Hildmann's Telegram account, 24 August 2020, https://www. bz-berlin.de/berlin/ mehr-als-70-objekte- auf-museumsinsel- beschaedigt.

52
Thanks to the Harun Farocki Institut, Alexander Kluge, and Eran Schaerf.

Cana Bilir-Meier, *This Makes Me Want to Predict the Past*, 2019 | Installation view, *Tell me about ~~yesterday~~ tomorrow*

Mohamed Bourouissa, *Shoplifters*, 2014 – 2015 | Installation view, *Tell me about ~~yesterday~~ tomorrow*
VG Bild-Kunst Bonn, 2019

Notes Toward a Phraseology
of the Many

I.   "WE ARE THE MANY."
      – THE OCCUPY MOVEMENT, 2011

It may seem a very long time ago, but just before a regional epidemic developed into the pandemic that has taken the lives of too many while deeply affecting the lives of many others, a phrase had been haunting the globe: We are the many. Some people may think that something about this phrase is, or was, extremely troubling, if not frightening, whereas others may find this phrase is, or was, a most joyful one. It probably depends, firstly, on whether you think of yourself as belonging to the many or not and secondly, on whether you believe that the times of the many are definitely over now or still yet to come, albeit in a radically different form. In any case— and indeed now more than ever—the phrase "we are the many" raises a number of questions and issues. What are we saying when we say that we are the many? If we say that we are the many when we assemble, who are the others that are not considered part of our assembly? What about the meaning of a series of other phrases which seem similar to the phrase "we are the many", phrases such as "we are the people" or even the phrase "we are the 99 %"? What kind of concept of the many emerges from the interwoven histories of all these phrases? Are representatives part of the many which they represent, or do representatives belong to those others of the many, whom a history as long as the history of the concept of "the many" itself, has given the name of "the few"?

To say that "we are the many" could be understood as a poetic phrase of protest against the positions and actions of others whom we outnumber or claim to outnumber. We are the many. Depending on contexts and constellations, the others could be very different groups. However, whatever the context or the constellation, the idea seems to be that we who are the many and who outnumber others, should be able to determine what is to be done in, by and for the political community in which we outnumber or claim to outnumber those others. If we insist that we are the many, it seems that we suppose that, if it were true that we are the many, it should have particular consequences, depending on what it means to be the many in the context and constellation within which we insist that we are the many. To say that we are the many could mean that we are the majority. But what does that mean? In so far as the political community in which we are the many is organized as a parliamentary democracy and given the role of majorities in it, this could mean that we expect parliament to follow or to decide what we, who are the many, want or propose. However, can a parliament indeed be supposed to follow a self-declared majority of people who are not in parliament? Is this what we are when we say that "we are the many": a self-declared extra-parliamentary majority which claims that it should be listened to?

It seems that we may have encountered the phrase "we are the many" in contexts and constellations where a self-declared extra-parliamentary majority derives political claims from the fact that, although it is not in parliament, it constitutes a majority of the population and thus something to be reckoned with, also by parliament, whatever the actual majority in parliament may be. If we say that we are the many, we sometimes mean to say that we are more the majority than the majority in parliament, even if that parliamentary majority derives its claims from the fact that it was (once) elected by (some of) us. However, it should come as no surprise that, in some contexts and constellations, the phrase "we are the many" turns out to be a contestation of parliamentary democracy itself. In that case, none of us who are the many seems to expect anything from parliament and its elected members, as their majority seems to be a very different one from the one that we say that we are. If there is something troubling about the phrase "we are the many," then it probably is this radical ambiguity or the ambiguity of its radicality. If we say that we are the many, do we actually demand something from those who are considered to be our representatives in parliament, or do we, to the contrary, believe that we as the many can only be represented by ourselves, an idea which runs through all four volumes of Negri and Hardt's theoretical trilogy, examining the concept of the multitude.[1]

The phrase "We are the many" is a simple phrase which is not that simple. For one thing, to say that "we are the many" is not the same as saying that "we are many". The definite article "the" which precedes the word "many" turns it into a noun. We are not just many, we are the many. As the word "many" is usually not used as a noun, but as an adjective, which qualifies nouns, the expression "the many" may sound slightly artificial, as if it were some more or less recent rhetorical invention. A hasty genealogy could have it that the phrase "we are the many" appeared around 2011/12 in the midst of the so-called Occupy movement, as an alternative to a slogan which many may remember as its most important one: "We are the 99%." In a sense, the Occupy movement, which was launched in the United States with the occupation of Zuccotti Park near Wall Street on September 17, 2011, and went global with hundreds of protests in cities worldwide on October 15, 2011, could be considered, next to the Movement of the Squares in Greece and the May 15 Movement of the Indignados

1
See Michael Hardt and Antonio Negri, *Empire,* Cambridge (Mass.) 2000; id., *Multitude. War and Democracy in the Age of Empire,* New York 2004; id., *Commonwealth,* Cambridge (Mass.) 2009; id., *Assembly,* New York 2017.

in Spain, which had both also occupied squares, as part of a Euro-American version of the Arab Spring movement earlier that year, the key event of which was the occupation of Tahrir Square in Cairo.

As for the phrase "We are the 99%" as the rallying cry of the Occupy movement, it could be read as a response to the title of an essay by Joseph Stiglitz. His article "Of the 1%, by the 1%, for the 1%" had been published in *Vanity Fair* six months before the beginning of Occupy Wall Street.[2] Stiglitz warned that the growing inequality between the 99% and the 1%, who not only have a disproportionate share in income and wealth, but also in political power, will eventually undermine the legitimacy of representative democracy. As most American elected politicians themselves belong to the 1%, today's so-called representative democracy is no longer, as president Abraham Lincoln's Gettysburg Address on November 19, 1863 solemnly promised, a "government of the people, by the people, for the people", that would "not perish from the earth", but has become a government "of the 1%, by the 1%, for the 1%," as the title of Stiglitz's essay suggests. Therefore, to say, with the Occupy movement, that "we are the 99%," is also to say that "we are the people", as in that famous phrase that defines democracy as the "government of the people, by the people, for the people." To say that "we are the 99%" is to say "power to the people" without using the words "power" and "people," thereby avoiding some of the troubling connotations of these concepts.

At some point during the Occupy movement, the phrase "we are the many" would become yet another way of saying that "we are the 99%." Due to its numerical vagueness, the phrase "we are the many" would help the Occupy movement to avoid tiresome discussions over the question as to whether or not the self-proclaimed 99% were indeed really 99% and not rather somewhat less or somewhat more. Thus, Paul Krugman suggested that, though he thought it was a great slogan, it would be more precise to say that "we are the 99.9%," as the title of one of his op-eds said: "If anything, however, the 99 percent slogan aims too low. A large fraction of the top 1 percent's gains have actually gone to an even smaller group, the top 0.1 percent—the richest one-thousandth of the population".[3] By this move, however, Krugman also diminished considerably the number of the few who should, according to the argument he developed in this op-ed, pay more taxes. Rather than "aiming higher", the many would be aiming lower, if we were to follow Krugman's definition of "the few" as the "super-elite."

For George Caffentzis, the rejection of parliamentary democracy was an important aspect of the Occupy movement's politics: "You simply have to be bodily at the center of the circulation of cities

2
Joseph E. Stiglitz, "Of the 1%, by the 1%, for the 1%, in: *Vanity Fair*, March 31, 2011.

3
Paul Krugman, "We Are the 99.9%,"in: *The New York Times*, November 25, 2011, p. A35.

to practice this politics. Its opposite, representative politics, is being rejected by millions of people. Let's remember where representative politics comes from, i.e., re-presentation. Your re-presentative presents you in order for you to be absent from the political debates and decisions. So actually what appears to be a politics of presence is really one of absence."[4] However, whenever we say that "we are the many," as the Occupy movement did, our claim should be situated philosophically within the horizon of a parliamentary conception of democracy in which majorities are supposed to rule because they are majorities, even if, or precisely because we express our disagreement with an actual majority in parliament by saying that we are the many, not the majority in parliament. When we claim that "we are the many", we distance ourselves from a political belief system in which it doesn't count at all whether one constitutes a majority or not. Even if we may contest a particular parliamentary majority by saying that we are the many, or even if we contest the way in which majorities are constituted in a particular parliamentary democracy by saying that we are the many, there remains something parliamentarian about the phrase "we are the many." We seem to share the idea that a majority, even if it is a constructed one, may legitimize particular political claims, as is the case in parliament. If many people take to the streets while shouting "we are the many," they seem to consider themselves as representing the many others who are not there. As the idea of representation is not entirely absent from the claim that "we are the many," as we consider ourselves, many as we are, to be representing the many others who for one reason or another cannot be there, the assembly of the many in the streets is not entirely different from the way parliament represents the many who are not there either. Therefore I cannot agree with George Caffentzis when he writes: "The parliaments and council chambers are temples of absence, while the Tahrir Squares of the world are places where a general will is embodied and in action."[5] Rather than thinking of Parliament and Assembly as absolute opposites, we may want to consider them, with Judith Butler, as one another's necessary supplements.[6] For The Invisible Committee, as they despise parliamentary democracy, the aim cannot be to become the majority, even if they too want to become many and get organized: "If we are everywhere, if we are legion, then we must now organize ourselves, worldwide."[7] To say, or to suppose that "we are legion," is to say or suppose that "we are many," without claiming to be the many. The international hacker and activist collective Anonymous, which in its very own way joined the 2011 protests of the Occupy movement, regularly describes itself by the phrase "We are Legion," whereby Legion is written as a proper name.

4
George Caffentzis, "In the Desert of Cities. Notes on the Occupy Movement in the US", in: Kate Khatib, Margaret Killjoy and Mike McGuire (eds.), *We Are Many. Reflections on Movement Strategy from Occupy to Liberation*, Oakland-Edinburgh-Baltimore 2012, p. 393.

5
Ibid., p. 397.

6
See Judith Butler, *Notes Toward a Performative Theory of Assembly*, Cambridge (Mass.)-London, 2015, pp. 154–192.

7
The Invisible Committee, To Our Friends, (translated by Robert Hurley), South Pasadena, 2015, p. 19.

For those who may wonder why Legion is presented as another name of Anonymous, the answer could be, unexpected as this may sound, in the Gospel according to Saint Mark. There you will find a particular phrase in the strange story of the so-called Gadarene swine, to which the Anonymous slogan clearly refers. When asked by Jesus for his name, the Gadarene man who is possessed by demons, tells him, as the famous phrase in the Gospel according to Mark (5,9) goes: "My name is Legion. For we are many," upon which Jesus exorcises the demons that took possession of the man, by transferring them to swine, upon which these swine run from a cliff and drown in an act of collective suicide.[8] It seems as if the members of Anonymous, given their notorious battle with the Church of Scientology, which in the tabloid press has often been suspected of practising exorcism, like to identify themselves provocatively with the demons who are many.

Given that the Occupy movement has embraced the slogan "We are the 99%" as its catch phrase, which would often be replaced by the phrase "We are the many" for the reasons we explained, the Anonymous collective aka Legion, when it joined the Occupy movement, should be considered as constituting itself as "a many" among "the many," without supporting a particular belief in the importance of building majorities. One can be many and still be a minority, even a minority which does not care to become a majority. And thus it happened that at one and the same Occupy demonstration, one would see people wearing signs saying "We are the many" and other people wearing signs saying "We are legion. For we are many."

As the phrase "Our Name is Legion. For We Are Many," which Anonymous regularly uses as a slogan, signals, there is a long history of the concept of the many. However, there is more than one genealogy of the concept of "the many" to be drawn, dating back to its first appearance not about ten years ago, with the Occupy movement, but some two thousand five hundred years ago. Apart from the intriguing Christian lineage, there is also a complex ancient Greek lineage. Indeed, "the many" is, first and foremost, a literal English translation of an expression with a long-standing tradition in ancient Greek philosophical and historical discourse on politics: *hoi polloi* (οἱ πολλοί). Whether in Plato, Aristotle, or Thucydides, *hoi polloi* are the many, who are said to rule in a democracy, whereas *hoi oligoi* are the few who rule in aristocracy (which, if they do so self-interestedly, turns into an oligarchy). In the nineteenth century, English literati with a classical education would snobbishly use the transcribed version of the Greek expression *hoi polloi* in order to refer in an extravagant, unordinary way to the "ordinary people."

8
In the 1550 edition called *Stephanus Textus Receptus*, the third edition of the Greek New Testament by the Parisian printer Robert Estienne, the word for many is πολλοί: "Λεγεὼν ὄνομά μοι ὅτι πολλοί ἐσμεν".

It might be that we used to say that we are many, whereas today we would rather or also say that we are the many. To say that we are the many, rather than that we are many, could be understood as a subtle form of radicalization. To say that we are the many no longer allows that others claim that they are many too. To say that we are the many is not just to claim that we are more than the others. It is also to claim that the others are few. Moreover, to say that we are the many implies the claim that the others are not only few, but that they are the few. As the few have to be few in order to be the few, one could also wonder if the few should be particularly few in order to count as the few. If we are the many, then the others are the few. Being the many, we consider the few as our other. What we as the many have in common, then, is that we do not belong to the few. Therefore our initial phrase could be considered as only the first part of a phrase which says: "We are the many, they are the few". The radicalization to which the expression "the many", with its unusual definite article, is pointing, comes with the antagonistic articulation of a division between two different groups.

II. "YE ARE MANY—THEY ARE FEW."
– PERCY BYSSHE SHELLEY, 1819

9
Slavoj Žižek, *In Defense of Lost Causes*, London-New York 2008, p. 192.

10
Percy Bysshe Shelley, *The Mask of Anarchy*, lines 372–376.
We quote from and refer to the numbered lines of the poem in: Percy Bysshe Shelley, "The Mask of Anarchy. Written On the Occasion of the Massacre at Manchester," in: id., *Selected Poems and Prose*, (ed. by Jack Donovan and Cian Duffy), Milton Keynes, 2016, pp. 357–368.
An editors' note says that the edition is based on "MWS's [Mary Wollstonecraft Shelley's] fair copy with corrections by PBS [Percy Bysshe Shelley] which was sent to Leigh Hunt on September 23, 1819 and which is now in the Library of Congress (MMC 1399)" (p. 760).

Ever since its appearance during protests of the Occupy movement, the phrase "we are the many" has made a few remarkable comebacks at other occasions and in quite different constellations. Thus, since 2017, the phrase "We are the many" could be heard at a great many campaign meetings of the British Labour Party, whose Manifesto for that year's parliamentary elections was entitled "For the Many, Not the Few", which was also Labour's campaign slogan. With this slogan, we should bring in a third, Romantic lineage to our genealogy of the concept of "the many": Percy Bysshe Shelley's poem *The Mask of Anarchy*, which according to Slavoj Žižek is "arguably the greatest political poem in English."[9] For many people in the Anglo-American world who consider themselves to be "the many," to say that they are "the many" is almost impossible without evoking a reference to the closing stanza of this particular work of the radical-democratic writer that Shelley was:

> *"'Rise like lions after slumber*
> *In unvanquishable number—*
> *Shake your chains to earth like dew*
> *Which in sleep had fallen on you—*
> *Ye are many—they are few.'"*[10]

On September 5, 1819, during his stay in the Villa Valsovano in Livorno, Percy Bysshe Shelley had heard about the local authority's brutal military repression of a very large workers' assembly on August 16, 1819, at Saint Peter's Field in Manchester, during which a dozen people died, while several hundred were wounded. The aim of the assembly had been to demand, among other things, a radical parliamentary reform that would ensure parliamentary representation of the inhabitants of cities such as Manchester, who were most often unrepresented in the House of Commons. At that time, the so-called "radical" movement for parliamentary reform was considered by the authorities as dangerously insurrectionary.[11] Unlike the phrase that we have been repeating here "again—again—again," according to which we say that "we are the many," Percy Bysshe Shelley addresses himself in *The Mask of Anarchy*—through a voice which his poem seems to attribute in an allegorical way to the Earth—to others, to the workers, telling them that they are many: "Ye are many." With this poem, written shortly after the so-called Peterloo Massacre, Shelley proclaims himself to be someone who, despite seeming to belong to the few, nonetheless deeply sympathizes with the many, supporting their peaceful revolt against the powers that be.

It would take more than a decade before modest reforms in parliamentary representation would be enacted by the so-called Reform Act or Representation of the People Act in 1832. The Reform Act would extend the franchise only in a limited way, restricting the right to vote to men with certain possessions or leases. It still did not allow women, Jews, and most workers to vote. Only in that same year 1832 would Shelley's poem be published for the first time, a decade after his accidental death by drowning in the Gulf of Livorno. In his preface to this first edition, Leigh Hunt explains why, as a matter of prudence, he decided not to publish the poem as an insertion in *The Examiner*, of which he was the editor, when it was sent to him on September 23, 1819.[12] In this preface, Hunt also informs his readers that Shelley took the issue of parliamentary reform very much to heart and even wrote a draft of a philosophical essay on the matter, which would remain unpublished until 1920.[13] With his poem *The Mask of Anarchy*, Shelley had supported the workers' call for parliamentary reform, encouraging them by reminding them that they clearly outnumbered their opponents: "Ye are many—they are few." In his essay *a Philosophical View of Reform*, Shelley would specify that parliamentary reform implies the necessity to extend the franchise so as to include the many, both men and women, as one may infer from his careful use of the word "individual(s)."[14]

11
See Ortwin de Graef, "Spectre Disorder: Neuro-Marxism and the State of the Soul", in: *Marxism and the Future. Proceedings of the Third Sino–British Bilateral Forum on Marxist Aesthetics*, Shanghai, 6-8 April 2013, p. 109.

12
Leigh Hunt, "Preface", in: Percy Bysshe Shelley, *The Masque of Anarchy. A Poem, (Now First Published, With a Preface by Leigh Hunt)*, London, 1832, pp. v–xxx. One should note that, even in 1832, the editor still decides not to mention the subtitle that Shelley had given to his poem: "Written On the Occasion of the Massacre at Manchester". In a sense, the generic, editorial subtitle "A Poem" is a mask for a heavily loaded political reference.

13
A large part from Shelley's unfinished essay *a Philosophical View of Reform* is published in: Shelley, *Selected Poems* (see note 19), pp. 636–651.

14
Ibid., p. 650.

If democracy as we know it is in fact, technically speaking, parliamentary democracy, which requires simple or qualified majorities for its decisions, we could believe that the main aim of those who consider themselves "the many" is to make clear that, in the parliamentary culture that is theirs, political decisions should take into account what they want. Today's parliament seems to be confronted with two main critiques, which sound mutually exclusive: on the one hand, there is the critique that parliament all too often fails to listen to what the many want. On the other hand, there is the critique that parliament often makes wrong decisions as these depend on the majority rule, which says that a law will be adopted if it is supported by the many in parliament. A majority, however, is no guarantee at all that the law in question will be just, right, or good. One may object that the many (in the streets) are not necessarily the many in parliament and that the contradiction is only an apparent one. However, even if there is no contradiction, there is at least the problem that the many in the streets do not seem adequately represented by the many in parliament. One would expect that a parliament is only considered legitimate insofar as it is representative. In order for a parliament to be representative, one could expect that the majority in the population should be reflected by the majority in parliament. Considering, however, the composition of parliaments all over the world, it is easy to see that such assemblies do not necessarily mirror (their) populations. Not in terms or race, class, and gender, and not in terms of opinions either. If a parliament speaks in the name of the people, should it not also represent it? One of the problems with the concept of parliamentary representativeness, however, is that it is understood in two very different ways. In a formal sense, a representative in parliament is representative due to the simple fact of being duly elected as a representative. He or she represents his or her entire constituency and therefore also those who did not vote (for him or her) by the simple and formal fact of being elected by that constituency. In a sense which one could term 'aesthetic', however, representatives are said to represent certain categories of citizens. Representatives are identified as belonging to the same category of citizens: women, people of color, gay people, elderly people, etc. Along these lines, some people expect parliament to be (also) representative in the aesthetic sense of the term. They expect parliament to look like a representative sample of the people it formally represents. Could it not be that we also say that we are the many when we find diversity in parliament is missing? What exactly is the relationship between the many and minorities? Could it be that the many is the name of a majority that is constituted as an assembly of minorities?

III. "WE ARE NOT THAT FEW."
– BERTOLT BRECHT, 1938

We are the many. As this phrase has been moving around the globe, it has been speaking to us in many different languages. Thus it also speaks to us, for instance, in German, saying: "Wir sind die Vielen". Therefore, the genealogy of the concept of "the many," the philosophical story about how "the many" became a concept, is also a story about translations, both so-called literal translations and translations which reconfigure the meaning of certain expressions, adapting them to different contexts and constellations. One of the troubling aspects of the concept of the many is that we may be the many here, in this particular context and constellation, while at the same time, at another place, in another context and constellation, we might be the few. At the same time, we may be the many for now, in order to become the few later on. Or we find ourselves in a seemingly desperate situation, as if we are very few, in order to become the many at a later moment in time. Due to the situatedness and temporality of the many, the concept of the many is intrinsically unstable. It is never clear once and for all who the many are. Who the many are is contingent on contexts and constellations.

In situations of political despair, we wonder whether we are many enough to resist, or whether we have become all too few. Among the many persecuted German writers, artists, and intellectuals who had to flee or stay away from Germany after the Nazis seized power in 1933, were the Marxist playwright and poet Bertolt Brecht, the German-Jewish, leftist novelist Lion Feuchtwanger and the communist writer Willi Bredel, author of *Die Prüfung*, the first novel on a Nazi concentration camp, published in London in 1934. In 1936, the three men would become the editors of *Das Wort*, an anti-Fascist literary review by and for German exiles. The review was published in Moscow, distributed worldwide outside of the German Reich and existed until March 1939. In its June 1937 issue, the editors made the following announcement: "Recently, there was this message from England, that one had discovered a great contemporary political poem, which was probably inspired by Shelley. However, this work was THE MASQUE OF ANARCHY and is included in the complete editions of Shelley, but not in all others. —In what follows, we present the last part of this poem […]".[15] What follows then is the German translation of the second part of Shelley's poem by German-Jewish lyricist Alfred Wolfenstein. The translation carefully avoids all references to "England", which might explain why the translated excerpt does not begin with the

[15] "Vor kurzem wurde aus England gemeldet, man habe eine große Zeitdichtung entdeckt, die vermutlich von Shelley herrühre. Aber dieses Werk war THE MASQUE OF ANARCHY und ist in den vollständigen Shelley-Ausgaben enthalten, freilich nicht in allen anderen. – Im folgenden bringen wir den letzten Teil dieses Poems," [Editors' note to Percy Bysshe Shelley] "Sie sind wenige — Ihr seid viel!", in: *Das Wort. Literarische Monatsschrift*, Moscow, no. 6, June 1937, p. 63; our translation.

very first lines of the speech— "Men of England, heirs of Glory,"
—but with the famous second quatrain of the speech (which the
very last quatrain of the poem repeats):

> *"Auf! In löwenstarker Zahl!*
> *Werft der Unterdrückung Qual*
> *Ab, die euch im Schlaf befiel:*
> *SIE SIND WENIGE – IHR SEID VIEL!"*[16]

16
Percy Bysshe Shelley,
"Sie sind wenige —
Ihr seid viel!", [German
translation by Alfred
Wolfenstein], in: *Das
Wort. Literarische
Monatsschrift*, Moscow,
no. 6, June 1937, p. 63.

Wolfenstein's German translation of the last line of the quatrain—identical with the poem's last line—with its inversion of its two constitutive
parts, puts the accent on the last word, which is "Viel", as a translation of
"many". This German translation of the poem's last line also functions as
the editorial title of 'Shelley's article' in *Das Wort*. With its exclamation
mark, this title turns the ballad into a manifesto: "SIE SIND WENIGE
– IHR SEID VIEL!" By erasing all references to the original location
of the events described in Shelley's poem, the aim of the translation's
publication seems to have been to demonstrate the actuality of Shelley's
poem, here and now, whereby this "here" is unmistakably a Europe which
is threatened by Nazi Germany, and whereby "England" has become
a destination for many refugees. In a move to supplement this effort,
the editorial introduction acts as if, upon "the discovery" of the poem
in England, the first impression was that it was a *Zeitdichtung*, a poem
about its "now" and thus about the late 1930s, a poem which somehow reminded one of Shelley's style. Only upon a second look, thus the ironical
statement, did it become clear that in fact it was *The Mask of Anarchy* by
Shelley himself. In this way, both the German editors and the translator
used *The Mask of Anarchy* as a mask for their own critique of the tragic
times that they were experiencing. While Fascism meant the end of freedom and democracy, Shelley's poem could be read as—and was presented
as—encouraging the many to fight against it.

In 1938, the publication of Wolfenstein's translation in *Das Wort*
would reinvigorate the German left's dialogue with Shelley's poem,
as nobody less than Bertolt Brecht took the defense of Shelley in the
(in)famous debate on realism, to which an essay by György Lukács
had given rise.[17] In an implicit response to Lukács, Brecht wrote, in
an article which was meant for publication in *Das Wort*, but would
remain unpublished until 1955: "It may be a good idea to introduce to
the reader at this point a writer from the past, who wrote differently
from bourgeois novelists and yet must still be called a great realist:
the great revolutionary English poet P. B. Shelley. If it were the case
that his great ballad *The Mask of Anarchy*, written immediately after

17
György Lukács,
"Marx und das Problem
des ideologischen
Verfalls," in: *Internatio-
nale Literatur/Deutsche
Blätter*, 7, 1938, pp.
103–143.

the bourgeoisie's bloody repression of the riots in Manchester (1819), did not fit the usual descriptions of a realist mode of writing, then we would need to make sure that the description of the realist mode of writing is indeed changed, broadened and completed".[18]

In a footnote to his reference to Shelley's poem in this text, added after 1947, Brecht mentions the following fact: "I used the ballad as an example for my poem 'Freiheit und Democracy'."[19] Indeed, the structure and rhythm of Shelley's poem would define to a very large extent the form of a poem which Brecht wrote in 1947 and whose complete title is *Der anachronistische Zug oder Freiheit und Democracy*. The title has an obvious playful pseudo-anagrammatic relationship with the title of Shelley's poem in German translation: *Der Maskenzug der Anarchie*. Brecht's "anachronistic parade" describes a procession of members of society amidst the ruins of post-war West Germany. Its destination is Munich, "the capital of the movement." The parade includes a whole series of people who, in their respective professions and positions, had been supporters of the Nazi regime, but who are now supposed to be considered as the promotors of 'Freiheit' and 'Democracy,' the two main slogans of the parade. Among them are, for instance, teachers, doctors, and scientists, as well as others in high positions.[20]

Brecht's poem *Der anachronistische Zug oder Freiheit und Democracy*, for which in the 1950s both Hanns Eisler and Paul Dessau would write a musical score, states that a state is not necessarily democratic when it presents certain formal characteristics, such as parliamentary elections and a free press.[21] In the late 1940s, former enemies of democracy were still in high positions in West Germany, which prided itself on having become truly democratic again, defending "Freiheit und Democracy". Throughout the German text of the poem, Brecht writes the word "Democracy" in English, as a *Fremdwort*. This suggests that Brecht was extremely sceptical about the way in which, after the Second World War, the Western Allied Forces in general and the United States in particular were "accompanying" the democratization processes in West Germany. After all, during the last year of his American exile, he had experienced vividly to what limited extent a parliamentary institution of the United States considered politics as the space for the peaceful conflict of opinions. On October 30, 1947, the year in which he wrote the poem *Der anachronistische Zug oder Freiheit und Democracy*, Brecht had been interrogated by the House Un-American Activities Committee. The interrogation confirmed his impression that for the United States, parliamentarism was good as long as certain (anticapitalist)

18
Bertolt Brecht, 'Breadth and Variety of the Realist Mode of Writing', in: Id., *Brecht on Art and Politics*, (Edited by Tom Kuhn and Steve Giles. Part Five edited by Stephen Parker, Matthew Philpotts and Peter Davies, Translations by Laura Bradley, Steve Giles and Tom Kuhn), London, Methuen, 2003, p. 221.

19
"Ich benutzte die Ballade als Vorbild für mein Gedicht 'Freiheit und Democracy'"; ibid., p. 82 n. 1 (our translation).

20
See Bertolt Brecht, "Der anachronistische Zug oder Freiheit und Democracy," in: id., *Gesammelte Werke. Band 10. Gedichte 3*, (werkausgabe edition suhrkamp), Frankfurt 1967, p. 945.

21
Whereas in 1947, Brecht had expressed his anger with the presence of former Nazis in official positions in West Germany, in 1953, he would sarcastically express his disappointment with the German Democratic Republic in the poem *Die Lösung*, included in his *Buckower Elegien*. See Bertolt Brecht, "Die Lösung," in: id., *Gesammelte Werke. Band 10. Gedichte 3* (see note 20), pp. 1009–1010.

parties are banned and freedom of expression was necessary as long as certain (Marxist) ideas were not expressed.

Whenever the democratic character of real existing parliamentarism is put into question, chances are high that some people will plead for certain forms of direct democracy, such as referendums. However, as a procedure to learn what the many want, a referendum is not necessarily more democratic than parliamentary elections. Structurally, one could even argue that referendums are more compatible with dictatorships than parliamentary elections. There have been cases in which a referendum was anything but the democratic expression of the many, but rather the confirmation of its utter insignificance. On April 10, 1938, in order to democratically legitimize the German military annexation of Austria which had taken place one month earlier, a referendum was organized in Austria which asked whether people agreed with the "reunification" (Wiedervereinigung) of Austria with the German Reich and whether they voted for the list of "our leader" Adolf Hitler. The graphic design of the ballot gave a clear indication as to what the correct answer was: the circle in which the cross mark for 'yes' was supposed to be put was much larger than the circle for 'no'. According to the official result of the referendum, 99.73% voted 'yes.'

The depressing result of the Austrian referendum explains the title of a theatre piece by Brecht, which premiered one month later in Paris, on May 21, 1938.[22] Based on eight scenes from the theatre piece *Furcht und Elend des III. Reiches*, on which Brecht, in cooperation with Margarete Steffin, was working in the Danish town of Svendborg, Slatan Dudow directed a piece which he entitled *99 %*, subtitled *Ein Zyklus aus der deutschen Gegenwart*, with music by Paul Dessau, in which, among others, Helene Weigel and Ernst Busch participated. Although Brecht, in a letter to Dudow of April 24, 1938, considers *99 %* as the title of the performance "a little bit too funny" ("ein wenig zu witzig"), he accepts it, not without stressing the importance of the theme of growing anti-Fascist resistance throughout the piece. One should not have the impression that the piece simply accepts that 99% of the people are Fascists; what is important is that there are 1% which resist. The epistolary exchange between Brecht and Dudow will lead to the addition of a scene, which deals specifically with the Austrian referendum and which Brecht and Steffin had just finished writing.[23] In this scene, which is entitled 'Volksbefragung' ['Referendum'] and is situated in a proletarian home in Neukölln—the Berlin neighborhood where Steffin grew up as a workers' child—on March 13, 1938, two workers and a woman, while hearing on the radio how Hitler is

22
See Walter Benjamin, "Das Land, in dem das Proletariat nicht genannt werden darf: Zur Uraufführung von acht Einaktern Brechts," in: id., *Gesammelte Schriften. Band II.2*, (ed. by Rolf Tiedemann and Hermann Schweppenhäuser), werkausgabe Band 5, Frankfurt, 1980, pp. 514–518.

23
For our references to the correspondence between Bertolt Brecht and Slatan Dudow, see the detailed editorial comment in: Bertolt Brecht, *Werke*. Große kommentierte Berliner und Frankfurter Ausgabe. Band 4. Stücke 4, (ed. by Werner Hecht, Jan Knopf, Werner Mittenzwei, Klaus-Detlef Müller), Berlin-Weimar-Frankfurt, 1988, pp. 529–530.

celebrated by cheering crowds in Vienna, discuss the risks of distributing leaflets against the upcoming referendum. At first, the mood is rather low. Whereas the woman is eager to do what is necessary, the two workers are undecided:

> "*THE OLDER WORKER: [...] Doesn't this actually sound like ONE PEOPLE?*
> *THE WOMAN: It sounds like twenty thousand drunks who got their beer paid for.*
> *THE YOUNGER WORKER: Maybe we're the only ones saying this, what do you think?*
> *THE WORMAN: Yes. We and others like us. [...]*"[24]

At the end of the scene, however, the three take courage from the conviction that they are not that few and decide to act:

> "*THE OLDER WORKER: We're not so very few.*
> *THE YOUNGER WORKER: Then what should we put on the leaflet for the referendum?*
> *THE WOMAN (thinking): The best thing would be the single word: NO!*"[25]

Given that, in 1938, Bertolt Brecht also translated large parts of Shelley's *Mask of Anarchy*, one may consider the phrase "Wir sind doch nicht so wenige" as an ironic modulation of Shelley's phrase "Ye are many". Thus we discover the phrase "We are not that few" as a particular variation of the phrase "We are many", which we keep encountering in different contexts and constellations. When the elder worker in Brecht's scene 'Volksbefragung' says "We are not that few," his aim is exactly the same as when the voice in Shelley's poem says "Ye are many." These two phrases do not simply make an informative statement on the quantity of a group. First and foremost, these are performative speech acts, which are supposed to encourage a particular group to act. Whereas the phrase "we are many" may sound like a simple, self-conscious confirmation of the size of the group to which one belongs, the phrase that says that "we are not that few" is a particular negation of a phrase that says, in an affectively negative way, "we are few." Now, to say that "we are many" could be another particular negation of the phrase that says that "we are few." Therefore it cannot be excluded that one of the meanings of the phrase "we are many" is… "we are not that few."

24
Translated after Bertolt Brecht, "Furcht und Elend des III. Reiches. 27 Szenen," in: id., *Werke* (see note 23), p. 442.

25
Ibid.

Sebastian Jung, *Art intervention on the NSU trial* | Installation view, Criminal Justice Center Munich

Emeka Ogboh, *Sufferhead Original – Munich Edition*, 2019 | Installation view, *Tell me about ~~yesterday~~ tomorrow*

Technology and Democracy

Technology is a way of thinking and acting. It has the constructive potential for imagining and shaping a different form of democracy and society. How can processes and developments be speeded up and made more transparent, permeable, participative, and just? How can government and representation be thought of differently? How should markets be changed so that property and possessions are no longer obstacles to the good life for as many as possible?

There can be no progressive politics without technology, or in opposition to it. With this in mind, one can begin to form a different view of technology, one that accords with neither the cult of the technologically feasible, as embodied by Silicon Valley, nor an intuitive aversion to all technological change that blocks all economic and above all democratic innovation. Between these two positions lies a broad range of options for progressive policies. It becomes a matter of re-envisioning the fundamentals of democratic practice for the digital age. This calls for a structured approach and the ability to change, democratic innovation, different institutional forms, and alternative market structures.

The question is whether there is a way to place technology at the heart of democracy, so that it obeys neither the extractive logic of present-day capitalism nor the Chinese model of a state-run and authoritarian digital surveillance apparatus, elements of which have by now been adopted worldwide. Is there possibly even a specifically European answer to the questions posed by the technological revolution; is there a chance to rethink and reposition Europe in the spirit of responsible individualism?

The European sense of citizenship has been carried over from the Enlightenment into the present day and offers the possibility of democratic innovation even in the digital age. An essential element in this is that the concept and function of the state need to be redefined in the wake of decades of the dominance of neoliberal thought. The state is not necessarily something opposed to its citizens. Ideally, the state <u>is</u> the citizen, is a construct created by citizens. The citizens themselves are agents who can—and must—actively intervene so that democracy remains vital and the economy develops in an innovative and equitable manner.

Such a state would be fundamentally different from the one we know today, for today democratic thought and action lag far behind the technological possibilities. In the political reality of most Western democracies there is a gulf between political aspirations and political reality, one that has profound systemic consequences. People turn away from the system and take refuge in past realities that promise protection. Institutions cling to an outdated sense of power because they fear change, and this is just as true of political parties as it is of the traditional media and large industrial concerns, most of which continue to be dominated by elderly white men who were shaped by the analog age and have no interest in permitting change.

Yet something very fundamental has changed. Power works differently in the digital age: communication works differently, the market works differently, identity, individuality, the state, the nation—all work differently, so that essential elements of basic democratic order need to be rethought in the twenty-first century. And in fact there have long been such innovations as the block chain and peer-to-peer technologies that make it possible to shape more decentralized, more individually controlled economies and societies.

Still, a problem for progressive positions is the fact that present-day discussion about the Internet and digital possibilities is overshadowed by a negative reality that the Harvard professor Shoshana Zuboff has termed "surveillance capitalism"[1]—the power of companies to limit one's liberties by digital means. No-cost services like e-mail, search engines, and social networks are paid for with information that the concern offering them can store, evaluate, and analyze. This form of surveillance is then sold as a prognostic tool, one with which a person's actions and demands can be predicted. One's personal data become just another product.

The consequences of the integration of data are already especially apparent in authoritarian states. In China, for example, pedestrians might be filmed crossing a street against a red light, then their movements and facial features analyzed and compared with data banks. Their misdemeanor is then entered into a scoring system that determines whether they are admitted to university or given an apartment. Technology is thus more powerful and more effective than any kind of policing, for it is omnipresent.

But nothing has to be this way. Technology does not fall from the sky; it is not the tool of abstract forces. It is politically and socially negotiable, and therefore a part of our culture. Emancipation will come from the appropriation and modification of technology itself. Everything could be different. The search for radical alternatives, for new structures, practices, and institutions that might make possible a different, more vital, direct democracy, presupposes a democratic or democratized technology.

1
Shoshana Zuboff,
The Age of Surveillance Capitalism, London 2019.

The Brazilian thinker Roberto Mangabeira Unger speaks with emancipatory optimism of a "high-energy democracy," in contrast to our present "low-energy democracy," in which fear and the avoidance of missteps become the driving forces maintaining the status quo of government, state, and market, as if in their present form all possibilities for social and political innovation have been exhausted. Democracy is a commitment to change, and not all of those who wish such change bring a message of doom and destruction—known as disruption.

Technology, perceived as enigma, fate, or threat, is thus a part of the present downward spiral in democratic practice. It appears like an external force that uncontrollably determines our lives. But technology has a history; it has agents with interests and intentions of their own. Technology is always embedded in a power structure; it traffics in power. Describing technology as something beyond anyone's desire and control only serves to weaken democracy, in that it robs it of its ability to act.

The election of Donald Trump in 2016 and the Brexit vote in the same year only heightened this impression. The two events were interrelated, as is shown by personnel and technological connections: the firm Cambridge Analytica worked for both Trump and the Leave campaign, using massive amounts of data from Facebook in order to manipulate voters. Real political, economic, and social developments were at the bottom of both events, and with what we now know it can be claimed with relative certainty that both contests would have turned out differently had the destructive power of digital technologies been properly recognized.

The two events also show that there are reactionary forces at work creating a new world order—nationalistic, protectionist, anti-multilateralist, and destructive of human rights. In league with authoritarian regimes in countries like China and Russia, both of which have created their own forms of capitalism without essential democratic control, they are creating the pattern for a form of government for the twenty-first century, one that shrinks the role and rights of the individual and establishes a kind of neo-feudalism—a rigid class and surveillance society governed by advanced technology.

What is so far lacking is a genuinely progressive alternative, a coherent political philosophy, a plan. Yet it is true of our time that the faster circumstances change, the more difficult real change becomes. Thinking lags behind reality, technology is swifter than democracy, and the chances for concrete utopias are lost thanks to a failure to translate thought into action. This has always been the case in revolutionary times.

2
Evgeny Morozov,
*To save everything,
click here: The folly of
technological solutionism*,
New York 2013.

Such is the danger when solutions to our present-day problems are seen to lie above all in the resources and potential of technology, or "solutionism,"[2] as the political and technological thinker Evgeny Morozov has called it—the faith that technology can solve all problems, possibly even those it has itself created. What is more, that solutionism is entirely based on the rationality of technology; it excludes other important arguments and considerations that might help us imagine a different world, a different society, a different technology.

Left out of the discussion are economic and political approaches in particular. It appears that in the crucial debates of our time, people fail to recognize how important, effective, and powerful politics is—or can be. The British theorist Mark Fisher has referred to the assumed absence of an alternative to an economic system that has declared the time for thinking in terms of possibility to be over as "Capitalist realism."[3]

3
Mark Fisher,
*Capitalist Realism:
Is There No Alternative?*,
London 2009.

Technological developments have too long been regarded as something that takes place outside the coordinates of the democratic decision-making process. But democracy, the great conversation, must open itself to technology, just as technology—the concerns, the developers—must open itself to society, to everything that has to do with the ethics of its innovations, to possible misuse and the social consequences when technology concerns accelerate material redistribution and a change in living conditions at an unprecedented speed. This view, going beyond the individual and focusing on the issue of the whole, must be practiced again if solutions for existing and future technological challenges are to be found.

On the part of politics, what is needed is the self-reliance that comes from professional competence, the involvement of experts, and an openness to technological problem solutions. And as for the technology sector, a pause is needed, with a recognition that not all of the world's problems can be solved by technology—indeed, that many of these problems were only created by technology.

Ultimately, in all of this there is the question of how we wish to live. What is important to us as a society? How do we see the rights of the individual and mankind's future? For the climate crisis shows how urgent these questions are. The time remaining to us for the consumption of fossil energy can be calculated. We will have to change our economies, our behavior, and our political system. And we need technology in order to adapt our lives, our consumption, and our habits to a sustainable use of resources.

Our democracy depends on this adaptation. If we fail to react, parts of the earth will become uninhabitable owing to heat waves, drought, floods, and other climate conditions. The time window is not hypothetical, but can be calculated scientifically. It is defined by the so-called "carbon budget," which shows how high our greenhouse gas emissions are annually and how many years remain for us to reduce our emissions so as not to exceed the goal of 1.5 °C of global warming.

In this complex model, all the emissions caused by man are added up; at the moment, if one includes not only energy consumption but also transportation, agriculture, and industry they come to roughly 42 gigatons, or 42 billion tons of carbon dioxide. The Special Report of the Intergovernmental Panel on Climate Change (IPCC) from 2018 estimates the remaining budget to be 420 gigatons if we do not wish to exceed the 1.5 °C.[4] According to this calculation, we thus have ten years in which to reduce emissions to net zero. A single decade for complete decarbonization.

For this reason, every political objective has to be considered ecologically if it hopes to meet the challenges of our time. Our system of government needs to be judged by how democratically elected parties and governments intend to divert climate catastrophe. For defending democracy means defending peoples' living conditions. Our society has to change more in a decade than it has in the century since 1850, when Europe changed from an agrarian to an industrial society. This ecological transformation—the ideas of the proponents of the Green New Deal in the United States have shown this—will bring much more than a decarbonization of our infrastructure, buildings, consumer goods, and our financial system. Only a transformation of that magnitude can make possible a more just and more transparent society, a more democratic way of life.

That, if you will, is the utopian, the actual-utopian dimension of this project, the necessity of thinking beyond actual circumstances. In Germany, precisely, any sense of possibility is lacking, which is becoming dangerous and politically problematic. When thinking is reduced to the reality, reactionary ideas gain the upper hand. Politics requires imagination. Politics requires a notion of what an alternate, better world could look like. But to get there, there is no map with which to orient ourselves. The tool for rational, empathetic comprehension is the compass, as the American writer Gideon Lewis-Kraus has called it, "a sense of direction."[5]

4
IPCC (Intergovernmental Panel on Climate Change), Summary for Policymakers, in: Valérie Masson-Delmotte et al. (eds.), *Global Warming of 1.5 °C, An IPCC Special Report on the impacts of global warming of 1.5 °C above preindustrial levels and related global greenhouse gas emission pathways, in the context of strengthening the global response to the threat of climate change, sustainable development, and efforts to eradicate poverty*, Geneva 2018, pp. 3–24.

5
Gideon Lewis-Kraus, *a Sense of Direction. Pilgrimage for the Restless and the Hopeful*, New York 2012.

Thus the direction has to be clear. As societies and as individuals we will have to risk something in order to change something. We will lose a great deal in order to gain something else. These are times of resistance and of opposition, times of systemic thinking and doubts about the system. We are many, but we don't feel it.

What we envision is the possibility of a democratic-digital revolution from below, a technological grass-roots movement that once again adopts the cybernetic thinking of the 1960s. We are all in this together. Only together can we prevail. Power to the people!

Diamond Stingily, *Entryways*, 2019 | Installation view, *Tell me about ~~yesterday~~ tomorrow*

Lawrence Abu Hamdan, *Once Removed*, 2019 | Installation view, *Tell me about ~~yesterday~~ tomorrow*

Arthur Jafa, *APEX*, 2013 | Installation view, *Tell me about ~~yesterday~~ tomorrow*

What Do You Represent?

It is with a somewhat heavy heart that I google the words "Frederick Adolf Reinhardt: What does this Represent, 1946". For those unfamiliar with the cartoon that shows up in the Google search results, it was produced by the American abstract artist "Ad" Reinhardt for *PM* newspaper in New York. It was one of many cartoons he made between 1942 and 1947 about the question of modern art and its supposedly disturbing effects upon established values. The cartoon is divided into two parts. In the upper section, we see a man tilting towards a hanging panel that carries cuneiform script. He has turned towards the viewer and wears a hat, a business suit and a wide-eyed grin that implies we will share in his mockery of this unintelligible nonsense. "Ha Ha. What does this represent?" he moronically exclaims. In the lower image, the hanging panel has been transformed into a sketchy likeness of an abstract painting with something of the style of a Kandinsky painting. The painting wears a scowl drawn onto its right-hand side, from which a nose and an accusatory pointing arm and finger have knocked our mocking viewer sideways with the retort: "What do you represent?". Underneath the drawings is the sentence: "A painting is not a simple something or a pretty picture or an arrangement, but a complicated language that you have to learn to read." While this cartoon is relatively famous, it is less often reproduced alongside its equally important accompanying panel. This second panel turns our attention toward what we might call "the obligations of the viewer." The now confused-looking man in a hat finds a rope placed around his neck. He is clearly the man from the first panel. The rope is held with a ring enclosing a dollar sign. His eyes are reduced to twin vortexes of confusion and resignation. Around his head are the words: "Rich Man? Poor Man? Beggar? Indian Chief? Progressive? Good Guy? Trade Unionist? Professor? Reactionary? Wise Guy? Money Grubber? Dope?" And underneath is the following sentence. "After you've learned how to look at things, and how to think about them, clear up the problem of what you personally represent…"

Self-referentiality in art and related cultural production is structurally critical—meaning it is critical of the structures of art, and at the same time it is evidence of critical thinking within the self and in relation to the collective. Self-referentiality demonstrates self-awareness and consciousness of the relative status of that which has been produced. Humans have always made things that sit in the wide gulf between function and organized superstition (various religions), and the "art" that results is something in a constant state of negotiation and reconsideration. Of course, some art is also functional and some art is produced in the service of magic, religion, and various consciousness-raising structures, yet still remains art. The functional or proselytizing potential of art always embodies a substructure of self-conscious production values, techniques, effects, and affects that allow us to read across art produced for various, often contradictory, reasons. Which is why we are capable of going to a museum which holds paintings of crucifixions, poor people eating dinner, rich aristocrats with heavy eyelids, and blurry pictures of trains steaming across viaducts—and are still able to find some common artness in their varied execution. Crucially overlooked in anxious claims to art's self-regard is that artists also communicate with and develop new languages in relation to each other. Some are quite indifferent to comprehension or excessive management of desire—attempts to corral and control art's content—and this is something that only a repressive society would want to hinder. A lot of contemporary art conforms to the adage, "artness is the whatness of all art"—to succinctly ruin James Joyce's rather more elegant "Horseness is the whatness of allhorse".

> *"Aquinas and his followers distinguished between the essence of a thing (its "quidditas" or its "whatness") and its existence, a distinction that the artist must bear in mind to reach beauty in the work of art. We should not forget that: "the epiphany was the sudden revelation of the whatness of a thing, the moment in which the soul of the commonest object… seems to us radiant."*[1]

1
Rafael I. García León, "Reading *Ulysses* at a Gallop", in: *Papers on Joyce 3*, 1997, pp. 3–8, 8.

In the summer of 2020 I made an exhibition in Tokyo. Making use of the phrase *Horseness is the Whatness of Allhorse* as the title of the exhibition, I wrote:

> *"Joyce brings animal form to an abstract philosophical concept—testing universal claims with the example of a living thing. There is some irony in this gesture, for the process also renders the animal as philosophical abstraction. The phrase Horseness is the Whatness of Allhorse is a permanent reminder of the limits and potentials of art in pursuit of the essential "whatness" of an object in relation to the "artness" of the art work. It is a resolutely modern phrase that is embodied (as a horse), made comprehensible and rendered absurd at the same time. It is philosophy brought to the racetrack and tested against the reality of the city and the farm."*[2]

2
Liam Gillick, Introductory text to the exhibition "Horseness is the whatness of allhorse" (June 5 to July 4, 2020, Taro Nasu Gallery, Tokyo, Japan), see https://www.art-it.asia/en/partners_e/gallery_e/taronasu_e/209616 (accessed on October 12, 2020).

The self-referentiality I write of is not limited to contemporary art or the world that emerged around it. Self-referentiality can be found at every historical phase of human production. It is particularly notable in the making of what we might call the drive to create art, in its broadest sense. In the caves and on the plains, something was produced—often in the presence of others. Think of the process of art in the company of others: the making of marks and the emerging of carved, scratched, or painted images as a procedure of unveiling, revealing, and sharing in abstract creation. The ancient artist would either produce art to entrance the other, to leave behind a message or produce art as a collectively shared process. To tell stories, to show off and to cleave off the excesses of consciousness, dreams, and desires. Processes of play in regard to revealing and emerging are those that take place when we demonstrate the production of an artwork. When we watch an image emerging at the interface of a human and a surface, the process of emergence and that fact bind and unbind the producer and the witness. An ancient wanderer might come across artistic messages in the form of images and signs upon the landscape and read them in a way that is non-linear, but also one that requires a recognition that another human has already passed this way and wants to leave behind a demonstration of skill or an ingenious design merely to entertain the other. In a related way, the encounter with an ancient artwork at the moment of production required a recognition that something was about to be produced by another human, and within the nuances of that production, one might find moments of recognition and alienation from the producer of the work at the moment of execution. It is this process of simultaneous recognition, estrangement, and revelation that provokes a quality of interest in the apparently non-functional artistic production of another human. This does not imply there is no "use" in art. There is a big difference here between function and use. All art has some kind of use value. Even if there are moments when the ability to read across every nuance of an artwork might require an immersion into the points of emergence, reference and lack that are embodied within it. Art is partly about recognition, and that can also be powerfully expressed negatively as "I do not understand this thing," "This thing makes me uncomfortable" or "This thing is making fun of me and my values."

Nationalistic and neo-fascist structures today are currently fighting a "culture war" against forms of subjective art and cultural assertion that are often inherently self-referential and can require complex reading, including music, literature, and fashion—purely because these threaten the pseudo-universalizing desires of the existing dominant culture in advanced industrialized countries. All complex expressions of creative subjective assertion contain elements of self-referentiality. It is required in order to speak within many-layered alienated groups and refine motifs towards the creation of new languages of expression, and therefore mount endless challenges against the boredom provoking the anti-human quality of approved art forms—which are incapable of expressing the thoughts and ideas of alienated groups. All complex expressions of self-referentiality are against the "transparency" desired by neoliberal political structures. All attempts to quash art forms that are viewed as incoherent and self-referential signal that one is living in a society that requires the establishment of a "them and us" in order for the dominant culture to keep its dominant position. The cartoon by Reinhardt may be by a white man and drawn in the 1940s in the nascent empire of the United States, but its message, that by reading apparently self-referential forms and attempting to understand them we must also ask who we are,, remains a foundational aspect of why we must protect cultural forms even when they make us uncomfortable. This is not the same as alt-right claims for "free speech". We know that such claims are quite the opposite to what they intend. Free speech pleas are generally invoked to protect the "speech" that seeks to hinder or obscure the forms of cultural expression that make the speaker uncomfortable—to shout down and drown out nuance and difference. Claims that free speech is being suppressed proliferate when others develop new languages to describe oppression—and that includes artistic production—and those new languages appear threatening to the established "order".

All authoritarian governments attempt to introduce the notion that there is a decadent art that is self-obsessed and self-referential—and pitch that against "universal" values of representation that are inherently evading unique, different, and new human stories, experiences, techniques, and languages. The creation of semi-autonomous worlds of creative habits and codes threatens the oppressive pseudo-universalism of the dominant class. And at the same time summons worrying implications for those who attempt to instrumentalize art and reduce it into a force for "social good".

So what of those who are anxious to achieve the watchword of advanced bureaucratic liberal political structures—particularly in Europe: accessibility. Let us first deal with the political and technical aspect of this word. Ensuring accessibility in racial, economic, and class terms is a never-ending task that requires clearly articulated political outcomes. But when we think of accessibility in relation to artistic content—those who worry that art is too self-referential to allow access to its strange codes and reference points—then we have a problem. Those who worry in this regard often believe that art has a potential to change things, and also that it has the duty to educate and improve humans. No study of art history could be made and result in such assumptions. Neither the reason it was made in the first place nor how it was produced, received, or understood. The twentieth century in particular was driven by art that was evasive, petulant, super-subjective, hard to read, and often dismissive of the notion of art and artists as good citizens. It is arguable that the first decades of the twenty-first century have invoked new demands that artists are indeed good citizens and art does hold the potential to change things. Encountering art is to come face-to-face with a series of questions about who you are in relation to this thing, structure, or affect. There are many questions to be asked of the surrounding context, by artists and non-artists alike: who makes the decisions about what is shown where, and who can gain access to it—and this is where the focus of attention should be. It is the "art world" as a surrounding structure of administration that often makes overreaching claims about arts potential and the curator or administrator's unique ability to break down the supposed barrier between art and the poor alienated public. To over-reach art and create an imaginary ethical demand upon it to satisfy the requirements of an increasingly large bureaucratic sphere of administration is as destructive to human self-realization as those who attempt to universalize an approved art that negates all of its self-referentiality in favor of an inoffensive neo-nationalist consensus.

I accept that contemporary art is a matrix of paradox—that's what makes it interesting and a fractured mirror of our time. In this regard, it sits in a strange symbiotic relationship to philosophy and cultural theory. Contemporary art is a product of philosophy and theory, and feeds it at the same time. Modern philosophy has always looked at human artistic production as a way to interrogate new forms of human consciousness and desire. But art does not always look at philosophy for the same reasons. It looks to philosophy and theory in order to find new ways to disrupt or confirm the very structures of thought that it feeds off. Contemporary art is applied philosophy that seeks to find a form for questions about reality, existence, and the human potential, and to create languages that account for contradictions and lacks in the theoretical framing of existence. In order to do this, art tends to make reference to other art. Trying to imagine an art that could do otherwise results in an easily dismissible philosophical paradox. This does not mean that all contemporary artists are students of philosophy, or that the ones who are well-read even understand or apply philosophy in a logical or effective manner. The two developed together and work off each other with often wonderfully creative or catastrophic results. All contemporary art is rooted in some philosophical aspect that can be described—even if the intention of the artist is to deny that very possibility. And when artists are "good students," they do not necessarily make the most interesting art. Philosophy about aesthetics is sometimes used as a guide for making terrible paintings. Mid-century musings on the culture industry are censoriously twisted into moral frameworks for producing installations in biennales. Neither of these things necessarily advances art or philosophy. There is a productive tension between the art and the philosophy. At best, forms of new philosophical reflection and creative acts of art-making produce something in the gap of that which is already known and, most importantly, they reflect on what has already been produced and divine new paths. To produce without awareness or reference to that which has already been produced would suggest a sense of delusion that was against other humans. This does not exclude the possibility of deliberately attempting to ignore everything else that had already been produced. That's the paradox of the contemporary artist.

Nearly ten years ago, Dieter Roelstraete quoted Thierry de Duve's book *Kant after Duchamp*[3] in his essay on a similar theme to this in the art magazine *Frieze*:

> *You descend to Earth. Knowing nothing about it, you are unprejudiced [...] You start observing humans—their customs, their rituals and, above all, their myths—in the hope of deriving a pattern that will make Earth-thought and its underlying social order intelligible. You quickly notice, among other things, that in most human tongues there is a word whose meaning escapes you and whose usage varies considerably among humans, but which, in all their societies, seems to refer to an activity that is either integrative or compensatory, lying midway between their myths and their sciences. This word is art.* "He continues to quote a later passage: *"these symbols that humans exchange in the name of art must have [...] the undeniable function of marking one of the thresholds where humans withdraw from their natural condition and where their universe sets itself to signifying"*. In other, more elegant words still, art appears to have *"no other generality than to signify that meaning is possible"*.[4]

3
Thierry de Duve,
Kant after Duchamp,
Cambridge (MA) 1996.

4
Dieter Roelstraete,
"Echo Chamber.
Is today's art too
self-referential?", in:
Frieze, Issue 148, June–
August 2012), https://
www.frieze.com/
article/echo-chamber
(accessed on September
24, 2020)

While Roelstraete develops this into a text against both the proliferation of managed expectations around art and the development of a new form of excessively self-referential art, I would venture to develop some more nuanced implications and add them to his argument. Managed expectations about what art can do are supposedly a way of increasing access to an ever more demanding self-referentiality in art itself. Roelstraete worries about whether artists can be "understood". This is maybe a "natural" problem for someone like Roelstraete who trained as a philosopher, but a strange one to be concerned about. You never know, an art work that could not be understood might render it useless in the back and forth between the confusion of art and the academic practice of philosophy. Yet to police "understanding" would involve a number of philosophically unobtainable developments, and that I am sure he would agree with. First, it would require knowing a limit to understanding and secondly, it would involve finding the border to misunderstanding. In either case, "understanding" would require policing and defining. A better position might be to remove the requirement that public funding for art should include a proviso that it is for the public good via its educational potential, and secondly take a much more serious look at the political and economic framing of contemporary art's expansion—namely the rise of the art fair on one capitalistic extreme and the often overreaching claims of various Biennale foundations where good social work struggles to live up to the desires expressed in the catalogue. Any attempt to otherwise police self-referentiality towards better understanding would deny access to new and potentially uncomfortable voices, right at the moment when the political drive exists to engage, not only with new audiences, but more importantly, with new forms of production. Truly creative movements are initially hard to commodify and difficult to instrumentalize at the moment of conception. They also tend to feed off themselves in terms of rapid development of ideas within a small group. It is that moment that should be protected and funded. Conforming definitions of intent, understandability and a limit to self-referentiality into clear terms of production and reception should be rejected out of hand, as they will always affect the least-entitled creators the most.

Brenda Draney, *Tulip*, 2019; *Vacuum*, 2019; *Ingrid*, 2019; *Wake*, 2019 | Installation view, *Tell me about ~~yesterday~~ tomorrow*

I Speak From Experience
(Writing While I'm High)

I wish that I had paid better attention to the streets and the stores and the way people crowded around a lovely distraction. I wish that I had savoured the way I hugged someone I had just met.

I wonder how it might be in the next days and the next days. Are small children afraid now? Teenagers and young people scoff at us. This virus has the advantage in patience. We are only animals responding to what we experience around us, which, in this case, are the alarm bells of news channels, social media, and emptying store shelves. It's a sound not triggering to the young. They only see our panic and our weird behaviour as we buy up toilet paper and whatever else.

I was sitting on the stairs surrounded by hand sanitizer and Gregg was on the phone. His pitch was high. He is going to get the atomizer and some more anti-bacterial spray. I got to a hair appointment. He made jokes about people dying and the end of the world.

I am trying to catch what this has been. People are working hard to make sense of the mostly unknown parts of the pandemic. But we can all feel what is real.

The cracks are the most important. And they always show. I am like a dog with a bone. I can see something is different. It doesn't make sense to me. Some people can live with the unknown and accept they may not understand it. Something just shifted and I can't let it go. I have to define it and know it; name it. We are hard-wired to see human faces and make them correct with our vision. It's primal. And it is the same way we see the flaw in the pattern.

I had just gotten back from Lethbridge, Toronto, and Ottawa. Canada was beautiful and the winter was loosening its grip, in spite of the last few snowfalls we always get. As I made my way back to the Northwest, it got quieter, more distant, and the jokes were fewer.

As I settled back into Edmonton, I found a changed world. Gregg was marvelling at the new demand and how extraordinarily everyone was behaving. I couldn't talk much about it. Robert was trying to track what was going on: borders were closing, in China there were curfews and soap and a nurse he knows and a report.

I don't know what I was expecting.

Sometimes I'm overcome with a kind of frantic feeling to collect the photos and tickets to events of the kind we may not see again. I'm referring to all the things that are so casual to us and that are destined to change.

We have just been hit by a wave.

One of my anthropology professors at the University of Alberta (I think that his name was Higgs) said that we might think of ourselves as an archipelago of islands and technology as the water surrounding us. His point was that we are becoming increasingly disparate islands as the water rises. We are surely seeing this now. Yet this distancing might be something that also connects us the way a funeral might bring a family together. We are only as healthy as the most vulnerable among us.

I don't know what I thought would happen, but this too feels a little lonesome. So, what shall I do now? We are marching into a place no one told us about.

I'll try to catch all the things I was thinking about before everything changed. It will have changed too. Some things are unimportant now while others have new meaning. I could not have imagined the danger there is now depicted in the camping tents and the hospital beds that I painted years ago.

Maybe the reason young people are so casual is that everything is sort of a first time for them.

Paul Dean from Fogo Island gave a talk in Lisbon. He described an earthquake so catastrophic and global in scale that it brought religious doubt. Historians now can trace the earthquake's ripples in the earth and in the cultural records. I keep thinking about it. What will they see of us? What might be revealed? What we valued? Or what we became dependent on?

How long has it been now? All the measurements have their own agenda. There is the media. There are the closed parks. There is my sister working from home. How long have we been standing here with our collective mouths agape? How long have we been wading into the brown flood waters? We have just been hit by a wave.

I was speaking with Sarah today. She lost her father three weeks ago and so I tried to be a bit careful with her. She was seeking hope. "There are dolphins in the Venice canals!" she said. She thought we would all become sweeter, kinder, and more thoughtful about our values because of this. Such a sentiment is shared by so many others. Social media posts declare things like: This is nature taking the earth back! There is less pollution now! We are spending time with family. We are eating together and making healthy food.

This all makes me secretly angry. It may well be the disparity through which we experience this pandemic. White settlers called the smallpox epidemic 'the divine plague.' It might also be the danger of hope.

I don't know when we decided that we should try to be happy.

Sandi had a student and she took her to a group for children. It was to help with some serious issues this young girl already had to navigate. Sandi was not impressed. The young lady was aggressively optimistic, and coercively happy. Sandi and I agreed it was maniacal. The young teacher had the children sit in a circle and hold a 'hopeappotomous' and tell the circle what hope meant to them. Sandi was cringing. She thought perhaps she would have to have a conversation with the girl to undo some damage. When the girl was handed the 'hopeappotomous' she thought for a moment before she carefully said, "Sometimes… I want to punch hope in the face."

"You know what? Me too," Sandi replied.

I don't know when we decided that we should try to be happy. I don't know when we decided to 'cure' other feelings. I speak from experience, writing while I'm high. I know it is difficult to sit in the feeling, even if it is temporary. We don't know if it gets worse!

My mom would laugh at that. Her laughter is related to me in the way I used to cut myself, the way she lived off a loaf of bread for two weeks, the way it would get so severe it was clean. Anything but survival has sort of fallen away. You can use it as a strength. Focus becomes clear. You know you can walk through the flood waters because you did it before, in a way.

No atheists are in foxholes.

This is the terrible game I can't quite stop: Name the Living Ones You Love. There is Mom, Auntie Bertha, Uncle Gordon, Cathy… You have to stop. You can never take a name off the list once it is quietly spelled in your mind.

You have to stop.

I get a little afraid sometimes of what might be on the other side of this.

I am moving in mud.

A month passed in a sort of stasis. Then I started painting. It was so beautiful. I felt so grateful. I was surprised by how easy it was to start. I expected it to be like moving in mud. It is the only thing I remember doing with any clarity. It is the thing I am certain about. It is what I have to offer. I cried.

Now, I don't want to go to the studio. I go and I don't do anything. Everything is so much work. I am moving in mud. And I am afraid this one true thing will never come back. I tell myself that it will come back, in some form.

Another month has gone by, impossibly. I am still in the same place. I feel as though I am in a fast motion movie of flowers blossoming, trees greening, and plants bending to the light. I have been here the whole time.

My friend and I have been playing a game via text messages during the pandemic. We text smells and memories: truck stops and French fries, school desk cleaner and the inside of your arm, Mom's purse and mint gum. These things defined my whole world at one time.

I wonder if everyone has forgotten about me. I know it is an indulgent kind of whining. My world has just gotten so small. It is like when I was a child. I am from a small town in Canada. It is northern even by our standard.

I want to like how I am anywhere I am.

I know my family tells stories you don't hear. We tell stories you don't value, but they live on out of necessity. These stories tell us who we are and they tell us who we belong to. They live like water in the cracks, slowly, and modestly changing the path.

It's why I talk too loud, have too many opinions, and laugh too easily. I am big and loud like construction work. I feel out of place most of the time because I am. There are few places I belong; not completely in the small town. But not in the art conversations where I find myself only seeing the deficits I could never make up for.

He makes me wish I was cooler and more beautiful and less giant and loud. I want to love myself. I want to like how I am anywhere I am. That seems so radical sitting here now. The longing I feel is for another kind of me. But you cannot shake off your own history and all that it gave you. And I feel like it is a betrayal of myself and my family to hope or long to be something else. I am my mother and my sister and my aunts and my *kohkom*[1] and my grandmother and my uncles and all my family. I am proud of that. I feel so grateful and fortified in so many ways. But I am unsophisticated, giant and awkward.

1
Kohkom means grandmother in the Cree language.

Some people can write and make work that is so much less emotional or personal. I seem unable to do that. Accessing my resources has never been a clear path. Sometimes I had to understand how elements in my life could be a resource and not a shortfall. I use everything I have. I bring everything because I never know what I will need. The stakes are high.

The larger narrative is like a beautiful coat that doesn't come in your size and is too delicate for your climate. The smaller personal narratives fit. They are thick and warm. They will do for my weather. I could never lose those smaller narratives because they are vital to my world understanding. It is like when my uncle's friends fixed a car window with a coat hanger. It was funny and it worked. "It was Indianized!" he laughed.

Sometimes I feel like such a burden. A fuckup. I don't know what to do and I have a paralysis. She doesn't understand me somehow. She understands her business and her business to tie up the loose ends.

MAX CZOLLEK

Max Czollek is a writer and journalist. He is a member of the Poetry Collective G13 and co-editor of the journal *Jalta—Positionen zur jüdischen Gegenwart*.

CLÉMENTINE DELISS

Clémentine Deliss is Associate Curator at the KW Institute for Contemporary Art Berlin. From 2010–2015 she directed the Weltkulturen Museum in Frankfurt. She is a Fellow of the Institute of Advanced Study Berlin. Her book *The Metabolic Museum* was published by Hatje Cantz and KW in 2020.

SIMON DENNY

Simon Denny, born in New Zealand, is an artist and a professor of Time-Based Media at the HFBK Hamburg. He makes exhibitions that unpack the social and political implications of the technology industry and the rise of social media, startup culture, blockchains, and cryptocurrencies, using a variety of media including installation, sculpture, print and video.

BRENDA DRANEY

Brenda Draney is a Canadian artist and Cree from The Sawridge First Nation. In her work she provides a glimpse into the human experiences of memory retention, preparedness, isolation, sexuality, dominance, and trauma.

GEORG DIEZ

Georg Diez is a writer and journalist. He has worked at various German media, written numerous books, and spent one year as Nieman Fellow at Harvard. At present he is the chief editor at *The New Institute*.

LIAM GILLICK

Liam Gillick is an artist based in New York. He exhibited in the German Pavilion at the 2009 Venice Biennale and is the author of numerous books and essays including Industry and Intelligence: Contemporary Art Since 1820.

MARINA GRZINIC

Marina Gržinić is a philosopher, theoretician, and artist based in Ljubljana, Slovenia. She serves as a professor and research adviser at the Institute of Philosophy at the Scientific and Research Center of the Slovenian Academy of Science and Arts.

ANDREAS HUYSSEN
Andreas Huyssen is the Villard Professor Emeritus of German and Comparative Literature at Columbia University in New York. His research and publications focus on international modernism in literature and the arts, Frankfurt School critical theory, contemporary visual arts, and cultural memory politics in transnational contexts.

ISMAIL KÜPELI
Ismail Küpeli is a political scientist who focuses mainly on conflicts in Turkey and the Near and Middle East. He is currently writing a dissertation on the "Kurdish question" in Turkey at the University of Cologne.

DIETER LESAGE
Dieter Lesage is a Belgian-German philosopher and writer. He teaches political theory, philosophy, and art research at the Royal Institute for Theatre, Cinema and Sound (RITCS) at Erasmus Brussels University of Applied Sciences and Arts. He lives in Berlin.

CATRIN LORCH
Catrin Lorch is an art historian and journalist. She works as a feature editor at the *Süddeutsche Zeitung* in Munich.

SVEN LÜTTICKEN
Sven Lütticken teaches art history at the Vrije Universiteit Amsterdam. He is the editor of books including *History in Motion: Time in the Age of the Moving Image* (2013), *Cultural Revolution: Aesthetic Practice after Autonomy* (2017), and the forthcoming *Objections (Forms of Abstraction, Part 1)*.

VANESSA JOAN MÜLLER
Vanessa Joan Müller is an art historian, author of numerous works on contemporary art, and curator of various solo and group exhibitions. She lives and works in Vienna.

KARAMIA MÜLLER
Karamia Müller is a scientist and lecturer at the School of Architecture and Planning of the University of Auckland, New Zealand. Her research focuses on the meaningful 'indigenization' of design methodologies invested in building futures resistant to inequality.

ANDREA PETŐ

Andrea Pető is Professor in the Department of Gender Studies at the
Central European University, Budapest, Hungary, Doctor of Science
of the Hungarian Academy of Sciences, and Doctor Honoris Causa
of Södertörn University, Stockholm, Sweden.

PIOTR RYPSON

Piotr Rypson is Professor at the Polish-Japanese Academy of
Information Technology and senior curator at the Jewish Historical
Institute (Warsaw). He has published 10 books and over 200 arti-
cles. He recently curated an exhibition on the 100th anniversary of
Poland's independence.

MONIKA RINCK

Monika Rinck has authored a number of books published by various
houses since 1989. Her most recent titles are *Alle Türen* (kookbooks),
Champagner für die Pferde (S. Fischer Verlag), and *Wirksame Fiktionen*
(Wallstein Verlag). (See also: www.begriffsstudio.de).

DIRK RUPNOW

Dirk Rupnow is a professor at the University of Innsbruck's
Department of Contemporary History and the current dean of the
Faculty of Philosophy and History (s. https://www.uibk.ac.at/zeit-
geschichte/mitarbeiterinnen/rupnow.html.en)

PHILIPPE SANDS

Philippe Sands is professor of law at University College London and
a barrister at the Matrix Chambers. His book *The Ratline: Love, Lies and
Justice on the Trail of a Nazi Fugitive* was published by W&N in 2020.

NICOLAUS SCHAFHAUSEN

Nicolaus Schafhausen is Strategic Director of Fogo Island Arts and
Shorefast. Before that, amongst other things, he was director of the
Witte de With Center for Contemporary Art, Rotterdam, and the
Kunsthalle Wien, Vienna, as well as curator of the German Pavilion
at the 52nd and 53rd Biennale di Venezia.

DOROTHEA SCHÖNE

Dorothea Schöne is the artistic director of the Kunsthaus Dahlem,
Berlin. She has curated numerous thematic and monographic exhibitions on postwar Modernism. In her research she focuses on art from
the Nazi dictatorship and the postwar period.

GÉRALDINE SCHWARZ

Géraldine Schwarz is a writer, journalist, and documentary filmmaker. She is also a committed European. She has published and intervened in numerous countries on such themes as memory work, democracy, and populism. For her book *Those Who Forget* she was awarded the European Book Prize in 2018.

NORA STERNFELD

Nora Sternfeld is a professor of art education at the Hochschule für bildende Künste Hamburg (HFBK). She is associated with trafo. K and schnittpunkt. Aussstellungstheorie & praxis (Vienna), and freethought (London). She writes on contemporary art, exhibitions, educational theory, the politics of history, and anti-racism.

NIKO WAHL

Niko Wahl is a historian and curator in Vienna. He has worked at the Austrian Historical Commission and as curator for Vienna's Jewish Museum and Wien Museum, the Mauthausen Memorial, and elsewhere.

MIRJAM ZADOFF

Mirjam Zadoff is the Director of the Munich Documentation Centre for the History of National Socialism and teaches at the Ludwig Maximilian University in Munich. She previously held the Alvin H. Rosenfeld Chair for Jewish Studies and was Professor of History at Indiana University Bloomington.

This publication is being published in connection with the exhibition of the same name presented in the Munich Documentation Centre for the History of National Socialism from November 28, 2019, to October 18, 2020.

Editors
Nicolaus Schafhausen and Mirjam Zadoff

Authors
Max Czollek
Clémentine Deliss
Simon Denny
Georg Diez
Brenda Draney
Liam Gillick
Marina Gržinić
Andreas Huyssen
Ismail Küpeli
Dieter Lesage
Catrin Lorch
Sven Lütticken
Karamia Müller
Vanessa Joan Müller
Andrea Pető
Monika Rinck
Dirk Rupnow
Piotr Rypson
Philippe Sands
Nicolaus Schafhausen
Dorothea Schöne
Géraldine Schwarz
Nora Sternfeld
Niko Wahl
Mirjam Zadoff

Editorial office
Andreas Eichmüller
Lukas Graf

Copy editor and proof reader
Jane Michael, Munich

Translations from German
Russell Stockman, Vermont, U.S.A.; Nicholas Grindell (essay by Monika Rinck); Jon Cho-Polizzi (poem by Max Czollek, first published in *Jewish Currents*)

Photos
Orla Connolly
Jens Weber
© NS-Dokumentations-zentrum Munich
© VG Bild-Kunst (pp. 13, 90/91, 122/123, 142/143, 144/145, 182/183, 194/195, 207, 221, 268/269)

Picture editor
Juliane Bischoff

Design and typesetting
Boy Vereecken with Antoine Begon

Published by
Hirmer Verlag
Bayerstrasse 57–59
80335 Munich
www.hirmerverlag.de

Project management Hirmer Verlag
Rainer Arnold

Lithography
Reproline Mediateam, Unterföhring

Printing and binding
Eberl & Kösel, Altusried-Krugzell

Type
Adobe Caslon Pro

Paper
Maxi offset 90 g/m²

Bibliographic information published by the Deutsche Nationalbibliothek
The Deutsche National-bibliothek lists this publication in the Deutsche Nationalbibliografie; detailed bibliographic data is available on the Internet at http://www.dnb.de

ISBN
978-3-7774-3543-5

© 2021 NS-Dokumentationszentrum, Munich; Hirmer Verlag, Munich; the authors

© Verlagshaus Berlin, Berlin, for the original text taken from Max Czollek, *Jubeljahre*

Supported by the German Federal Cultural Foundation

KULTURSTIFTUNG DES BUNDES

NS-Dokumentationszentrum München

Eine Einrichtung der Landeshauptstadt München

Printed in Germany